Non-Cooperation: The Dark Side of Strategic Alliances

Non-Cooperation: The Dark Side of Strategic Alliances

Wilma W. Suen

First published 2005 by
PALGRAVE MACMILLAN
Houndmills, Basingstoke, Hampshire RG21 6XS and
175 Fifth Avenue, New York, N. Y. 10010
Companies and representatives throughout the world

PALGRAVE MACMILLAN is the global academic imprint of the Palgrave Macmillan division of St. Martin's Press, LLC and of Palgrave Macmillan Ltd. Macmillan® is a registered trademark in the United States, United Kingdom and other countries. Palgrave is a registered trademark in the European Union and other countries.

ISBN-13: 978–1–4039–4565–5 hardback
ISBN-10: 1–4039–4565–9 hardback

This book is printed on paper suitable for recycling and made from fully managed and sustained forest sources.

A catalogue record for this book is available from the British Library.

Library of Congress Cataloging-in-Publication Data
Suen, Wilma W., 1970–
    Non-cooperation: the dark side of strategic alliances / by Wilma W. Suen.
        p. cm.
    Includes bibliographical references and index.
    ISBN 1–4039–4565–9 (cloth)
        1. Strategic alliances (Business)–Management. 2. Business networks– Management. 3. Joint ventures–Management. I. Title.

HD69.S8S84 2005
658′.044–dc22   2005043178

10   9   8   7   6   5   4   3   2   1
14   13   12   11   10   09   08   07   06   05

Printed and bound in Great Britain by
Antony Rowe Ltd, Chippenham and Eastbourne

For my parents

Contents

List of Tables

List of Figures

List of Abbreviations

AOL	America Online
API	Application programming interface
BA	British Airways
BGS	Ballard Generation Systems
CATV	Cable television
CDG	Charles de Gaulle Airport
CEO	Chief Executive Officer
CSA	CSA Czech Airlines
DoJ	Department of Justice
EU	European Union
GM	General Motors
GPUI	GPU International
HP	Hewlett Packard
HTML	Hyper-text mark-up language
IBM	International Business Machines
ICE	Internal combustion engine
ICP	Internet content provider
ICT	Information and communications technologies
IE	Internet Explorer
ISP	Internet service provider
ISV	Independent software vendor
IT	Information technology
JVM	Java Virtual Machine
KLM	KLM Royal Dutch Airlines
LEV	Low emission vehicle
LOT	LOT Polish Airlines
NSP	Native Signal Processing
OEM	Original equipment manufacturer
OS	Operating system
PC	Personal computer
PDA	Personal digital assistant
PEMFC	Proton Exchange Membrane Fuel Cell
R&D	Research and development
SAS	Scandinavian Airlines
SUV	Sport utility vehicle

XML   Extensible markup language
ZEV   Zero emission vehicle

Acknowledgements

This book is the culmination of over half a decade's work in the area of business strategy related to alliances. It would not have been possible without the support and assistance of countless individuals, in the private sector, government, and academia, whose insights, suggestions and critiques have been instrumental in shaping this work. Their contributions strengthened the analytical framework, and any errors in interpretation are mine.

There are several individuals to whom I am particularly indebted. Benjamin Gomes-Casseres at Brandeis University responded with an enthusiastic 'yes' when I approached him to join my dissertation committee as an external reader back in 1999. Ben embraced the idea of applying international relations theory to corporate alliances, and played a vital role in challenging how and where I thought these two concepts intersected, and helping anchor my ideas about alliances in the larger historical context. Ben has continued to be a valuable mentor and sounding board, with a shared interest in the practice and theory business alliances. I also want to thank Lee McKnight at Syracuse University for being an integral part of this project since the very beginning. Lee has been an unwavering supporter, reading numerous versions of this manuscript and various case studies over the years, and providing invaluable comments.

I am grateful to my industry interviewees, particularly at British Airways, for sharing their experiences in alliances, and for their frank appraisals of their firms' relationships. Others, in the management consulting and equity research communities, have complemented these with their broader scrutiny of alliance activities. These commentaries added depth and colour to the case studies. I want to thank Brock Friesen for opening doors for me in the airline industry, and for bringing me into a major global alliance to work on a novel concept – alliance-, rather than firm-level, strategies. Brock, and Louise McKenven, also provided a rare and valuable opportunity to deal with intra-alliance dynamics first-hand, an experience I am extremely grateful for. Furthermore, I want to acknowledge the work of the US Department of Justice, Antitrust Division, whose trial proceedings released a torrent of primary documents without which the Microsoft case studies simply would not have been possible.

My thanks also go to Brian Job and faculty and staff of the Liu Institute for Global Issues at the University of British Columbia for providing office space and access to library resources. Their generosity made the task of finishing this book infinitely easier. Thanks also to Jacky Kippenberger at Palgrave Macmillan for her enthusiastic support of this book.

I want to thank my parents for making sure that I stayed on track to finish this manuscript on schedule, and to my friends for cheering me on throughout the process. Last, but not least, I would like to acknowledge the Social Sciences and Humanities Research Council of Canada for its financial support during the early stages of this work.

Wilma W. Suen
Vancouver, Canada
January 2005

Foreword

The alliance field is already congested with books and articles that all too often follow well-worn paths. This book is different. It aims to redress some imbalances in the conventional wisdom in the field and to introduce new perspectives. As such, it justifies our attention in a crowded field.

Let's consider first the imbalances that it seeks to redress. As I see them, there are three: (1) irrational exuberance about alliances; (2) the rule of economics in analysis of alliances; and (3) the elevation of 'the alliance' to a goal in itself. In each case, the imbalance in conventional wisdom of managers and scholars is not an old, well-established one, but one that emerged over the last ten to fifteen years. But that makes such wisdom no less stubborn.

First, consider the irrational exuberance about alliances. Most recent books and articles, especially those written for managerial audiences, take a distinctly optimistic approach to alliances. In some, alliances are the wave of the future, or the solution to complex issues of global or technological competition, or simply a smarter and leaner way to organize work.

This kind of optimism stems from several sources. In the 1970s, alliances were not generally seen in such a positive light, not by scholars and certainly not by managers used to command-and-control organizations. So, the early work on alliances often took a contrarian approach, touting benefits rather than dwelling on risks. Companies were told to use alliances to compete across borders, to develop new technologies faster, and even to learn from competitors.

This exhortation stuck. But for traditional managers, it was not an easy prescription. Some firms, like IBM and GM, entered into their first alliances kicking and screaming. But, then, as their traditional strategies failed, they began to switch wholeheartedly to new organizational models, including alliances. Others followed. By the time the technology boom appeared in the 1990s, alliances were being formed at a dizzying pace. And, as is human, every alliance was launched with optimistic projections and hopes. No wonder so many put aside their old fear of what Peter Drucker had then called 'dangerous liaisons'.

Into this exuberance steps Wilma Suen with a book not about the virtues of cooperation, but on what she calls the dark side of alliances:

xv

non-cooperation. Why the gloom? Did we hit a wall and are alliances now failing at alarming rates? No. But, the discussion needs balance. In part, this is achieved here by re-focusing our attention on the downsides and risks of alliances. In part it is achieved simply by asking us to examine not 'what makes alliances work' but 'what keeps alliances from not working.' This book's explicit focus on the motivations behind defection and non-cooperation helps us understand the other side of the coin that we always knew was there, but which most did not study in detail.

The resulting study does not aim to be pessimistic, but instead realistic. In this it borrows from the field of international relations, where *realpolitik* denotes a distinct and dominant approach of scholars and diplomats. This leads us to the second imbalance that the book attempts to redress: an over-reliance on the analytical tools of economics in the study of alliances. To be sure, this imbalance has been under attack for some time, but mainly from scholars using approaches from sociology, psychology, and history. This book adds international relations to the mix.

The political science perspective in this book introduces concepts of power and interdependence to the discussion in new ways. These terms had been common in the early work on alliances, but seem to have faded away as transaction-cost minimization and governance efficiency became dominant themes in the literature. But notions of the relative bargaining power of partners and the use of power to punish or reward alliance members were never far away; here they come to the fore again. The book goes deeper into these concepts than most works that focus on economic efficiency or the sociology of networks.

The realist view of alliances proposed in this book also helps to redress a third imbalance. In international relations, the realist keeps the interest of states front and center; international organization and international harmony are never ends in themselves. Thus too with alliances in this book: they are seen as tools of firm strategy, not goals.

This focus on firm interests is eminently reasonable, of course; how could we ever have thought otherwise? Apparently this was not hard to do, if one looks at much recent alliance literature and advice. Along with the optimism about the form came the elevation of alliance survival, partner satisfaction, and alliance harmony to the status of goals. So, scholars set out to measure results of alliances in terms of the alliances themselves, rather than in terms of the contribution of the alliances to a firm's performance. And firms created managerial positions and offices charged with forming more alliances and keeping them going; in the process they sometimes lost track of the underlying strategic reasons behind the alliances. Here too, we need to regain some balance and perhaps to return to fundamentals, as this book helps us to do.

Finally, this book gives us some new concepts and terminology. In re-introducing the concept of power into the alliance discussion, it allows us to think more deeply about two related concepts. The first is interdependence, a core concept in international relations but one that also has roots (and slightly different meanings) in economics and organizational studies. In this book's view, interdependence comes in two varieties: natural and constructed. This is an important distinction.

Natural interdependence in an alliance exists when the actions of one partner affect those of another, e.g. because their technologies depend on each other. It is embedded, so to speak, in the nature of the technology and markets of the partners. Constructed interdependence is a bit different: it is created consciously or unconsciously by the partners in the way they structure their alliance and in the commitments that they make as part of the alliance. This type of interdependence also leads to one partner being affected by the actions of the other, but only because the partners choose to tie themselves to each other through the alliance.

These two forms of interdependence are clearly related. Constructed interdependence can lead to commitments that in later periods may appear as 'given' or 'natural'. For example, when one firm commits its technology to be compatible to the technology of a partner, it is constructing interdependence. But later, when the compatibility commitments have become engrained in the firm's technological approach, a 'natural' interdependence on the partner firm will remain, regardless of the state of the alliance. Microsoft and its partners are a case in point. Conversely, a natural interdependence may beget constructed interdependence, as the airline cases show.

The second concept related to power that the book re-introduces into alliance thinking is the distinction between the motivation to act and the ability to act. The argument here is that firms may have a motivation to defect, but lack the power to do so. But the distinction is more general than this. Two firms may share a motivation to work together, but lack the power to do so, due to third-party commitments. Or a firm may have the motivation to acquire or ally with another firm, perhaps in another country, but lack the power to do so due to regulatory constraints. In other words, the efficiency goals of a pair of firms cannot always be met in practice, due to constraints, resources, or political conditions. Once again, this book asks us to think more broadly about alliances than most economic models do.

All this is great grist for the mill of alliance scholars and managers. But the book adds one more ingredient: rich case evidence, sometimes on well-known players and sometimes on new players. The case study of Microsoft is probably the first to ask alliance questions of the extensive data unearthed by the US Justice Department in its antitrust case. The book wisely enriches this evidence by also examining Microsoft's alliance strategies in emerging technologies. The case of Ballard Power Systems is new to the alliance literature, though the venture itself has long stood as a model of a multi-party alliance in an emerging technology. Finally, the airline cases – a well-known industry, to be sure, but one on which this book adds substantial evidence and some first-hand insight.

For these reasons, perspective, concepts, and evidence, this book deserves to be studied by alliance scholars and managers alike. It has earned its spot not only on our bookshelves, but on our desks and in our classrooms. Its success will depend on our willingness to open our minds.

Benjamin Gomes-Casseres
International Business School
Brandeis University
January 2005

1
The Dark Side of Strategic Alliances

Strategic alliances are a key element in a firm's portfolio of management tools, and considered a source of competitive advantage in many industries. Even firms initially wary of cooperative competition have adopted alliances in response to changes in their operating environments. However, alliances introduce new risks as firms depend on partners for vital resources, share control of key programmes and link their success to their partners' actions. The risks are real: over half of alliances fail. This has serious consequences for a firm's performance, and for the development and commercialization of new technologies.

But, why do alliances fail? Many of the explanations relate to challenges in alliance-management and operations. Taking a broader view, alliance failure is often about failures in cooperation, be they unintentional or intentional. The alliance literature focuses on activities that tilt the balance in favour of building and maintaining alliances, such as partner choice, goal setting, integrating operations, or creating trust. This presumes that so long as we address these technical issues, firms will cooperate. Nonetheless, non-cooperation occurs even where alliances achieve their stated goals, and in spite of operational successes.

Alliance managers must avoid being seduced by the language of cooperation, and take a realist (and realistic)view of alliances. Alliances are a tool used to implement a firm's strategy, and do not represent a paradigm shift in inter-firm relations. Despite alliance-level goals, each firm is responsible to its shareholders, and cannot be expected to act in the alliance's interests when it conflicts with its own. Given the opportunity, firms will exhibit strategic behaviour in strategic alliances. And, if firms choose to partner because it is the most appropriate tool at a given time, once the circumstances change, they may not remain.

This book focuses on the dark side of strategic alliances, the why and how of non-cooperation. What factors motivate non-cooperative impulses? What allows firms to act on them? The book disaggregates the influences on the firm's attitudes toward alliance into their levels of influence and highlights the linkages between them. It introduces measures of power and interdependence to determine which firms are able act on non-cooperative impulses.

In our case studies, why was Microsoft able to 'persuade' its partners in the personal computer (PC) industry to act against their own interests, but faced defections in its cable television (CATV) and mobile phone partnerships? Why do airlines not object when their partners invite their competitors to join their alliance? How has Ballard's alliance survived several realignments of its structure? These cases show that firms act to protect their own interests, and suggest that how indispensable a firm is determines whether its partners ignore its interests, and whether it can impel partners to act in ways that benefit it. The lessons learned have implications for how firms structure relationships and tasks within an alliance.

Firms may be bound by 'natural' interdependence between their resources, but where this is insufficient, they can increase their ties by 'constructing' interdependence. This raises new questions – how much structure is enough? And, can there be too much? The Swissair Group found, too late, that it had created a structure that increased its exposure to its partners' financial weaknesses, leading to its own collapse.

The challenge of non-cooperation is even more pressing in uncertain economic climates. Slow growth, pressures to improve financial performance, and difficulties accessing capital markets strain firms' relationships with their partners. As firms concentrate on improving their bottom lines, the temptation to reap short-term gains at their partners' expenses can become irresistible.

This book's primary goal is to remind managers to take a realistic view of firm behaviour in alliances, and provide them with an approach to break down and identify the factors that influence their partners' attitudes toward alliance, in the hopes of forestalling non-cooperative behaviour. Furthermore, it gives managers a framework to assess how much the firms in their alliance need each other's resources, and identify which ones have the ability to act on non-cooperative impulses. For firms not yet in alliances, the framework provides a structured approach to partner choice, and to evaluate their partners' and their own contributions to the group. This will allow them to determine whether there is sufficient natural interdependence to bind the parties, or whether they need to create stronger ties.

What is a strategic alliance?

First, we need to be clear about what a strategic alliance is. In the past, 'strategic alliance' referred to a specific form of inter-firm relationship, but today, there are as many definitions of what an alliance is as there are alliances. The term has been applied to such a wide range of cooperative activities by both academics and practitioners that it has lost its meaning.[1] Moreover, as cooperative structures have evolved and become more complex, defining and categorizing strategic alliances has become an even bigger challenge, spawning an extensive literature specifying alliance characteristics and describing alliance-types.[2] The growth of multiparty alliances has further complicated the issues of definition and taxonomy.[3]

The definition of alliance used in this work draws from both the necessary and sufficient conditions set out by Yoshino and Rangan – independent firms, shared benefits and control, and continuous contributions – and Gomes-Casseres' contributions with respect to control.[4] Although the Microsoft case studies in the PC industry push the boundaries of our definition, for our purposes, a strategic alliance is a cooperative venture between firms situated on the continuum between markets and hierarchies, and is distinguished by several characteristics:

- the firms remain independent
- the relationships are not solely transactional, so that contributions are made continually
- partners bring resources, share risks and benefits, but have limited control
- they are a means to address the challenges raised by incomplete contracts, agreements which cannot be written to specify all future scenarios

A multiparty strategic alliance is composed of three or more firms. Structurally, the multiparty alliances in this study are groups of firms bound to each other through networks of ties, rather than constellations revolving around a central firm. However, the reality is that the distinctions between the different multiparty alliance forms are becoming blurred, with the emergence of hybrid groups. The airline industry has one of the cleanest distinctions – a firm either chooses a global alliance, or a constellation of bilaterals. But, even there, airlines supplement their global alliances with bilateral partners to target tactical markets.

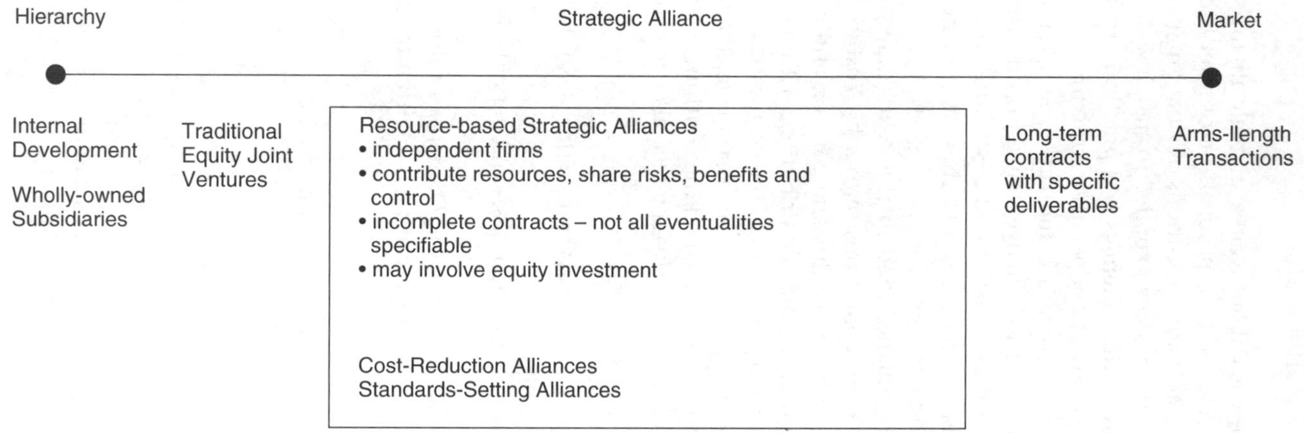

4

Hierarchy ──────────── Strategic Alliance ──────────── Market

Internal Development
Wholly-owned Subsidiaries

Traditional Equity Joint Ventures

Resource-based Strategic Alliances
- independent firms
- contribute resources, share risks, benefits and control
- incomplete contracts – not all eventualities specifiable
- may involve equity investment

Cost-Reduction Alliances
Standards-Setting Alliances

Long-term contracts with specific deliverables

Arms-llength Transactions

Figure 1.1   Strategic Alliance: Between Markets and Hierarchies

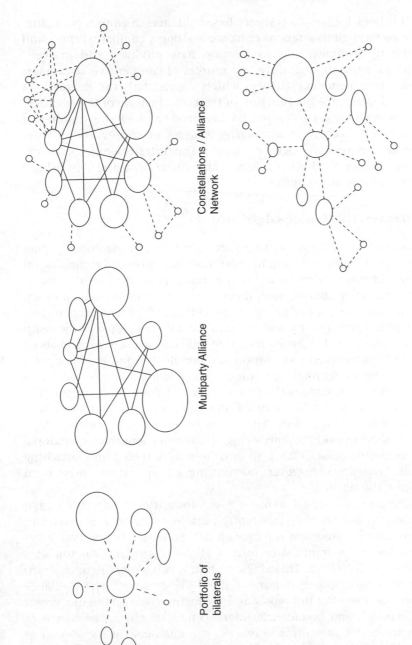

Figure 1.2 Multiparty Alliance Structures

Constellations / Alliance Network

Multiparty Alliance

Portfolio of bilaterals

This book focuses on resource-based alliances: members pool tangible or intangible assets to enhance a group's competitiveness and generate revenues, and to develop new products and markets. Alliance partners, therefore, are sources of competitive advantage. Resource-dependence theory, which argues that 'the degree of a firm's dependence is a function of the critical nature of the resources in the exchange to the parties involved, and of the number of and ease of access to alternative sources of supply...'[5] provides the genesis for the focus on power and interdependence as key determinants of whether a firm is able to act on a desire to behave opportunistically or defect.

Alliances: the double-edged sword

Firms enter into alliances to achieve goals more expeditiously than they could on their own, or in order to share market and technological risks. However, in choosing to ally, firms make a number of tradeoffs – giving up control, accepting constraints on their freedom to act, committing to a set of partners and cutting off other opportunities, sometimes permanently. But, cooperation does not represent the death of competition. For firms, therefore, alliance management is about optimizing between cooperation and conflict,[6] impulses which arise from a firm's rationale for joining an alliance and management's imperative to maximize the firm's returns.[7] So, although cooperation may be necessary to achieve a firm's goals, management's role is to identify ways to get 'more' for its firm. For example, by lobbying for a larger share of work, or convincing partners to adopt their operational or technological standards, so as to minimize their firm's switching costs. Sometimes, however, maximizing a firm's returns may mean leaving the alliance.

Alliances are critical tools in many industries' competitive environments, but are they inherently unstable? Not only do they face significant management and operational challenges – made even more complex in the multiparty form – alliances are built on top of a number of fault lines. These include: firm versus group interests, short- versus long-term orientations, rigidity versus flexibility in alliance structure, differing firm goals and competitive environments, power differentials and asymmetric interdependence. Given the extent of relational risk that firms must take on, alliances can be viewed as a residual option, adopted *in the absence of other acceptable choices at a given point in time and under certain conditions.*

Thus, alliances may be seen as temporary commitments to be disposed of if the conditions that favour cooperation change, or if the benefits fail to meet the firms' expectations. The calculus of cooperation versus defection is different for each member of the alliance, just as defections have different effects on the other firms in the group and their ability to achieve their objectives.

Since an alliance's competitiveness is a function of its portfolio of resources, defections have a negative effect on its performance and likelihood of success, although the impact depends on whether the defector possessed a unique and vital asset. For individual alliance members, a defection's impact varies, since each partner relies on the others' resources to a different degree. Defections also increase transactions costs – to separate the defector's contribution to common assets, or to buy them out, for the remaining firms to audit their vulnerabilities, and to search for a substitute.[8]

However, defections also have symbolic value – just as some firms contribute 'legitimacy', defections can signal a lack of confidence in the alliance's product or strategy. This could lead other members to hedge their bets, by reducing their own resource commitments or pursuing other options. Other groupings may target the alliance's membership. Thus, defections can result in a domino effect which ultimately destroys the alliance.

Non-cooperation has serious implications for the small- and medium-sized enterprises found in many technology alliances. They are more likely to rely on outside resources to bring their products to the market, and are unlikely to have the financial capacity to secure these through mergers and acquisitions or internal development. These firms need alliances the most, but are also the most vulnerable. Not only do they depend on their partners' resources, they often lack other lines of business to fall back on if their alliances fail.

Saying 'We', Thinking 'Me'

The study of strategic alliances raises questions about the appropriate level of analysis. Should the focus be on the alliance or the firm? While we speak of alliance success and failure, we have difficulty specifying what it really means. We know that an alliance that has not achieved its publicly stated goals, or which has collapsed under a series of defections, has failed, but what is success? Should an alliance be considered successful if the benefits from joint activities flow disproportionately to one or two members? Alliances do not have their own bottom lines; traditional measures such as net profits, stock price, or cash flow reside at the firm level. This leaves open the possibility that the alliance-level metrics we can count, such as longevity, numbers of members, or total revenues, are the 'wrong' things. In extreme cases, an alliance can achieve its goal, such as commercializing a new technology, but the firm that invented it no longer operates.

But, if we agree that alliances are a tool of firm strategy, then it is obvious that the firm is the appropriate level of analysis. This book takes the firm's perspective, since *it* decides whether to cooperate or not. Firms in resource-based alliances rely on each others' contributions and the resulting synergies to achieve their goals, and thus have a stake in the alliance's performance. Ultimately, though, the firm is a profit-maximizing actor judged on its own performance.

While it is easy to agree that alliances should be viewed from the firm's perspective, from a practical standpoint, it is difficult for alliance managers and representatives to do so, and extremely difficult for those in alliance institutions to keep in mind. Experience in the field shows that individuals who are only involved in alliance activities find it easy to criticize member firms for being obstructionist or for lacking vision. But, an objective observer might say that the 'obstructionist' firm should be praised for understanding how to use its alliance to maximum effect.

Organization of the book

While not denying that firms cooperate and build trust, and that successful alliances do exist, this book argues that the realist perspective underlying the assumptions about firm behaviour suggests that firms are better off not to expect their partners to cooperate. By focussing on the dark side of alliances, it reminds alliance managers of the damage that non-cooperation, and in particular, defection, can have on their interests, and potentially, to their firm's survival.

Chapter 2 examines *why* firms behave as they do in alliances. If alliances are supposed to be beneficial, why does non-cooperation occur? The assumptions about the firm borrow from the realist perspective in international relations to show that firms can choose to cooperate and be self-interested at the same time; an alliance may be the most expedient tool to achieve its goals under the given circumstances. Alliances, therefore, are not a strategy, but a tool to implement the firm's strategy. The assumptions about the firm relax the view that economic returns are the only consideration; firms are also concerned with strategic positioning and therefore care about relative returns. So, a firm may choose not to pursue an alliance initiative, even if it is beneficial, because it would rather retain a capability in a function for the future.

This chapter breaks down the influences that motivate firm behaviour, a number of which have been identified elsewhere in the alliance literature, according to their levels of analysis, and highlights the oft-ignored firm-internal considerations. It reminds managers to examine the alliance in the context of a firm's overall operations, and that factors extraneous to the alliance also affect how the firm views it.

The power and interdependence framework presented in Chapter 3 provides a structured approach to examine the *how* in non-cooperation: the conditions under which firms in a resource-based alliance are able to defect. Power and interdependence are a barometer of a firm's ability to pursue its interests independently of its partners. They are functions of the type and uniqueness of the resources contributed to the alliance, the firm's financial position, and the extent to which partners are technologically or operationally integrated. All things being equal, the more powerful the firm, and the less dependent it is on its partners, the more able it is to pursue its interests. However, having the ability to act does not mean that the firm will do so.

The framework, combined with industry knowledge, allows managers to identify the sources of power in their alliance, determine their firm's importance to its alliance and its partners, identify who needs whom more, and whether their firm has the ability to respond to non-cooperation.

The three sets of case studies – Microsoft, Ballard and international aviation – illustrate contrasting alliance environments: industry type, alliance size, extent of structure, and vertical versus horizontal relationships. The Microsoft cases illustrate how a firm can use its power to defend its position by behaving opportunistically and threatening defection. At the same time, Microsoft also illustrates the contextual nature of power. Its source of power in the PC industry, the Windows operating system (OS), is of limited value in the new industries it is trying to enter. Ballard Power Systems' vehicular alliance typifies technology-based alliances between start-up companies and established firms, and is an excellent example of an alliance which appears to have done everything right. This alliance reminds us that any analysis of power and interdependence is only a snapshot at a point in time. Relative power and interdependence changes as assets become less unique, as operations become more integrated, and as different resources are critical at different stages of a project's development. The airline alliances may foreshadow future trends in alliance structure. In the meantime, they highlight the importance of interdependence in binding firms to their alliances – but also show that, depending on the tools used, these ties may lead to unintended consequences.

These cases illustrate the challenges managers will face as they examine their own alliance relationships, and as they build their alliances. The cases show how resource contributions differ between industries, and more importantly, how context-specific power resources are: in some environments, even firms as feared as Microsoft can be (temporarily) curbed. They also reinforce the message that the elements outside of the alliance are critical to how firms view their participation.

The conclusions shed light on a number of questions, including power and interdependence's relationship to firm behaviour, the nature of firm power, and alliance size and composition. Beyond specific instances of defection or non-defection, the findings have implications for how firms structure relationships and tasks within their alliances, and present new directions for academic research.

Given the limited number of case studies, and practitioners' general reticence to speak about the dark side of strategic alliances, this book does not purport to provide a definitive answer to the question what drives non-cooperation in strategic alliances. The situations and the alliance dynamics illustrated in the case studies should resonate with alliance managers, and are meant to provoke reflection about their own alliances... and hopefully, encourage them to share their experiences.

2
The Challenge of Non-Cooperation

If alliances are vital for firms to achieve goals they cannot reach on their own, why is there non-cooperation? Cooperation is not a denial of a firm's self-interest or its goal of profit maximization. In the international relations sphere, Morgenthau contended that states pursue alliances for expediency's sake, not principle.[1] Applied to the business context, alliances are a means for a firm to achieve a goal more expeditiously, share risk, or access resources it does not possess. This perspective implies that strategic alliances are not meant to be permanent institutions, but rather, are temporary constructs created in response to a particular situation or environment. As such, the marriage analogy used by many observers is not accurate because it implies permanence. Instead, alliances might resemble a game of musical chairs as firms juggle their partners to access the most valuable assets.

The focus on the dark side of strategic alliances brings their role into perspective. Alliances are a means rather than an end. They are one tool, among many, that firms can choose from to implement their strategy. So, cooperation does not represent a new paradigm in interfirm relationships. Firms ally to improve profitability, reduce risk and achieve things that they cannot do on their own. If an alliance does not meet its goals, or if it is no longer relevant to the competitive environment, firms cannot be expected to remain for the sake of belonging to a group.

This chapter and the next provide a structure for alliance managers to identify the influences on a partner's attitude toward the alliance, and ascertain which partner(s)' non-cooperative behaviours negatively affect their firm. This chapter can be read on its own as an analysis of the factors in the firm's and alliance's environment that motivate non-cooperation. Chapter 3 introduces a framework to determine the extent of interdependence between partners, whether there is room for firms to engage in non-cooperative behaviours, and whether a firm has points to exert leverage over its partners.

Assumptions

Cooperation amongst firms has been explained from a number of perspectives which identify different levers to modify firm behaviour. Economic approaches, for example, focus on changing incentives, while sociological approaches look to social norms of fairness and reciprocity, and relational approaches argue that internal norms of reciprocity develop over time.[2] The management literature has applied these approaches to questions of structure, governance, operations and evolution; this work is split according to whether researchers believe that the competitive or cooperative imperatives are stronger, and again according to the stage at which these measures can be applied. The divide is a fundamental difference in beliefs about the nature of inter-firm relations, and the possibility of changing managerial attitudes regarding the firm's imperative to compete. Both strands, however, seek to identify ways to change a firm's cost-benefit analysis, whether through an implied threat to pre-empt defection, by providing larger absolute returns by increasing the size of the pie, via monitoring and control devices, or by promoting processes which engender trust.

This work sees alliances as economic, rather than social, constructs, and favours the economic-based approach. But it does not deny that other elements play a role in influencing behaviour. It takes a realist view of alliances – that they represent a new tool that firms have adopted rather than a paradigm shift in inter-firm relationships, and that we should not be seduced by the language of cooperation into ignoring the firm's fundamental interests.

The assumptions about the firm and its environment draw from the realist perspective in international relations, economic and management theory, and shape a firm's desired action as it negotiates the delicate balance between factors that encourage cooperation versus those that lead to self-interested behaviour. These influences come from the firm's operating environment, the alliance's competitiveness, intra-alliance relations, and the firm's internal requirements.

If the firm exists to own and control the deployment of resources and to further its owners' interests, then the more strategic an issue is, the greater the firm's desire to control rather than share power.[3] In hierarchies, control is explicit, but in the loosely-structured world of

Table 2.1   Assumptions

Assumptions about the Firm

• Firms are profit-maximizing actors.
• Firms have both financial and strategic/positional goals, so are concerned about both absolute and relative returns from alliance.
• Firms choose to cooperate because the cost of using an alliance to pursue their goals is lower than doing it independently, at that point in time.
• Benefits from the alliance can be quantifiable (e.g. stock price, profits, cash flow, ROI, ROE) or intangible (e.g. strategic positioning, legitimation/reputation).
• Firms re-evaluate their participation in alliances, according to whether the returns from cooperation or non-cooperation are greater. This is also influenced by environmental, inter-alliance, and intra-alliance factors.

Assumptions about Intra-Alliance Relationships

• Conflicts of interest are inherent to alliances.
• Two levels of objectives co-exist, the alliance's and the individual member firms'.
• The alliance's success/failure is not directly related to a member's success/failure.
• Alliance members compete against each other to maximize their share of the benefits, and to increase their influence within the group.
• A firm's value to the alliance is a function of its resource contribution.
• Interdependence between alliance partners is asymmetrical.
• Sub-groups may form within the alliance.

Assumptions about Inter-Alliance Relationships

• The alliance competes against other alliances or firms.

---

alliances, firms have influence from owning resources, holding equity stakes, and being able to reward other alliance members.[4] Resource-based alliances are characterized by shared control, and a reliance on others to provide vital assets. Thus, except when trying to set technical standards, when the firm's goal is to marshal as many supporters as possible, alliances appear to be a residual option: firms choose alliances and the relational risk they represent because it is the least costly option at a certain point in time, because a firm-based solution is not available or the technology or market risks are unacceptable.

From a financial perspective, economic and management theory assume that firms are profit-maximizing actors, organized to ensure that managers run the business for the owners' benefit.[5] Managers choose courses of action which maximize the firm's returns, and assess whether and how far to cooperate to achieve that goal. But to protect shareholders' interests, managers must look beyond financial returns and ensure the firm's long-term competitiveness through its strategic positioning and by retaining the skills and financial resources necessary to react to future changes in its environment.

The firm's economic and strategic goals reflect an environment remarkably similar to that which states operate in, and allow us to draw lessons from a rich history of political alliances and integrate these with economic and management theory's assumptions about the firm.

The realist tradition[6] in international relations asserts that states are the primary actors in an anarchic environment, and that they will act to enhance their own power and prospects for survival. States may cooperate if it is in their interests to do so, but only as long as circumstances do not allow for more independent action, and the linkages do not violate accepted behavioural norms.[7] In essence, cooperation is a necessary evil, and this utilitarian view assumes that rational actors want to win, will try to influence others to act as they desire, and will exploit situations to their own advantage. Thus, self interest drives both the actor's decision to join a group and its actions within a coalition should the individual's and group's interests conflict.

States that believe that they are responsible for their own survival will be sensitive to their position relative to others. Staying ahead economically is important since economic power can be translated into military power – as a case in point, the Soviet Union lost the Cold War because it could no longer keep up with the US' investment in the military. By implication, cooperation is possible only where the distribution of gains preserves the pre-alliance distribution of power. After considerable debate in international relations over whether absolute or relative returns are more important, there is agreement that although cooperation increases every party's returns, this does not end distributional conflict.[8]

A more nuanced view has emerged that argues that the issue is whether a relative gain is cumulative or positional. Cumulative gains affect whether a gain today allows a party to compete effectively in the future, and how difficult it would be to recover its position after a relative loss. Similarly, Tucker's 'Partners & Rivals' model differentiates between short-term welfare payoffs and long-term positional payoffs, and argues that although parties are not overly-concerned with gains considered to be one-off shocks, they are concerned if relative gains affect their long-term position.[9]

Relative gains may be even more salient in the business environment than in international relations. Since a firm's prospects for long-term survival are a function of financial returns and strategic positioning, relative gains are important within an alliance of rivals and potential rivals. Unlike states, firms operate in an environment where hostile takeovers are routine, where a dominant position can be protected by standards and intellectual property rights, and where firms can cease to exist.

A relative gains argument is also implicit in Hamel and Doz's view of alliances as learning races to reduce a firm's reliance on its partners, thereby shifting the power distribution within the group.[10] Relative gains are key to strategic positioning: in fast-changing technology industries characterized by network effects and increasing returns, falling behind today may lock the firm out of the industry's future. It is also in the interest of maintaining this skill base that Porter and others argue against alliances for fear of 'hollowing out' the corporation, and allowing the firm's internal capabilities to atrophy.[11]

Realism's implications for business is that alliances are a pragmatic response to changes in the environment, and the most appropriate tool to achieve a goal at that point in time. It encourages us to relax the assumption that firms are driven solely by net present value considerations, to take into account strategic goals. Firms, like states, prefer to have more influence over the alliance's direction, rather than less, and would prefer to be less dependent on their partners as this reduces their relational risk. Even absent a merger or acquisition, a firm whose partners contribute significant assets will find that it has ceded its sovereignty, as partners gain seats on its board and a voice over its future direction. Although there is no agreement over whether absolute or relative returns are more important to a firm, we cannot dispute that differences in relative returns can impact power and interdependence within the alliance.

Alliance environment

The assumptions about the firm show that conflicts of interests are inherent in alliances, and even when parties agree to cooperate, they have different interests or goals, and may disagree over how to operationalize an agreed-upon goal. This work assumes that there are two levels of interests within an alliance, that the alliance's and individual members' interests may not be congruent, and that the alliance's success or failure to achieve group-level goals may not be directly related to a specific member's success or failure.

While members cooperate to achieve an alliance level goal, they compete for a larger share of the benefits and for greater influence within the group. Hamel, Doz and Prahalad subscribe to the view that collaboration is merely another means of competition, and 'strategic alliance[s] can strengthen both companies against outsiders even as it weakens one partner *vis-à-vis* the other.'[12]

Additionally, each member's value to the group varies according to the importance and uniqueness of the resources it contributes. Concomitantly, an alliance member relies on each of its partners to a different degree. As a result, firms which have closer relationships may form sub-groups within the alliance, which may create yet another level of divergent interests.

Industry environment

At the industry level, this work assumes that the alliance competes against other alliances and firms, to the extent allowed by regulation and competition laws. It also assumes that the alliances will take actions to weaken their competitors, for example, by trying to 'poach' other alliances' members.

Cooperation and non-cooperation

Although we refer to cooperation and non-cooperation, a firm's choice of action encompasses a continuum of possible behaviours. As Figure 2.1 illustrates, these range from risking the firm's own interests in order to encourage others to cooperate, to not taking actions which could benefit their partners, to actions which hurt partners, and ultimately, exiting an alliance to compete against former partners. The type and scope of non-cooperation varies considerably: defection is a one-off event whereas opportunism, if undetected, may continue indefinitely; and where alliances pursue multiple activities, a firm may cooperate in some areas, but obstruct others.

Although the terminology of non-cooperation has normative connotations, the negative implications only apply if we look at the firm's actions from an alliance or partner point of view. Taking the firm's perspective, we would commend management for using the alliance effectively as part of its competitive strategy, and for protecting its interests. But, we should also recognize that non-cooperation will have consequences.

We are primarily concerned with the most transparent and serious form of non-cooperation, defection, although the case studies will

17

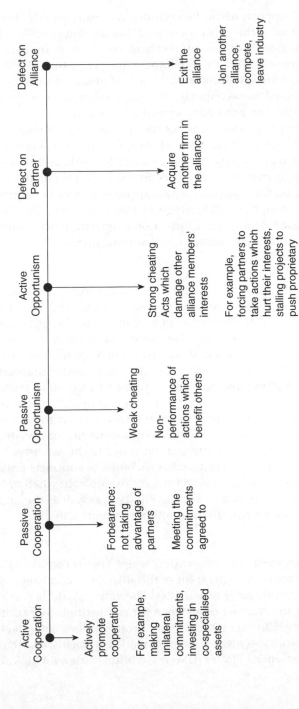

Figure 2.1 A Firm's Choices of Action in an Alliance

also illustrate opportunistic behaviour. We also need to keep in mind that not all forms of non-cooperation are unexpected – large firms often cooperate in one market and compete in another, and partners compete within their alliances by presenting alternative approaches to projects. So, the dark side of alliances only encompasses unexpected non-cooperation which takes place within the scope of activities the firms have agreed to cooperate on.

Non-cooperation is important because it has ramifications for the alliance and for the firm's partners. At the minimum, non-cooperation may erode the trust needed for the alliance to work, and widen the existing fissures between the members' interests. Not bringing the best resources forward, for example, may hamper the alliance's competitiveness, so that its members will receive a smaller return from the alliance than they bargained for. Significantly, non-cooperation may also spark retaliatory measures that weaken the alliance further.

Cooperation

Although the answer to the question, 'what is cooperation?' appears self-evident, there is a spectrum of cooperative behaviour, just as there is a spectrum of non-cooperative behaviour. I distinguish between active and passive cooperation. Passive cooperation is meeting the commitments that the firms have agreed to, or 'coordination effected through mutual forbearance.'[13] On the other hand, active cooperation, adapted from Axelrod and Keohane's study of inter-state relations, requires firms to adjust behaviour to the actual or anticipated needs of partners,[14] or, in the business context, take actions that promote cooperation, such as making unilateral commitments, or investing in co-specialized assets.[15] Active cooperation is tied to the extensive literature on trust in alliances. Trust makes incomplete contracts possible, and helps determine alliance structure, for example, in whether firms use formal measures of power, such as equity,[16] as well as the number and types of measures required to monitor partners' activities.[17]

Competition

Competition amongst alliance partners is not always considered non-cooperation or contrary to the spirit of the alliance since alliance agreements cover a specific range of activities. Therefore, anything outside of the purview of the contract is left open for competition. For example, Ford and DaimlerChryster (Daimler) cooperate in developing fuel cell vehicles, but compete across a number of market segments, and Daimler is working with General Motors (GM) on hybrid vehicles. All indications are that they will continue cooperating in one segment of the value chain while competing in end products even after the technology is commercialized.

Even within an alliance, maintaining channels for competition is important since they are subject to competition law. The airline industry is a case in point: except on routes where partners pool revenues and costs, for which they have received antitrust immunity, carriers expect their partners to try to 'steal' their customers through service enhancements, or fare reductions. However, this does not mean that consistent and extensive price undercutting would not increase tensions or would not lead to retaliation in other areas.

Alliance partners compete within the alliance – while they may agree on the goals to be achieved, there is not necessarily agreement on how to achieve these. This is an issue in horizontal alliances, where all the firms possess similar capabilities. For example, if the firms agree to integrate some aspects of their operations, each would likely want the others to adopt their technologies or standards in order to avoid the switching costs of changing their own operations, or to protect their constituencies.

Furthermore, only the traditional conceptualization of competition, that for customers, is transparent to the partner. A second view of competition articulated is tied a firm's desire to improve its relative position in the alliance, and reduce its dependence on the alliance or its partners. Another form of competition, therefore, is to develop or acquire capabilities provided by your partners, for example through learning races. This type of competition, too, is expected and legitimate within the context of the alliance, although some alliances try to dampen this behaviour by implementing knowledge-sharing processes.

Although there is a distinction between competition, which is 'legitimate' and expected, and opportunistic behaviour, this distinction is sometimes blurred. The line varies from industry to industry and from alliance to alliance. In the airline industry, for example, the area of cooperation is defined relatively narrowly. Given the very broad scope for legitimate competition, there is relatively little scope for opportunistic behaviour.

Opportunistic behaviour

In an alliance environment, opportunistic behaviour, defined by Williamson as 'self-interest seeking with guile',[18] refers to acts of non-cooperation short of defection, which take place within an area of expected cooperation. The range of behaviours can be divided into 'strong cheating' or 'active opportunism' – actions that damage another party's interests, and 'weak cheating' or 'passive' opportunism, the non-performance of an action which benefits other parties.[19] Opportunism, which is often not transparent to a firm's partners, suggests that although a firm engages in self-interested behaviour, it still values the alliance enough to remain in it. Therefore, the intent is to maximize the firm's own returns, at its partners' expense, not destroy the alliance.

Opportunistic behaviour affects alliance members in different ways. It may negatively impact one or more of the firm's partners, have no impact on others, and may even benefit the group as a whole, for example, by bringing in a second source for a key resource, or diluting a dominant partner's power. But, rampant opportunism can have a deleterious effect on the alliance's competitiveness. If it is obvious that a member is holding back knowledge or free-riding, others may become more reluctant to contribute, making the group less competitive. Or, if a partner becomes intransigent over how to operationalize a proposed project, the delay not only defers the benefits to the group, but could allow competing alliances to gain a first-mover advantage.

Although this book's focus is on non-cooperation by firms, alliances are also capable of opportunism. For example, although adding new members may strengthen the alliance's portfolio of resources, new entrants may negatively affect some incumbents' interests, particularly if they are direct competitors or if there are overlaps in skills and resources.

Defection

Defection or exit is the ultimate form of non-cooperative behaviour. The negative impact on the remaining members and the alliance depends on the firm's contribution and the extent of interdependence. If the firm contributed a unique and vital resource, the alliance may no longer be viable, as is often the case in technology alliances. On the other hand, if the firm only affected a small portion of the alliance's activities, and other firms can make up the loss, the effect may be negligible. The direct impact on individual firms will vary according to the extent of their bilateral ties. Some members may be indifferent to the firm's participation, but where competitors co-exist within an alliance, an exit may benefit the remaining firms, since their resources are now more valuable to the alliance's resource pool. The ramifications of exit also depend on whether the firm exited to compete against the alliance, or to pursue opportunities in other businesses, and whether an exit triggers a domino effect.

A second form of defection, which does not entail exit, is unique to the multiparty setting. A firm may defect from a partner by acquiring it; the acquirer increases its share of contributions and returns in the group, and changes the structure of relationships within the alliance. Whether or not an acquisition is hostile, it may destabilize the alliance if the target firm contributed a key resource to partners who compete with the acquirer.[20] For example, Silicon Graphics' acquisition of chip designer MIPS Computer Systems raised the question of whether MIPS would serve the ACE Consortium's or Silicon Graphics' interests.

Although cooperation, competition, opportunistic behaviour, and defection are presented as disparate choices, the reality is that aside from exit, these behaviours are not mutually exclusive.

Influences on the firm's attitude toward alliance

The forces that lead firms to enter into an alliance also affect their views of whether alliances remain the appropriate strategic tool. Firms enter into alliances to access resources, manage risk, acquire a 'real option' amongst competing solutions, because of regulatory barriers, or as an opportunity to learn. Firms may decide to exit once they have achieved an internal goal, if the rationale for entering the alliance no longer exists, or the advantages of being in a particular alliance have changed. Or, the firm may find that it garners greater benefits outside of a group, for example by changing its business model.

If firms do not enter into alliances to be sociable or to build a community, but because the benefits of being in are greater than remaining outside a group, then, whether the alliance delivers on its economic promise is key. If the economic benefits do not come about, but alliances are still the ideal vehicle to pursue its strategy, a firm may need to change it portfolio of partners. But, will it be able to do so? If not, it may resort to behaving opportunistically in order to reap greater benefits from the current alliance.

Figure 2.2 sets out the layers of influences on a firm's views of its alliance. Industry-level factors such as technology and regulatory changes impact the alliance's value, for example, by rendering a technology obsolete or limiting the scope of cooperation. Macroeconomic factors also play a role, as they may affect the firm's need for short-term boosts to their financial performance. Alliance-competitive factors impact the size of the pie the members share. Intra-alliance factors are a function of how well the partners interact at several levels, encompassing operational, technical, and strategic issues.

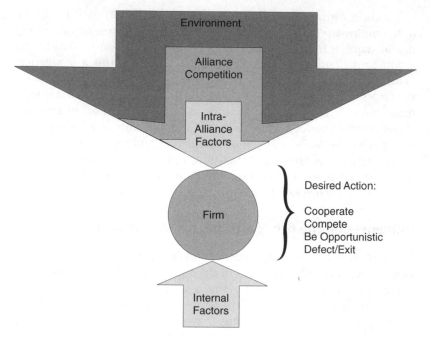

Figure 2.2   Influences on the Firm's Attitude Toward its Alliance

Much of the alliance literature is focussed on intra-alliance factors, leading to a significant amount of work on operations, strategic fit, trust, human resource management, and other issues to enhance co-operation. By contrast, the approach taken here looks beyond the alliance's operational effectiveness. We cannot treat the things that go on around an alliance as having little or no bearing on the firm's attitude. Neither can we ignore the competing claims for resources within a firm.

Gomes-Casseres brings together firm and alliance level competition, arguing that competition occurs between alliances and within alliances, where members compete for influence and a greater share of the benefits.[21] The two levels of competition influence each other. Alliances riven by internal rivalry are less likely to compete effectively against a more cohesive alliance, just as a weak alliance will lead to its members questioning their commitment to the group. Inter-alliance competition is one of the forces driving intra-alliance cooperation.

Arguably, the most important influences reside in the firm. These include financial considerations, whether the firm has achieved its goals (as distinct from alliance-level goals), how central an alliance is to the firm's core business, as well as the alliance's performance *vis-à-vis* the firm's other lines of business. However, firms do not make decisions in a vacuum. In traditional management frameworks, the external factors influencing a firm's decisions include its market environment and competitor behaviour. Within a strategic alliance, this scenario is even more complicated. Not only does the firm need to pay attention to environmental influences and firm-internal considerations, but alliance-level issues come into play.

Environment

Environmental influences are exogenous to the alliance's competitiveness or dynamics. These include factors such as the macroeconomic environment, regulation, or technological change, which can undermine the rationale for the alliance. The question alliance members face is whether an alliance is still needed in this new environment, and if so, whether the current set of partners are the right ones and whether the alliance is flexible enough to adapt or respond to changing requirements.

Environmental factors also influence a firm's desire to behave opportunistically. Slow growth, pressures to improve financial performance, and difficulties accessing capital markets strain firms' relationships with their alliances. As firms concentrate on improving their bottom lines, the temptation to behave opportunistically in order to reap short-term gains can become irresistible, even if cooperation yields greater returns over the long-run. Where members are constrained from investing in alliance-wide initiatives due to weak financial performance, the alliance may become uncompetitive, and less able to deliver value to its members; this can weaken other members' commitment to the group, which in turn, impacts the group's competitiveness.

Airline alliances are a case in point. The Star and Oneworld alliances were established in the late 1990s, followed shortly by SkyTeam, at the high-point of an economic cycle and a stock-market bubble driven by the new Internet economy. These alliances were designed to attract and retain high-yield business customers. Since then, the industry has been beset by recession, terrorism, war, disease, and the rise of a new business model. Instead of revenue enhancement, the best most alliance carriers can hope for today is revenue retention. The challenge all three alliances face is how to adapt their rules and processes to focus on enhancing efficiency, and finding cost savings, areas which had been more peripheral to their original design. But, it is not evident that the existing partners bring the right resources to achieve these new goals.

Government regulation plays a role in alliance formation and structure. In some industries, it creates the permissive conditions for cooperation; in others, it is the catalyst for alliance-formation.[22] In some industry environments, regulation determines who may partner, and what they may contribute, through competition law or regulations which favour one technological solution over another. In the airline industry, for example, alliances are sometimes seen as a 'second best' option absent the opportunity to merge. In the automobile industry, environmental regulation threatens to render their core competences in engine design superfluous.

Technological change is another key environmental factor that can render an alliance obsolete even prior to commercialization. Technological change's impact is completely independent of whether the alliance members meet their development targets. Firms who see signs that the alliance's current configuration will not be able to fulfil its mandate may exit quickly rather than waste resources.

Given the level of uncertainty at an alliance's inception, changes in industry conditions may mean that members' returns do not meet expectations. This will influence the firm's perception of the alliance's value, and can lead to either opportunistic behaviour or defection, although mechanisms to renegotiate the division of benefits may mitigate these urges. The industry environment can also affect a firm's decision to exit or not. For example, if alliance formation has created strategic gridlock, it may have not have an alliance to exit to even if it is unsatisfied with its current partners.

Alliance-competitive environment

In *Alliance Revolution*, Gomes-Casseres argues that alliance formation often spurs others to establish rival alliances, so that eventually, alliances may become the primary competitive unit in that industry. But, even if alliance is the dominant strategic tool, a firm may not be in the right alliance. Firms may try to defect to competing alliances if the returns from their existing group are lower than expected.

Gomes-Casseres' work on inter-alliance competition links the alliance's competitiveness to its members' actions within the alliance. Successful alliances are more likely to encourage loyalty than unsuccessful ones, even if the industry's economic outlook has deteriorated, because, all things being equal, a firm would not get a better return from alternative options. Moreover, the gains generated at the alliance level, or growth in the size of the pie to be shared, can blunt internal rivalry by focussing the members' attention on absolute gains. Firms in alliances that achieve their goals may also be more tolerant of opportunistic behaviour. For example, if demand grows so quickly that a firm cannot keep up, the fact that another member is encroaching on 'its' share of the market may be ignored, and even welcomed if it keeps a customer within the alliance.[23]

On the other hand, an alliance's inability to compete, however its members have defined competitiveness, can act as a catalyst for its members to seek other options, and adopt more individualistic attitudes to maximize their returns. Despite the fact that the alliance's success or failure is not directly related to individual members' returns, in a failing alliance, there is greater likelihood that returns do not meet expectations. The consequences are even more stark in many technology alliances, particularly in innovation-based industries characterized by 'winner-take-most' economics.[24] If an initial win becomes the basis for superior returns over the long-term, this raises the stakes for all the alliance's members; if a firm has tied its future to a group by developing co-specialized assets, then its alliance's failure may lead to the firm's failure.

Alliances compete for more than market share, they also compete for members. Alliances target valuable non-aligned firms to enhance their competitiveness or deny a resource to competitors. They may actively target disaffected members of competing alliances, poaching them to plug their resource gaps and weaken their competitors. But, they need to consider if the duplication of resources would create tensions within the alliance.

Intra-alliance environment

Perhaps we should not be shocked by the fact that over 50 per cent of alliances fail, but by the fact that almost 50 per cent do not fail. Alliances lie at the nexus of a number of cross-cutting forces: firm versus group interests, power differentials, and asymmetric interdependence. Additionally, members have different orientations toward cooperation versus competition, rigidity versus flexibility, and short- versus long-term returns.[25] The effects of these forces are manifested in the alliance's operations, structure and governance, growth and evolution.

Whether members of an alliance are able to work together is critical to the group's ability to achieve its goals, and to its members' attitudes toward cooperation. This has been dealt with in the extensive literature on alliance operations and management, which touches on issues as diverse as learning and technology transfer, human resource management, culture, and operational integration. But, operations is only one aspect of intra-alliance dynamics – firms may work well at an operational level, but still come into conflict, as happened in the Northwest Airlines-KLM Royal Dutch Airlines (KLM) relationship, where they resorted to legal action over ownership issues.

An alliance's structure and governance influences whether firms want to cooperate. On structure, airlines have pushed the boundaries in terms of the size and size distribution of members, the nature of their interactions, and now, by developing formal infrastructures. These are intended to be neutral bodies, but their existence raises the question of whether these bureaucracies develop interests separate from their members or push their own agendas. Does the alliance's governance provide opportunities for members to voice concerns or is exit the only option?[26] Some alliances are democracies – on paper. The reality may be closer to Orwell's *Animal Farm*, creating resentment as a few parties' interests are protected while others bear the costs of compromise. Opportunism and exit may also be dampened by a perception that the distribution of benefits is fair, and that renegotiations may be possible if the environment changes significantly. So, how flexible is the alliance? Ballard's alliance, for example, has restructured several times, with all three partners reiterating their commitment to the overall goal.

Changes in an alliance's governance affect its members' attitudes toward the group. For example, exclusivity rules limit what third parties a firm may work with. If the group's approach is to reverse the axiom 'my enemy's enemy is my friend' to 'my friends' enemies are my enemies', participation in the alliance may hinder a firm from pursuing other valuable relationships that help it compete in its market.

Alliance growth – in terms of membership and scope – can have a large impact on members' desire to cooperate. In some cases, new entrants who are supported by the majority may hurt the interests of a few. If alliances are not careful in choosing partners, the quality of the new entrants' resources and their financial stability may hinder the alliance's ability to achieve its goals. As the alliance evolves, there may also be disagreements over the scope of the group's activities, particularly if these require firms to give up control of what they perceive to be core functions, or if some firms do not benefit from pursuing these activities jointly because their switching costs outweigh the gains.

From a technical perspective, co-specialization arising from technical or operational integration creates natural exit barriers. Additionally, as the partners develop more bilateral ties and sub-groupings form within the alliance, it becomes more difficult for firms to extricate themselves from the plethora of commitments. Over time, attitudes toward cooperation may change, so that it becomes a social norm,[27] and may create a willingness to accept short-term losses in return for long-term gains.

Intra-alliance dynamics, or how the alliance's or partners' actions impact the firm, can have a significant influence on how it views the alliance. In multiparty alliances, firms are not only concerned with their bilateral relationships, but also with other dyads' impacts on them: there are instances where cooperation between two partners can have negative consequences for other firms in the group. Non-financial considerations may play a large role at the intra-alliance level. Non-cooperation by other members, for example, can undermine a firm's trust in its partners, even if it is not directly affected. Thus, a firm may be wary about cooperation even if its returns from the alliance meet expectations. Non-cooperation which directly impacts the firm's returns is even more likely to engender a desire to defect, particularly if its returns fall below expectations. Or, it may provoke tit-for-tat behaviour, sparking off a cycle of non-cooperation.[28] However, the firm may wish to defect even if its returns exceed its internal hurdle rates because of the principle of fairness or equity – instead of focussing on absolute returns, the firm may focus instead on what its returns would have been absent its partners' opportunistic behaviour.

According to the realist perspective, a firm will want to increase its influence in the alliance, control over its partners and reduce their influence over it, thereby reducing its relational risk. Thus, regardless of the financial returns, the firm may behave opportunistically in order to enhance its position. By implication, firms will also be concerned about relative rather than absolute returns, particularly as imbalances in returns can affect their relative power and interdependence over the long run.

Firm-level

Firm-level influences take into account the firm's financial return from alliance, as well as qualitative factors such as strategic positioning, reputation, market knowledge, and opportunities to learn. In fact, non-financial factors may play a larger than expected role – in practice, firms are often unable to quantify alliance benefits, either because the benefits are intangible, or because it is difficult to measure incremental gains, particularly if the industry is also undergoing rapid change. Additionally, gains from being in an alliance need to be netted against the opportunity costs of joining, such as severing other profitable relationships. However, we also need to look beyond the alliance to firm internal factors unrelated to the alliance's operations, which are particularly relevant in multibusiness firms.

The most obvious reason to continue cooperating is that the firm is meeting or exceeding its financial or strategic goals. From a purely financial perspective, a firm's choice of behaviour should be based on whichever course of action has the highest net present value, perhaps defecting to alliances which bring a bigger return. Alternatively, its decision may centre around whether the returns from alliance meet internal hurdle rates. Interestingly, firms may not exit even if the alliance has not met their expectations. Despite the fact finance theory dictates that sunk costs should be ignored when considering whether to go forward with a project, the alliance literature and alliance managers contend that firms are less likely to exit after making significant investments in an alliance, and where there are high exit and switching costs.[29]

A firm's reasons for behaving opportunistically or exiting may be completely unrelated to the alliance's performance. It may exit once it has achieved its alliance goals, such as learning a certain skill. Or, if the alliance is a real option against technology and market risk, once the risk has fallen to an acceptable level, the alliance rationale disappears. Moreover, an alliance is merely a tool of a firm's strategy, and being in an alliance does not mean that firms can avoid the difficult choices necessary to turn their businesses around. For example, there is speculation that Aer Lingus will pursue a low-cost carrier model to its logical conclusion, in which case, the Oneworld alliance would be far less relevant to its business. So, even if an alliance meets a firm's expectations, internal restructuring may have a much bigger impact on its finances and survivability. In Ballard's case, its partnership with Coleman Powermate was dissolved, after Coleman's parent company reorganized and refocused its business units.

Even where there is group-based competition, each firm still competes against its peers and will have specific requirements that may preclude cooperation with other alliance members. For example, even as Ballard collaborates with Daimler and Ford, it competes against other fuel cell developers to attract more automotive customers. So, it is not in its interest to tailor its technology too closely to Daimler and Ford's specific requirements. Airline alliances face similar issues: in order to provide service guarantees to all of their members' customers, they may have to base these on the lowest-common denominator, since benefits which are the norm in one market may be considered overly-generous in another, less-competitive one.

Firms may behave opportunistically in order to bolster poor financial performance in the short-run, even if this may damage relations with its alliance partners. Management may also take a 'bird in hand' approach, taking a tangible return today, by behaving opportunistically, rather than wait for an uncertain, albeit larger, return in the future.

Firms face resource constraints, and must choose between various priorities as part of their capital budgeting/resource-allocation processes. If a firm's other lines of business have better yields, it may divert its investments from the alliance to areas where it will reap a higher return. Moreover, a 'strategic' alliance is not equally strategic for all members. Firms which are in multiple alliances and markets may find themselves with divided loyalties or conflicts of interest between their various partners. In such cases, they must decide where their strategic direction lies and which partnership brings the greatest benefit.

Summary

These influences on firm behaviour provide a snapshot of some of the issues being addressed in the study of alliance interactions. While the business literature has always assumed that firms are self-interested actors, research into the conditions that determine cooperation/defection is just beginning. Much of the work focuses on cooperation, identifying strategies and tactics at the firm and alliance levels that promote trust. There is an implicit assumption that the logic of cooperation will trump a firm's temptation to behave opportunistically. The relative dearth of work on intra-alliance competition in multiparty alliances is surprising, given the assertions that alliance members compete for influence and position within their group. In fact, a multiparty setting may make opportunism more difficult to detect, and thus a greater temptation.

The influences on firm behaviour are about the impact on a firm's attitude toward its alliance and partners. Sometimes, though, firms cannot act on their desires. Firms might remain in an alliance even if the benefits are less than what they bargained for because there is too much operational integration. Or, they cannot exit because the economic trade-offs are too high, or because they are dealing with a monopoly supplier. In other cases, firms have walked away from long-term relationships, destroying their old alliance in the process.

This book argues that current approaches to understanding the decision to cooperate or not are missing a step. The literature highlights the influences on the firm, treating these influences as the independent variable, and the firm's behaviour as the dependent variable. My contention, however, is that these factors, which influence a firm's returns from an alliance or how it views the alliance with respect to its other options, generate a desired behaviour. While the current thinking applies when the firm's desired action is cooperation, it may not apply when the firm's desired action is non-cooperation. There is a missing intervening variable in this process: the ability to effect desired actions. This work focuses on the firm's ability to carry out a desire not to cooperate, which is a function of its power and interdependence with its alliance partners.

3
Power and Interdependence: the Firm's Ability to Act

This book contends that a firm's power and interdependence are key to understanding whether it is able to translate a desire not to cooperate into action. Why are some firms able to behave opportunistically or defect while others remain in alliances where their interests have clearly been ignored by their partners? For a firm that could be harmed by its partners' actions, what can it do to prevent this undesirable action from taking place? Both the capability to act and to defend or deter depends on its power and its interdependence. But, just because a firm has the capability to behave opportunistically or defect does not mean that it will.

While the concepts of power and interdependence are relatively easy to understand, identifying and weighting observable and measurable metrics to determine which parties are powerful or who is more dependent on whom is more difficult. This requires incorporating resource-dependence theory with industry- and firm-specific knowledge to assess which resources provide more leverage and what assets each partner needs.

The framework here gives managers a structure to examine their firms' alliances, and anticipate how these relationships may evolve, as different firms' resources become more valuable at different stages of a project's life cycle. Understanding power and interdependence also allows them to structure alliances to bind their partners more closely.

International relations theorists argue that in alliances, dependence is related to bargaining power and freedom to act, and the less dependent a party is (and the more dependent others are on it), the greater influence it will have over its partners because it would be more able to tolerate the alliance's dissolution than the others.[1] Interdependence can foster cooperation as firms recognize that they need each other to

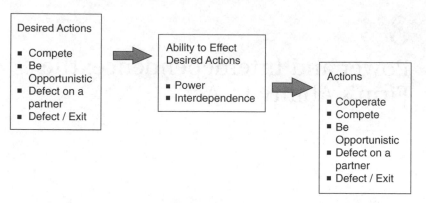

Figure 3.1   The Path to Non-Cooperation

achieve their goals, but may also trigger more conflictual relations, as firms try to reduce their dependence on the other parties.[2]

Power and interdependence are separate but related concepts which take into account both objective measures and relational ties. Their application to strategic alliances increases the concepts' complexity, as we look at a firm's position within an alliance, and what it does outside of it.

A firm's power and interdependence are a function of firm-specific factors, such as the type and uniqueness of resource being contributed, firm size, and the firm's options outside of the alliance. They also depend on relationship variables, such as where the firm sits on the value chain, the nature of the commitments made, equity, and alliance size. While the firms' resources and relative positions create 'natural' interdependence, firms may also 'construct' interdependence via contractual terms, such as non-compete clauses. But, interdependence can be limited by regulation, such as restrictions on investment, and constraints on foreign control or where firms may operate.

Power and interdependence are not static: just as the 'balance of dependence' between states varies over time,[3] this is also true amongst firms. The parties' power and interdependence shift as resources become less unique, as asset specificity increases exit costs, and as different firms own the most vital resources at different stages of development. A case in point is Microsoft's relationship with International Business Machines (IBM): in 1980, it was a start-up firm contracted to provide an OS for the PC. Today, it is indisputably the most powerful firm in the PC space.

Defining power and interdependence

The concepts of power and interdependence are addressed in several literatures. Network perspectives use structure to explain power differentials, arguing that it is a function of an actor's position within a group, as measured by the number of its connections to other actors (degree), its direct and indirect connections (closeness), and the number of relationships it sits between (betweenness).[4]

Resource-dependence theory, on the other hand, argues that owning vital resources determines influence and control. Power, therefore, arises from others' dependence on a firm's contribution.[5] The international relations literature also sees ownership of resources as a source of power, but also recognizes that a single definition of power is inadequate. What constitutes power differs according to the environment, with the result that who is powerful may vary significantly. In specific relationships, power also derives from asymmetries in interdependence, which measures the relative dependence of two actors.

Power

Power is commonly defined as 'the ability to get what is wanted, or to produce desired change', and more narrowly as the ability to get others to do something they would not otherwise do, at an acceptable cost to yourself,[6] or control over events and outcomes. But, this is only part of the equation. Power has both objective and relational aspects – power may be proprietary, in the sense of owning something that confers power. But, it cannot be fully understood without defining its domain and scope. In other words, power over whom and with respect to which things?[7] Additionally, when we speak of power, we must clarify whether we mean the resources or relationships that give a party the *potential* to influence, or the *exercise* of influence.[8]

Power, then, has many contexts and dimensions. When discussing power, we need to consider the objective measures, its instrumentality, and relativity. And, in the context of alliance structures, there is added complexity, as we need to separate a firm's power in general, from its power within an alliance.

One aspect of understanding power is to identify the objective measures, or measurable resources. In international relations, the traditional metric was military power – the number of tanks, aircraft, missiles, and so forth – but has since expanded to encompass economic power and ownership of strategic resources, such as oil. Similarly, in business, market capitalization and cash are generic and objective measures of power, that can be used to compare across industries and countries. In an industry-specific context, measures of power include indices such as market share.

A second dimension of power addresses the question of instrumentality. A power resource's usefulness depends on the context.[9] Owning a technical standard, for example, is not particularly useful in an unrelated market. Clearly some sources of power, such as cash or market capitalization, are far more fungible. Owning a unique technology resource may give a firm leverage over its partners, but having a large market capitalization allows a firm to acquire its partners, or a partner's competitors.

The use of the term power in the framework refers specifically to a firm's power within the alliance context – its potential to influence actors and activities in the group. The cases will illustrate how various firms have exercised this power. A firm's power in an alliance has both informal and formal aspects, and derive from both firm- and relationship-specific factors.

A firm's informal power is a function of its contribution to the alliance's goal, or how critical it is to the project. But, if power is about being able to get others to do what you want, then it is less about absolute values than what it is relative to others. Thus, informal power is affected by the number of parties in the group, and the weight of their respective contributions. To illustrate, if size is the key variable, then in a large alliance whose partners are about the same size, no one is likely to dominate. In contrast, one large firm amongst a group of small ones will give it the biggest voice. At the same time, power, in the sense of being able to shape events can also be affected by participation – firms whose resource contributions are not large enough to give them a significant voice can increase their influence by contributing more than their fair share in working groups and committees.[10]

Formal power in alliances comes from equity stakes between individual firms and alliance governance rules. In alliances, equity stakes can be used as a means to influence partners and reduce relational risk. While these may not be large enough to constitute control, they can give an investor a disproportionately large voice through seats on the board, guarantees of exclusivity, or vetos over certain types of decisions. More importantly, it gives the investor insight into their partners' operations, and greater rights to examine technology contributions.

The alliance's governance structure constitutes another element of formal power. Many multiparty alliances have established management committees and working groups composed of members' representatives. The voting scheme adopted, ranging from weighted voting, to majority vote, to consensus, can reinforce or blunt the more 'important' firms' power. However, whether these official structures are used as intended is likely to vary considerably; formal voting is sometimes considered a 'nuclear' option to be used only if consensus-building fails.

Although a firm's power in the context of an alliance is a function of its contribution and the structure of the alliance, the parts of the firm outside the alliance play a large role in determining the extent of its interdependence. Latent power is a function of more objective measures of firm power, such as size and financial strength, and give the firm the potential to threaten partners. While a pure-play firm may stake its entire future on the alliance, this is generally not true of multi-business firms, where the alliance only intersects with the tip of an array of operations. A firm's latent power plays a large role in determining the extent of its dependence.

Figure 3.2, which is representative of many alliances between technology-start ups and large firms, shows that within the alliance and in

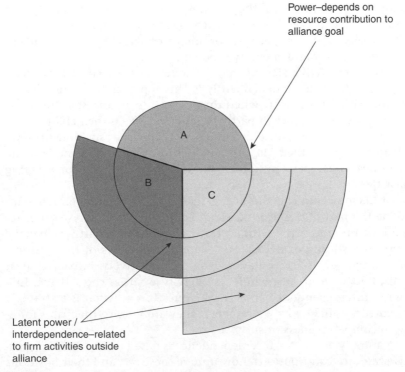

Power–depends on resource contribution to alliance goal

A

B

C

Latent power / interdependence–related to firm activities outside alliance

Figure 3.2 Power in the Alliance and Latent Power

the context of the alliance's goals, Firm A provides the most valuable resources and is the most powerful member in terms of the group's ability to achieve its goal. However, although B's and C's resources do not give them significant power in the alliance, they are instrumental in the general business environment, and give them the potential to produce a desired change. For example, they can invest in research and development (R&D) or manufacturing capabilities, or purchase key skills. The larger firms could also acquire Firm A to strengthen their portfolios, keep the technology from their competitors, or quash a future threat. The smaller firm, therefore, operates under the shadow of its partners' power to acquire, to develop competing resources, or to punish, and this could permit the larger firm to impel smaller ones to act in ways that benefit it.

Interdependence

Interdependence can be defined most simply as mutual dependency,[11] where one party's interests are impacted, positively or negatively, by another's actions, even if they do not have a formal relationship. For example, in a market, one firm's increase in market share may come at the expense of its competitors', or, increased sales of a good results in higher sales of complementary products.

A more restrictive view of interdependence is as a constraint on an actor's ability to act independently.[12] This approach better reflects the relationships firms create when they enter into alliances; as this book argues, their need for their partners' resources affects their ability to act on what they want. Interdependence, therefore, can bind firms in alliances to each other. The case studies show that while some firms are naturally interdependent, others bind their members by constructing new ties.

Unlike power in the alliance, calculations of interdependence include the part of the firm outside of the alliance, as these other resources provide firms with options should their partners behave opportunistically or defect. For example, the goals of the business unit involved in an alliance may be negatively impacted if it fails, but the firm, as a whole, is likely to weather the setback. In a sense, interdependence answers the question of 'what is a strategic alliance?' – alliances are strategic if they are vital to the firm's long-term competitiveness or survival.

'Naturally occurring' interdependence is based on the firms' respective resource contributions, how unique these are, and their positions on the value chain. For example, co-specialized technologies are naturally interdependent. This type of interdependence can be found in its extreme form in the independent software vendors' (ISV) relationships with Microsoft because of their need to interoperate with the Windows platform.

But, interdependence is also related to questions of alliance structure and governance. Firms have tried to redress imbalances created by naturally occurring interdependence, or the lack of resource-based interdependence, by constructing interdependence. 'Constructed interdependence' is based on contractual terms which bind the partners more closely together. These could include off-take provisions, anti-equity-dilution agreements, non-compete arrangements, requirements to share R&D, and rights to license. Constructed interdependence is similar to the network literature's approach to developing structures which increase exit barriers. Over time, however, the measures introduced could cease to be a prop by fostering natural interdependence; for example, exclusivity provisions can lead to co-specialized technologies or partners must rely on each other to perform key activities they no longer have internal capabilities in.

Interdependence in multiparty alliances is more complex because it occurs at two levels. The alliance layer addresses the extent to which a firm depends on its alliance's resources, and vice versa. But, the firm is also interdependent to a different extent with each of its partners. The different layers can be illustrated by the Ballard-Daimler-Ford alliance in fuel-cell vehicles: although each partner contributes to different parts of the value chain, Daimler and Ford are more interdependent with Ballard than each other. Similarly, in airline alliances, all the carriers benefit from increased traffic and feed generated by the group, but for individual members, the bulk of the benefits may come from one or two partners.

In a resource-based alliance, members are often more dependent on the alliance than vice versa, although it is also clear that some firms are more vital to the alliance's success than others. However, we need to think about interdependence in a broader context than just the alliance, and refer to external considerations. To illustrate, Ford and Daimler are dependent on Ballard only if the market is zero emission vehicles (ZEVs); if regulators allow low emission vehicles (LEVs), the automakers become far less dependent. While their interdependence changes, the relative importance of their resource contributions (or power) in the fuel-cell vehicle project do not change. By the same token, firm size also comes into play: while the alliance may encompass all of one firm's operations, it may be peripheral to its partner's operations, even if that partner is dependent on the other firm to achieve the alliance-specific goal.

At the bilateral level, even if an alliance establishes a base level of reciprocal obligations, as airline alliances do, the firms often have deeper and more interdependent relationships with some of their partners, forming closely-knit subgroups, but will not have direct ties with others. As a result, firms are far more concerned about the behaviours of some members. Moreover, these subgroups have serious implications for the alliance: if a member of the group exited, the others may follow because they are more tied to that firm than the rest of the alliance.

Interdependence can be viewed along several dimensions, but the two most relevant to our framework are 'symmetry' and 'degree', with degree interdependence at the core of our model.

Symmetry provides a snapshot of the parties' relative dependence. All things being equal, the less dependent party can potentially exert influence over the more dependent. Thus, it addresses the firms' relative power based on firm-specific assets, and where in the value chain the parties sit. At the alliance level, symmetry revolves around the firm's importance to the alliance's goal versus the alliance's importance to it. For example, Oneworld weathered the loss of Canadian Airlines well because a number of its members flew to all the major Canadian destinations, containing the impact to a relatively small percentage of customers, although these had a disproportionate effect on revenues. On the other hand, the alliance would be far less sanguine if British Airways (BA) or American Airlines were to leave, since these two carriers generate a significant percentage of its traffic, represent its largest markets and have extensive networks.

While symmetry provides a snapshot of the *status quo*, degree focuses on a relationship's impact on the parties, particularly if one acted to change the environment. Degree can be further broken into 'sensitivity' and 'vulnerability',[13] which reflect the short- and long-term impacts, respectively.

Sensitivity is about the immediacy of an impact on a firm and reflects short-term costs that accrue before that party has a chance to respond to the changed environment. In business alliances, sensitivity is a function of whether there is an immediate impact on revenues or cash flow. For example, the defection of a partner which provides technology at a pre-commercial stage will have no effect on revenues, and does not threaten the firm's ability to deliver its product. On the other hand, if a partner were the sole distribution channel, its exit would have an immediate impact on the firm's revenue, one that is potentially fatal.

Vulnerability has a longer time-horizon than sensitivity, and is more a question of the effect on a firm's competitiveness and strategic positioning. It measures how costly it is for a party to react to a shock to its environment, and may entail permanent changes in its practices. Vulnerability is a function of a resource's replicability and substitutability; for example, losing a distribution channel is much less harmful to a firm with many channels. But, it is also a function of the firm's own resources – how well can it absorb the search and switching costs involved in acquiring alternative resources? Thus, vulnerability is also a function of a firm's size, the range of its businesses, and its financial strength, and is further ameliorated by the number of options it has outside of the alliance, for example, if there are competing alliances it could join.

In technology alliances, the project's goal is often vulnerable because resources may be unique, but the firm's survival, the ultimate measure of vulnerability, may not be at stake even if the alliance collapsed. By the same token, a firm whose entire business relates to the alliance is more vulnerable than a multibusiness firm. From the point of view of a party wanting to change the *status quo*, vulnerability is a question of how costly it would be to end a relationship.

Vulnerability, which centres around a firm's exposure to and ability to cope with the negative consequences of a partner's actions, is influenced by a number of factors. Within the context of its alliance operations, the extent of co-specialization and asset specificity, along with the uniqueness of a partner's resource and its importance to the firm's contribution are critical factors. But, if we look beyond the firm's alliance activities, vulnerability is also a function of the firm's size, its financial strength, and the uniqueness of its own resources.

Measuring power and interdependence

Measuring power and interdependence, based on resource contributions, is an art rather than a science. Since resources can tangible or intangible there are no generally accepted measures or categories of resource contributions, even amongst resource-based theorists. As a result, studies have tended to be industry-specific, relying on proxy measures and secondary data to attempt to quantify resource contribution, and related issues such as resource imitability, substitutability, and criticality.[14]

Table 3.1   Approach to Analyzing Resource Contributions to the Alliance

Type of Contribution	Importance to Alliance (H, M, L)	Substitutability Within Alliance (Y/N)	Substitutability Outside of Alliance
Equity/Capital			
R&D/Innovative Capability			
Technology			
Manufacturing Capability			
Distribution Channels			
Management Experience			
Reputation/ Legitimacy			
Denies a resource to a competitor			

The key point in interdependence is that we are not concerned with the intrinsic value of a resource, but its value relative to another party's, which changes according to which alliance a firm is in. But, measures are, by definition, a snapshot of a situation at a point in time, while a resource's relative value changes as the alliance evolves and according to developments external to the group.

Power and interdependence in alliances are a function of both firm- and relationship-specific factors. Relationship-specific factors, such as equity investments, are easy to identify. Firm-specific factors relate to informal sources of power based on resource contribution. Table 3.1 provides a template to evaluate the types of resources needed to achieve the alliance's goal, identify the critical resources, to determine if there is resource duplication, and whether substitutes are available beyond the group. The template highlights the extent of naturally occurring interdependence, and gives firms a basis to determine whether they need to construct interdependence.

As this exercise shows, determining a resource's importance to an alliance is best shown on a scaled basis and requires industry-specific knowledge to rank and weight the categories of resources contributed. Similar challenges arise with respect to the issue of a resource's imitability (replicable) and substitutability (developing different things to achieve same goal)[15] – in some cases, replacing a partner is just a matter of minor switching costs, in other cases, it may involve significant re-engineering.

Power

What are the components of power in an alliance? From the resource-based perspective, power and influence in an alliance is primarily a function of the firm's contribution to the alliance's collective strengths.[16] The type of resources which are important depends on whether the alliance is horizontal or vertical, the alliance's goals, and the types of industries involved. Ultimately, power or influence conferred by resource contributions is a subjective measure, for example, over questions of whether technology or manufacturing skills are more valuable. Even if we can agree which one is more valuable, we are unlikely to be able to state *how much* more valuable.

Power is also a function of relationship-specific factors, which take into account the structure and size of the alliance, and a firm's relationships with its partners. Although equity, or formal power, is only instrumental on a firm-specific basis, it is relevant at the alliance level because it effectively increases the firm's weight within the alliance. Operational relationships, such as significant outsourcing agreements, can also be significant, as they give one firm influence over another. For example, if a number of members adopt one firm's technology platform, that firm has a bigger voice over alliance-level technology choices in the future.

But, a firm's power is also influenced by alliance governance. Alliances can be structured to give all parties an equal voice in decision-making. However, the actual decision-making process may not reflect that set out in their governance. For example, more influential firms could pressure the other partners to refrain from opposing measures they favour. The cases will highlight instances where more powerful firms have compelled the others to act in their favour, and in some instances, for less powerful parties to act against their own interests. As a result, the focus should be on resource contributions and formal ties.

Interdependence

How do firms measure interdependence, or the extent to which one firm is affected by another? In the context of alliance relationships, the capability to defect derives from the asymmetries in the relationship. The question, then, is who is less dependent, or most able to absorb a partner's non-cooperative action.

Power, based on the parties' resource contributions, presents a snapshot of a situation within an alliance, but interdependence takes into account resources and options generated by the part of the firm outside of the alliance, and one firm's ability to absorb the effect of another's actions. The challenges to measuring resources apply equally here, particularly as firms can only make deductions about their partners' portfolios of resources, whereas resource contributions are known. Moreover, while objective measures of firm power such as size and financial resources are not relevant to the measure of power within the alliance, latent power should not be ignored because these types of resources are more fungible than context-specific sources.

While firms are uncertain how dependent their partners are on them, they know, with certainty, how dependent they are on each of their partners, and on the alliance as a whole. They *know* the costs they will incur if a partner behaved opportunistically or defected, and they know how difficult and costly it will be to replace that resource. So, to operationalize the framework, financial impact can be used as a proxy for sensitivity interdependence, and affect on strategic positioning as a vulnerability measure. Firms should ask themselves what would the cash flow effects of their partner's actions be? Is the partner (easily) replaced or will there be significant search, transactions, and switching costs? However, as in the measures of power, there is a caveat, since strategic positioning is a longer-term view, an assessment at a single point in time is not the final word.

The effect of a partner's action, therefore, depends on the partner's firm-specific factors – the type and uniqueness of the resource contributed and where the partners sit on the value chain, but also on the firm's own factors, such as its financial strength, options outside of the alliance, or ability to make or buy the missing resource. But, they also depend on relationship-specific factors, which focus on issues such as the extent of operational and technological integration between the firms or the alliance, for example, or the commitments made, which make it easier or harder to exit.

Alliance level

A firm's ability to defect or behave opportunistically depends on how much it needs the resources the alliance brings and its options outside of the alliance. Can the firm make or acquire the key resource and compete on its own, or can it join a competing alliance? How strategic is the alliance to the firm's survival or long-term competitiveness? For the largest US airlines, for example, global alliances are valuable but may not be strategic since international traffic only accounts for a small percentage of their operations, and transfer traffic from the alliance is a fraction of that.

Relationship variables often serve to tie a firm to its alliance even if it can find an alternative source for the resources it needs. At the alliance level, relationship variables primarily have to do with the alliance's structure. Network density, or the numbers of linkages amongst the partners in the alliance, increase exit costs. Moreover, the depth of the relationship created by contract terms (transactions, shared R&D), operational integration, and technological co-/specialization all affect a firm's interdependence by increasing the difficulty and cost of replicating the alliance's set of resources. Additionally, some alliances set formal exit barriers in the form of financial penalties.

From the alliance's point of view, the primary consideration is a firm's contribution to its competitiveness. Not all firms and resources are equally important. However, the alliance is clearly more dependent on a firm that contributes a resource which is unique, for example technology, or access to a market – *and* which is important to achieving the alliance's goal. Firms which contribute to a peripheral market are likely to have a minimal affect on the alliance's competitiveness, even if the resource is unique.

The alliance's sensitivity and vulnerability to a member's exit is related to the type of alliance. In horizontal alliances, a firm's exit will have a revenue impact on the group, as the alliance may become less competitive, or weakened because of the loss of some service options. Within the alliance, some members will be more severely affected than others. On the other hand, in a pre-commercial technology alliance, there will be no revenue effect, but the alliance may be vulnerable, if it cannot replace the defector's contribution easily, threatening its ability to maintain a technological edge in what Doz and Hamel term a 'race for the future'. Post-commercialization, the alliance may be both sensitive, as it loses a key input, and vulnerable, if that asset cannot be replaced, since this reduces the alliance's value to the remaining members, and may trigger a domino effect, as occurred in the MIPS Computer Systems' ACE alliance.[17]

Bilateral level

Examining interdependence at the bilateral level shows the firm which partners are most important to it and which could hurt it the most. It may find, by disaggregating the alliance into its component firms, that just one or two partners are responsible for the vast majority of the value generated from partnership and that the 'alliance' is not that valuable. Alliance managers must understand the effect of firm- and relationship-specific factors, determine individual contributions, and assess whether contractual or non-contractual factors limit the other party's ability not to cooperate. Since interdependence is relative, they should view the relationship from their partners' perspectives as well, to determine who has leverage over whom, in what areas, and where they can develop or strengthen natural interdependence or build constraints on opportunistic behaviour.

In terms of firm-specific elements, the type of resource commitment partially determines a firm's sensitivity to its partner's actions. Reneging on commitments with cash flow implications, such as agreements to purchase or to provide capital, or which affect a partner's ability to deliver its product, have an immediate impact. The magnitude of the impact is also measurable, although its relative importance will depend on the affected firm's own resources, particularly its financial strength. In contrast, commitments that focus on technology development or knowledge transfer have few revenue effects in the short term, and give firms an opportunity to try to recover. By itself, sensitivity does not mean much, as it assesses the immediacy and magnitude of an impact, without addressing whether the firm has the ability to seek alternative options, *except* where the cash flow implications are significant enough to threaten the firm's survival, such as Swissair's collapse, which then triggered that of Sabena, its partner and subsidiary, and imploded the Qualiflyer alliance.

A firm's vulnerability, its ability to cope with a changed environment, or its freedom to exit the alliance, depends on firm- and relationship-specific factors. The more important and unique the partner's contribution, and the higher the switching cost, the greater the resulting vulnerability, particularly if the alliance is strategic to the firm. Vulnerability also takes into consideration the firm's internal capabilities: whether it has the financial or technological capacity to remain unaffected by, or to respond to, a changing environment. These factors include the firm's absorptive capacity,[18] or ability to learn, and the firm's size, whether it has different lines of business, and financial strength.

The relationship-specific metrics focus on the extent of the firms' technological and/or operational integration. The deeper the relationship, the harder it is to unravel, because of the switching costs, which can be quantified. For example, Northwest Airlines is responsible for KLM's sales and support in the US, and vice versa in Europe, making it very costly for either to build up a comparable network if the relation-

Table 3.2   Components of Degree Interdependence

	Measures
Sensitivity	Impact on cash flow (e.g. financing)
	Impact on revenues/ability to sell
	Size of impact
Vulnerability	**Firm Specific**
	• Type of resource
	• Importance of resource
	• Uniqueness
	• Cost of replacing
	• Capability to respond
	Relationship-Specific
	• Operational integration
	• Technology co-/specialization
	• Stage of technology development

ship ended. Relationship-specific factors add a temporal element to the equation. Not only do the firms' operations become more integrated over time, the financial commitment to the project becomes more expensive to walk away from.

Symmetry focuses on the relative importance of each party's resource commitments to the other. Why did the firm choose this partner and how important is it to its goal? Symmetry also takes into account whether substitutes are available, and if not, how well protected the partner's resource is, since learning from a partner gives a firm the potential to reduce its dependence. Additionally, if a firm can leverage its partner's knowledge into its other lines of business, the relationship may be more asymmetric than narrow alliance goals indicate, and raise the cost of defection. In addition to the firm's absorptive capacity, this capability is also dependent on the type of knowledge-based resource sought, and how well it is protected.[19]

Symmetry interdependence is also affected by a number of relationship-specific factors. The most basic question is the nature of the relationship. In an equity-based relationship, is the investment one-way or two-way, and is there a commitment to contribute more capital in the future? Or, is the relationship based on marketing and operations support, or joint R&D? Furthermore, what is the scope of the relationship – how much of the firm is tied to the alliance? The firm may also find that it is tied to its partner in other relationships besides the lines of business in the alliance being examined, which increases their interdependence.

More important is the extent of technological specialization or co-specialization or operational integration. For example, a transactions-based relationship is not very interdependent, even if their interactions may encompass design changes and improvements to products and manufacturing processes. Agreements for shared R&D, for example, require a better understanding of each other's skills, a greater sharing of information, and in some cases, sharing of personnel. If the alliance requires the development of co-specialized assets, and these assets amount to a significant percentage of the firms' operations, then they are tightly bound together. In other alliances, one partner may provide operations, logistics or information technology (IT) support, leading the other to become dependent on it for core functions, potentially de-skilling the firm in these areas.

Transitory nature of power and interdependence

Power and interdependence are not static measures. They change due to factors both within and external to the alliance. Different firms are more powerful as alliance projects move along the development process. In technology-development alliances, for example, the respective firms add value to different segments of the value chain, and at different points in time. Therefore, the firm that owns an innovative technology may be the most important member at the alliance's inception, but those that provide manufacturing capacity and distribution channels contribute greater value at commercialization. The firms' relative positions also vary due to changes in the firms' internal capabilities, and as the firms' resources and skills become less unique. Moreover, the firms can actively try to change their relative power and interdependence, through Doz and Hamel's learning races, for example. Or, they may try to duplicate capabilities that their partners contribute.

Relative dependence also shifts as technologies and operations become more integrated, and as firms relinquish other relationships to focus on alliance partners. Alliances open doors to new opportunities, but also close off other options, and thus, partners are likely to become more interdependent over time. One analogy is a regional free trade area, which increases total trade, but may divert trade away from non-member countries.[20]

Thus, assessments of power and interdependence are not written in stone, but are snapshots of relations at specific points in time. In analyzing relationships with their partners, firms should look ahead to assess how interdependent they would be at different stages of the alliance's development, both in terms of whose resources are the most critical, and the extent of asset specificity that arises from cooperating over a period of time.

Applying power and interdependence

This chapter presents a framework for firms to gauge their power in their alliances, and assess their interdependence with the alliance and individual partners. The analysis can be applied in partner choice and alliance design. How can a firm protect its interests and try to minimize the risk of defections or opportunistic behaviour? If there is significant naturally-occurring interdependence, does the firm need to construct interdependence? For firms already in alliances, the framework allows them to determine which partners they are most dependent on, and whether those parties have the capability to behave opportunistically or defect.

The metrics used to measure power and interdependence highlight how germane the resource-based perspective is to strategic alliances. Two key factors, the availability of alternative sources and the resource's criticality to a firm's success, illustrate the potential for coercive power to be exercised if one firm were dependent on another.[21]

However, while a firm has the capability to act on non-cooperative urges, it does not mean that it will act. While this model does not provide the tools for a detailed risk analysis for non-cooperation, managers can look to the influences on their partners' motivation to cooperate, as presented in Chapter 2, to provide an early warning signal that a situation needs to be more closely monitored. The question then becomes what carrots or sticks may be employed to influence that partner's decision, and whether the response needs to be made by an individual firm or by the group.

The next three chapters present a series of case studies of alliances and non-cooperation in the communications and IT, alternative energy vehicle, and aviation sectors. These cases highlight how firms use naturally-occurring and constructed interdependence in their alliances, as well as the dangers that come from over-compensating when constructing interdependence.

As Figure 3.3 shows, the cases are a study in contrasts. They provide examples of both horizontal and vertical alliances, and equity and non-equity-based relationships. The cases also illustrate the range of industries multiparty alliances are found in today: services, manufacturing-based high-technology, and non-manufacturing based high-technology, where

	EQUITY	NON-EQUITY
VERTICAL	Ballard- Daimler- Ford Microsoft non-PC	Microsoft in PC hardware / software
HORIZONTAL	Swissair - Qualiflyer	Airline industry in general

Figure 3.3   Overview of the Case Studies

network effects and standards are important. Of all the cases, Ballard's alliance is arguably the quintessential resource-dependent technology development alliance between a start-up and established firms, with some equity investment; it also contrasts the others in that it is pre-commercial and allows us to map the changes in power and interdependence over time.

4
Microsoft: Power and the Limits of Power

In the dark ages of computing, computer-makers were vertically integrated: a hardware firm, such as IBM, developed proprietary OSs and applications software, and sold it to the corporate customer. Since then, the computer industry has undergone two paradigm shifts – to personal computing, then networked computing – and is now transitioning to a third, based on devices that send and receive data.

The advent of the PC and Microsoft's approach to software as a product de-linked the hardware and software industries. As a result, the OS, rather than the hardware, became the platform for which applications software was written. As Microsoft's MS-DOS, and later, Windows, became the *de facto* industry standard, customers made buying decisions according to the OS; hardware became a commodity.

For individual users, the era of standalone computing gave way to networked computing. This was made possible when software firms developed 'middleware' and supported open standards to disintermediate the OS and applications software. The goal was to make users OS-agnostic, just as the OS had made users hardware agnostic. So, across the Internet, it became irrelevant whether a document was produced on a Microsoft Windows PC or Apple Macintosh platform. This, therefore, was a direct threat to Microsoft's core business, and the source of its influence over the industry's evolution.

Today, we are moving beyond connected computers to connected devices. The Internet, which was built on open standards, would be the platform and medium for these devices to communicate. The convergence of information and communications technologies (ICT), such as Internet-enabled mobile phones, e-mail capable personal digital assistants (PDAs), and on-line gaming, are a natural progression from communications between computers. Also being brought under this umbrella is 'content', the material which makes much of the communications valuable. These connections bring together a number of established industries with powerful incumbents jealously guarding their power. Interconnectivity is anticipated to move beyond deliberate human communications, to networked homes, for example, where a refrigerator might order groceries from the local store after doing inventory.

The case studies in this chapter are snapshots of an inflection point in the evolution of computing, and the challenges posed to the most central firm in that industry. With the emergence of technologies that threatened to make the OS irrelevant, Microsoft faced what Christensen terms an innovator's dilemma, and used its power over dependent partners in the computer and software industries to slow down the paradigm shift long enough to defend its position, and to try to co-opt the new technologies.

At the same time, Microsoft recognized that the next shift would follow rapidly, given the growth in Internet usage, more powerful microprocessors, greater communications bandwidths, proliferation of wireless technology and the rise of new models of e-commerce. It embraced the paradigm shift, using its financial resources to speed up the change, and establishing equity and non-equity alliances across a wide spectrum of industries to try to set the technological standards for the future of the Internet. It has introduced a wide range of Windows-based OS and server software for these technologies, including Microsoft TV, and Windows Mobile for PDAs and smartphones.

Why Microsoft?

The Microsoft cases provide valuable insights into why firms behave opportunistically or defect, the conditions under which they are able to do so, and highlight the limits to regulatory authorities' abilities to constrain power based on owning technology resources. It also illustrates how interdependence can be a tool to bind partners. In the PC-related industries, the other firms' natural dependence on Microsoft meant that there was no need to establish formal alliances; in contrast, formal alliances, sometimes cemented by equity, are the rule in the new convergence industries.

From its inception, Microsoft has been one of the industry's most formidable competitors. Its success rests in Bill Gates' business acumen – being the first to recognize that software had value and moving to a licensing model,[1] rather than on technological superiority. In fact, many major technology features, such as the graphical user interface, and even today's browser and media player, were pioneered by other companies. With Intel, Microsoft drove the pace of development in PCs, and in the process, eliminated the mini-computer industry.

Since 1988, Microsoft has been subject to a number of antitrust investigations, but it was not until its business model was threatened by the new Internet technologies that concerns about its exercise of power over its partners spread beyond the computer industry. The PC-focussed cases and the Netscape one represent two points on the value chain on which defensive and pre-emptive battles were fought.

The Microsoft cases also furnish some of the clearest lessons of how power and interdependence changes over time, and the contextual nature of power. Juxtaposing its positions in the PC and non-PC arenas clearly illustrate the relevance of power and interdependence to a firm's ability to influence a partner's decision to cooperate, compete, behave opportunistically or defect, and show how dependence can force firms to act against their own interests, and against their customers' interests. In Microsoft's case, other firms' perceptions of its power, combined with its reputation, created an environment where they recognized Microsoft's power and willingness to use it, and so do not act for fear of retaliation.

The Microsoft cases are important because of the implications for the future, not least for future competition between third party software which adds functionality to the PC and Microsoft's development of similar capabilities. Its relationships and management challenges exemplify some of the key themes in technology and knowledge-based industries, and the challenges to business strategy and government policy raised by the logic of network effects, the need for standards and industries characterized by increasing returns to scale. Even though the US Department of Justice (DoJ) won a landmark antitrust trial, labelling Microsoft a monopoly that had 'maintained its power by anti-competitive means',[2] it was a hollow victory: today, Internet Explorer (IE)'s market share is around 95 per cent. Nor has it deterred Microsoft from taking similar actions in other markets; in March 2004, the European Commission ruled that Microsoft unlawfully tied the Windows Media Player to the OS, a judgment which mirrors the US decision. Microsoft has also put search engines, and industry leader Google, in its sights, with plans to build a search engine into the next version of Windows. Additionally, having purchased an anti-virus software firm in 2003, there is speculation that eventually, it will add anti-virus capabilities to the OS.[3]

Influences on the firm's attitude

The key influences on firm behaviour in alliances in the ICT industries come from the industry environment, and from firm-specific priorities. Inter-alliance competitive factors will come into play as the market and technology for networked homes, interactive TV, and mobile handheld devices develop.

Intra-alliance factors are less relevant to these case studies. Microsoft's relationships with other stakeholders in the PC arena are informal partnerships. Microsoft, the PC original equipment manufacturers (OEMs), ISVs, Internet service providers (ISPs), and Internet content providers (ICPs) are part of an ecosystem where innovations in one market stimulate demand throughout the industry: a new OS needs more powerful processors, which boosts PC sales, and creates an upgrade cycle for applications software.

Environment

Some of the most important factors affecting cooperation in the ICT industries are industry economics and technological change. ICT exemplify those industries whose underlying economics exhibit increasing returns:[4] they are characterized by high up-front costs, network effects (exemplified by products and services such as fax machines, text messaging or photo-capable phones whose value increases with the number of users), and customer lock-in because of switching costs.[5] In software development, for example, it may cost millions to write an applications programme and to produce the first set of disks, but the marginal cost of producing another unit shrinks to approximately zero. This gives the firm more resources to support future R&D or to compete on price with challengers.

In a world of increasing returns, the leaders' positions become more entrenched, resulting to a winner-take-all environment, where one firm establishes a dominant position that others may not have the technological or financial resources to challenge. The situation is more urgent in ICT, given the need for standards – proprietary or open – and interoperability: a win in one arena may be leveraged into related industries. For example, having an OS standard benefits ISVs, who do not have to develop multiple versions of their programmes; this, in turn, reinforces the original standard. This dynamic means that where there is already an industry leader, such as in the PC market, firms have little choice but to cooperate. But, in areas characterized by both technical and market uncertainty, alliances are more likely to break apart and new ones form as firms jockey to develop the strongest package of technologies and features, and as technologies prove themselves. Alliances will also fragment as standards get set, and firms move quickly to drop partners who support a losing technology.

Technological change is also important – when a disruptive technology is introduced, firms that recognize the threat may behave opportunistically to support the challenger in hopes of breaking the existing dynamic. This was certainly the case in the support for Internet standards and middleware, and in the support for the open-source Linux OS.

Having lost antitrust investigations in both the US and European Union (EU), it is tempting to conclude that Microsoft's behaviour would be affected by regulation. But, the legal process moves more slowly than changes in the facts on the ground, so that even though Microsoft lost, it is still victorious in the marketplace. But, the two judgments could lead to regulation by civil action as competitors and erstwhile partners turn on it. However, even this threat may be receding: in 2004, Microsoft settled long-standing civil suits with a number of rivals, including Sun Microsystems, Novell, and the Computer and Communications Industry Association. The trials' greatest ramifications may be that they embolden firms to overtly partner and support developments such as Java to change the environment by rendering OS level constraints irrelevant. Or, they may support an alternative OS, such as Linux, even as they recognize that the Windows infrastructure benefits them; Hewlett Packard (HP) and IBM have introduced Linux-based laptop computers.

Alliance-competitive environment

The importance of inter-alliance factors varies amongst the case studies. For example, since there are no viable alternatives to Microsoft's OS in the PC arena, there is no alliance level competition. In the browser wars, inter-alliance competition was for customers, but also for partners. Microsoft tried to entice firms to defect on Netscape by offering them positions on the desktop which could enhance their revenues further. Alliance-competitive factors do play a role in the new industry segments Microsoft is targeting, as the technology develops (or fails) and firms compete to set and block emerging standards.

Intra-alliance environment

As with more formal partnerships in the airlines and fuel cell industries, Microsoft's and its partners' positional interests are not congruent. Microsoft's goal is to protect the OS' position as the foundation on which software applications, and its own fortunes, are built. The other segments of the PC and software industry want to reduce the OS' importance, for example through middleware, and with it, their need to operate according to Microsoft's standards. Even in the alliances or coalitions established to hold back Microsoft's advance into new industries, the partners often compete to support their own vision of an open standard.

Firm-level

Firm level factors which influence a decision to cooperate or not focus on the relative returns from these decisions, and whether the firm has the resources to compete on its own. In the current environment, the need for a standard OS and to sell computers with the OS pre-installed means that OEMs cannot defect from Microsoft. On the other hand, they can defect from software and service providers whose products do not enhance their competitiveness. In technology development, an alliance's importance to a firm's strategic direction affects whether it cooperates or not. Given the extent of merger and acquisition activity amongst new economy companies, firms may acquire resources which render the alliance superfluous. With the uncertainties in new product and technology development, firms are also more likely to adopt a real options model, dropping partners when the shape of the market becomes clearer.

Power and interdependence

Power

What resources confer power in knowledge-based alliances? In terms of informal power, the most critical resource is technology, particularly if it is superior to other providers in the industry, or not replicable because it is protected by copyrights or patents. In other cases, it may be expertise in processes. But, other resources are also important. Reputation can be critical for firms whose technologies Microsoft supports, and deadly for those it does not, as investors may be reluctant to invest in technologies that compete with Microsoft, or which are in sectors that Microsoft may enter. Market share, or an installed base, and ownership of the customer is also important, which is why, when Microsoft had to play catch-up in the browser market, it pursued America Online (AOL) for its membership base. Finally, content is a source of power in new converged industries: even if Xbox is a technologically superior games device, it will not be adopted without a range of popular games.

Alliances in ICT are different from other technology-based alliances in biotechnology or even automobiles, in that standards are critical. Standards reduce development costs for complementary products, and allow software producers to benefit from increasing returns to scale, as well as allowing products to interoperate. The one element which may trump all others in conferring power to a firm is ownership of a proprietary standard, with the caveat that this must be at a key point in the value chain.

Moreover, setting a standard creates an applications barrier to entry by raising the customer's cost of switching to a different platform. The Office Suite of productivity applications gives Microsoft an additional source of informal power, because it is the dominant applications package. If it does not support a competing OS, users would not switch. Finally, the OS is important in its own right, as the Windows desktop is the most direct distribution channel to the end user.

In terms of formal power, most technology alliances have yet to establish formal infrastructures although they may have formalized decision making processes. Formal power resides in equity investments in partners. For example, many of Microsoft's alliances in broadband delivery, enhanced television, and mobile media are equity-based. But, interestingly, it is also in this area that Microsoft's partners were uncooperative, indicating that equity is not the ultimate source of power.

Unlike the airline industry, latent power, in terms of market capitalization, is usable in ICT industries, and partnerships often end in acquisitions,[6] particularly if a technology has been proven. A second, and perhaps more important source of latent power, is cash. Microsoft's cash reserves of some $40B means that it is not very sensitive to its partners' actions. It also allows it to acquire competing technologies or partners who develop technologies which strengthen its position, and give it the ability to absorb or recover from strategic mistakes. For example, even though it underestimated the importance of the Internet, it was able to catch up to Netscape within six months.

Interdependence

Although Microsoft has hegemonic power in the PC industry, its relationships with OEMs, and ISVs are still interdependent because its partners also contribute valuable resources. These parties are part of a virtuous circle: the Windows standard encourages more ISVs to write software to it, which in turn enhances Windows' value. Although OEMs need Microsoft's OS to sell their product, Microsoft also depends on them to be its primary distribution chain. And, although an individual OEM's defection is not likely to hurt Microsoft, a coordinated response has the potential to. However, the relationships are unequal because the OEMs face a classic coordination problem in their desire to weaken Microsoft's hold over them. Microsoft's natural and constructed interdependence with its partners as it tries to extend its operations into non-computer Internet-capable products is much more obvious, as they clearly possess resources which Microsoft cannot replicate, or perhaps even purchase, given the size of some of the firms.

Measuring interdependence in Microsoft's alliances must take into account the nature and depth of the relationship, and extent of integration. To what extent is the relationship based on technological needs vs marketing and distribution? To what extent are the technologies asset-specific? Applications software is extremely asset-specific, as it is written to an OS, just as an OS is tailored to specific processors. However, where standards are necessary, the extent of interdependence between firms differs depending on whether a standard is proprietary or open. Interdependence is also affected by a firm's ability to protect its resource from being appropriated, and whether it can leverage a partner's contribution into other lines of business.

Microsoft in the PC market: exercising power

The consumer PC business is comprised of a set of firms bound by technical relationships which bring complementary resources that add value for the end user. As Figure 4.1 illustrates, to build the PC, OEMs work with microprocessor providers, traditionally Intel, and Microsoft for the OS. But, since PCs are commodity products, differentiation largely depends on the software features the OEM adds. These include functionality applications, such as Internet capability, which have become a core offering, and others include antivirus software, and in some cases, even productivity software such as word-processing and spreadsheet programmes.

In essence, the PC value chain comprises of two sets of partnerships: one in hardware development, where the OEMs rely on Microsoft and Intel to provide them with the key technological resources; and a second in the OEMs' relationships with software and content providers to differentiate their products.

These firms are also bound by technology. OSs are analogous to a central nervous system; they are the layer between the computer

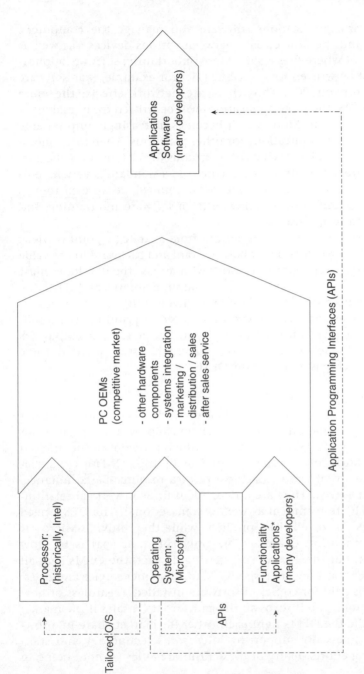

Figure 4.1 Relationships Amongst the PC Hardware and Software Industries

*functionality applications include critical software products such as browsers, media players

------- Technology Relationship

Application Programming Interfaces (APIs)

Applications
Software
(many developers)

PC OEMs
(competitive market)

- other hardware
  components
- systems integration
- marketing /
  distribution / sales
- after sales service

Processor:
(historically, Intel)

Operating
System:
(Microsoft)

Functionality
Applications*
(many developers)

Tailored O/S

APIs

hardware and applications software and manage the computer's processes and the flow of data between various devices,[7] as well as keep track of where files reside. More importantly, software applications must be written for a specific OS – for example, Mac software does not run on PCs. Thus there are network effects: the more popular an OS, the more applications will be written for it, making it even more popular. Moreover, it becomes increasingly unprofitable for ISVs to write applications for other platforms. Therefore, once a market tips toward a specific OS, a virtuous (or vicious) cycle begins, quickly entrenching its position. Once set, a standard is very hard to dislodge, even if a superior product is developed, because customers would have significant switching costs for software and training, and face a dearth of applications.

Control of the OS is also important from a strategic point of view, since it gives the owner power both forward and backward in the value chain. In order for software to work with an OS, the developer must provide ISVs with application programming interfaces (APIs), the synapses which allow the application to invoke software commands in the OS, such as displaying text on the screen or printing. As a result, ISVs are dependent on the OS-developer. By the same token, an OS also needs to be tailored to each microprocessor, without these changes, the chip is useless to the OEMs.

PC industry

The core of Microsoft's business is the Windows OS, and its success rests on a constellation of bilateral relationships with microprocessor developers, OEMs, ISVs and retailers, which grew out of the original IBM-Intel-Microsoft partnership to develop the PC. This constellation has many of the characteristics of a resource-based alliance, albeit with a twist. They are independent firms in vertical relationships which are technical as well as transactional. The OEMs need Microsoft's OS to sell their product, while they provide Microsoft with a distribution channel. The only common goal is to grow the market, but there is no risk-sharing. In fact, the OEMs bear all the downside, as they are responsible for customer service enquiries. Microsoft is paid for copies of software installed, regardless of how many PCs sold, and it reaps all the gains from OS sales if the market grows, while the OEMs fight each other for market share in a low-margin business. By supporting Microsoft's technology and standard-setting efforts, many of these firms are allies without being in an alliance.

Power

In the PC-related industries' ecosystem, power is a function of the type and importance of the resources contributed, industry structure, and whether formal sources of power exist.

The OEM PC makers' resource contribution is systems integration of hardware and, increasingly, software. Their value to Microsoft and Intel are as their primary distribution channels. Individually, their power is a function of their share of the PC market. They are also the primary distribution channel for some types of software applications, and a particularly important resource for ISVs and ICPs whose software is pre-installed, because this will likely take a sale away from a competitor. Finally, the OEMs are also the front-line customer service provider for hardware and software problems.

The microprocessor developers, historically Intel, provide a critical technology resource. The processor is the engine on which the OEMs build their platforms, and a key competitive resource. Intel successfully educated consumers that 'faster is better': the processor became more valuable than the box which housed it, giving Intel leverage over the OEMs. Thus, its contribution became not only technology, but also legitimacy. Intel's other contribution is to bring OEMs repeat sales, particularly of higher-end PCs, by continuously obsolescing current generations of chips. So long as microprocessor developers competed on functionality, defined as processing speed, Intel's position was extremely powerful, as there were few substitutes for its product. However, the demand for low-end PCs indicates that customers may have realized that even the most basic PC has all the capabilities they need. If so, then this type of technology lead may no longer contribute as much to a firm's power in the industry.

Microsoft provides the other critical technology resource. The OS is the technological link between the rest of the actors in the ecosystem. Its power lies in both its position on the value chain, and the fact that it owns a proprietary standard, and therefore the power to license ... or not. Microsoft's power is also a function of industry factors – while it is a monopoly, the other segments on the value chain are competitive markets. So, even if those segments provide critical resources to Microsoft, their fragmented markets do not allow them to use their leverage against it.

In its relations with ISVs, Microsoft has both informal and latent power. The informal power derives from their technological relationship, and in particular, the fact that it owns the APIs required to make the ISVs software work on Windows. Thus, Microsoft could use delay to good effect, treating cooperative firms better. The fear that competitors would gain an advantage creates an incentive for ISVs to cooperate. Microsoft's role as an applications developer enhances its informal power. Its products compete with the ISVs', and are a means to retaliate against uncooperative firms. Moreover, the ISVs' product may be at a disadvantage: Microsoft's applications are likely to work better on Windows since the developers can access the source code and they understand the OS' idiosyncrasies.

ISVs provide the value-added to owning a PC; the PC market would be much smaller if the only applications available were word-processing and spreadsheet programmes, instead of everything from road atlases, to education, to hobbies, to games. As a result, one of the resources it provides is support for the Windows standard, since the sheer volume of Windows-based applications help create an applications barrier to entry for any competing OS.

ISVs also provide the resources that allow OEMs to differentiate themselves, although these tend not to be expensive applications software such as office productivity packages, which are sold by retailers. This, however, may change – IBM distributes Lotus SmartSuite (which it owns), Dell bundled Corel WordPerfect Office, and Dell and Gateway bundled Office XP on some machines. As a group, ISVs do not have significant power over the OEMs, since the OEMs decide which features its customers would value. Individually, some ISVs have more power; for example, if an OEM wants to pre-install a particularly popular application, the ISV may be able to negotiate a higher licensing fee.

Browser developers and ISPs provide critical service resources, as features such as video players are becoming an expected part of a PC's functionality. For the ISPs, OEMs are critical because users are far more likely to choose a provider that is pre-installed and prominent on the desktop; Microsoft's own research found that 60 per cent of users did not download because it was too time-consuming.[8] Moreover, paying an OEM to pre-install its software is much less expensive and more successful than alternative means of distribution, such as 'carpet bombing' by distributing disks to every home. However, OEMs want their customers to have a choice of ISPs, so are unlikely to give any one exclusive rights.

Despite a complex web of relationships, Microsoft remains the most powerful actor in the OEMs' alliances, with Intel holding second place. Although the OEMs have technological relationships with ISVs, ISPs, and ICPs, which require them to integrate their software onto their

PCs, there is no asset specificity. Nor is the technology critical; the core of their relationships is a contractual agreement to distribute product. On the other hand, all the software, content, and processor providers have a technological relationship with Microsoft, and depend on Microsoft to provide APIs or to tailor the OS so that their products are even usable. Latent power, however, is much more spread out. Microsoft, Intel, and the OEMs tend to be larger than the ISVs, ISPs, and ICPs, and thus possess the power to acquire or develop the resources to compete.

Interdependence

The complex web of technical and commercial relationships between the various parts of the PC industry show how interdependent these industries are in supporting innovation and growth. However, the picture is very different at the firm level. Here, Microsoft is powerful and independent, due to the OS' critical function and to its financial strength.

Microsoft, Intel, the OEMs and ISVs are naturally interdependent along several dimensions: technology, position on the value chain, and in support of each other's markets. In this set of relationships, Microsoft is less sensitive and vulnerable, and the relationships are asymmetrical in its favour. There is significant asset-specificity as applications are written for an OS, which in turn needs to be tailored to specific processors. From the OEM's point of view, aside from Intel and Microsoft, who provide mission-critical resources, the other partners' role is to help them differentiate themselves, but with no expectation of exclusivity. Partners are expected to contribute unique resources, so that the OEMs do not waste finite storage space, or expend additional resources to test features.

Microsoft's relationships

In the Microsoft-OEM relationship, both parties are sensitive to the other's actions. Defection, for example, has an immediate revenue effect: Microsoft would lose the licensing revenue, and the OEM would not be able to sell its PCs without Windows. The impact would depend on whether the OEM had other sources of revenue, and the percentage of sales the OEM accounted for. But the two differ significantly in terms of their vulnerability, despite the fact that OEMs are Microsoft's primary distribution channel. Just as Intel successfully grabbed consumer mindshare with its 'Intel Inside' campaign, the latest version of Windows is what consumers look for. So, the OEM is vulnerable in that its customers would likely switch to competitors who have the relevant Microsoft product.

The relationship between Microsoft and the OEMs is heavily weighted in Microsoft's favour. In terms of firm-specific factors, the resources Microsoft brings to each individual OEM is critical to their ability to sell PCs, whereas no single OEM is critical to Microsoft's ability to achieve its goals. Microsoft is also the less dependent party according to relationship-specific factors. While Microsoft's relationship with the OEMs is contractual, the OEM's relationship is both contractual and technological. However, many of the OEMs have other activities which impact Microsoft's ambitions to extend Windows to both higher end computers and in Internet-enabled devices. These firms may be able to tilt the balance of dependence a little bit in their favour, since their decisions will affect whether Microsoft is able to set standards in these other arenas.

The microprocessor developers have a direct relationship with Microsoft since the OS needs to be tailored to each processor; this relationship is symbiotic since product improvements underlie the software upgrade cycle. By continuously improving processing power, Intel allows Microsoft and the ISVs to introduce greater functionality to their applications. Without this additional power, software innovations would simply degrade the PC's performance, as anyone who has upgraded an OS on an old PC has found.

The ISVs' relationships with Microsoft are primarily technical as they depend on Microsoft's APIs to make their programmes work on the Windows platform. Thus, they are both sensitive and vulnerable; they need to receive APIs in a timely manner, in order to release new versions of their products simultaneously with new Windows releases, since old versions of their software will not work with the new OS.

OEMs' relationships
In the relationship between the OEMs and ISVs, the ISV is more sensitive in that there is an immediate revenue effect if the OEM exits. The magnitude of the impact, however, will depend on the percentage of sales that OEM accounts for. For OEMs, the revenue effect is likely negligible, since customers are unlikely to make purchasing decisions based on a single feature. As a result, they are not vulnerable, but will still have search and switching costs, such as testing to ensure that any changes in features do not destabilize the system. Those ISVs who rely on OEMs to be their distribution channel are vulnerable to the OEMs' actions; if the OEM did not include its product, it may recoup some of

the losses through retail sales, but if it has been replaced, then the size of its market has effectively been shrunk unless customers have a compelling reason to buy its software.

The OEM is sensitive and vulnerable to the processor developer on both firm- and relationship-specific factors. A processor supplier such as Intel brings a vital and unique resource, so long as other chip-makers have not matched its technology's performance. Thus, not only would Intel's defection have an immediate revenue effect, in that the OEM may not have an alternate chip immediately, it may suffer further in terms of long-term competitive advantage if the substitute cannot match its performance. In addition, the OEMs' PCs are designed around a certain chip's characteristics, and thus there is asset-specificity on the OEM's part which increases its switching costs. The processor developer is sensitive to an OEM's defection, but may not be vulnerable. For Intel, if consumers base their purchasing decision on whether it is 'Intel Inside', losses in revenues may be made up by its other OEM partners. So long as it stays ahead of the competition and thus capitalizes on temporary monopolies in a performance standard, it retains its value to the OEMs.

On the other hand, an ISP is more vulnerable to the OEM than vice versa, particularly as OEMs may provide a choice of ISPs. Thus, an ISP which has been dropped will be reaching a smaller potential market; its vulnerability is a function of the OEM's market share.

Ultimately, however, except for the retailer, all of the firms in the PC ecosystem are vulnerable to Microsoft for firm- and relationship-specific reasons. Windows is both unique and vital to each of these parties' ability to sell. Regardless of the firms' internal capabilities, there is no substitute for Microsoft in the PC market. They are also vulnerable due to the nature of their technical relationships: the ISPs, ICPs, and ISVs, for example, need Microsoft's APIs, and many use Microsoft's developer tools to help them write software more efficiently. But, since intellectual property restrictions on these tools limit their ability to re-use chunks of software to port an application to other platforms, resource-limited ISVs do not bother, reinforcing their dependence on the Windows environment.

Behaviours

Microsoft's constellation of relationships in the PC and related industries are inherently competitive. But, given the preponderance of power on Microsoft's part, there is not much room for OEMs or ISVs to behave opportunistically or defect. In fact, the opposite may be true:

Compaq became a *Frontline Partner*, which gave it a lower licensing fee for the OS and more support from Microsoft, and hopefully, a competitive edge. On the other hand, IBM tried to break Microsoft's hold over PC OSs with its rival OS/2. This attempt failed miserably, despite hundreds of millions of dollars in development and marketing.[9] Such was Windows' importance that IBM could not risk selling PCs with only OS/2; instead, it gave the customer a choice, installing both OS/2 and Windows.[10] No other OEM has tried to defect from the Windows standard, though some are behaving opportunistically by supporting open source Linux systems.

Microsoft has behaved opportunistically toward its partners to protect Windows' dominant position. IBM testified that Microsoft offered to lower its licensing fees on Windows 95 by some $8 per copy if it would 'reduce, drop or eliminate OS/2', which would have saved it about $48M,[11] and that after it refused, Microsoft did not return telephone calls, and stalled the negotiations on the new Windows 95 license. IBM received its license minutes before the product launch, and missed out on the critical back-to-school sales season.

The antitrust trial also shattered some myths about Microsoft's relationship with Intel, which had been viewed as a cooperative venture to profit at the OEMs' expenses.[12] Intel's software unit had developed Native Signal Processing (NSP) software, which could be embedded in its chips to enhance the PC's multimedia capabilities. This would allow it to bypass Microsoft and establish a direct relationship with the software community, since ISVs could write software to the NSP. Intel executive, Steve McGeady, testified that the two firms clashed over NSP and Intel's support for Netscape and Sun Microsystem's Java language. Bill Gates pushed Intel to halt the NSP initiative, asserting that '"we are the software company here and we will not have any kind of equal relationship with Intel on software"',[13] and questioned why Intel had a software group whose work was detrimental to Microsoft. Microsoft threatened not to support Intel's next-generation Merced processor, and announced that it would work with DEC on its rival Alpha chip. Ultimately, Intel stopped work on NSP and shut down the offending business unit. Perhaps more significantly, Microsoft succeeded in pressuring OEMs to withdraw support from NSP, showing clearly that its relative position is strong enough that it can force OEMs to choose between two critical resource providers.[14]

Microsoft was also able to impel OEMs to take actions contrary to their own financial interests. It introduced provisions in licensing agreements prohibiting OEMs from modifying the start-up sequence,[15] arguing that all users should have a uniform Windows experience. As a result, Microsoft could guarantee that its products, such as IE and the MSN service, would be seen by the end user, and that competing products would be hidden. This provision took away the OEMs' ability to differentiate themselves, or to make the PC more user-friendly. For example, after HP reverted to the standard Windows 95 boot-up sequence, its service calls increased by 10 per cent, one-third of which were Windows issues. HP concluded that if it had a choice, it would not use Microsoft's OS.[16] IBM faced similar problems when a revised Windows contract prohibited it from displaying a welcome screen its research had shown would help novice users.[17] Compaq, a Frontline Partner, had to withdraw a video orientation demonstrating the PC's features.[18]

Many ISVs have tried to reduce their dependence on Microsoft. These include supporting efforts to reduce the OS' centrality by introducing middleware or even alternative OSs, in the case of Linux. However, these attempts have often proved futile; without critical mass, they still need to produce Windows-based products, and thus remain sensitive to Microsoft's actions.

The Java technology/programming language presents one such challenge. It allows users to run Java-based applications on computers with a 'Java virtual machine' (JVM), an intermediate layer that interacts with the computer's OS. The OS treats the JVM like a software application; Java-based applications treat it like an OS.[19] The Java challenge is led by Sun Microsystems, a computer company focused on high-end workstations and networked corporate systems; its focus on Java and the goal to make software platform-independent is a pre-emptive strike against Microsoft's attempt to bring Windows into the higher-end computing sphere, which would allow interoperability between hardware platforms on Microsoft's terms. It was supported by IBM, Compaq, Oracle, and Cisco, amongst others, which contributed some $100M to a Java Fund to help start-up firms that wanted to adopt Java.[20]

The Netscape challenge

Microsoft's ability to use power to overcome strategic errors is most evident in its response to Netscape and the rise of the Internet. Microsoft used its financial resources to acquire a necessary technology and destroy Netscape's revenue stream by offering its IE web browser for free, forcing Netscape to give away its Navigator as well, then use its informal and formal power over OEMs, ISVs, and ICPs to recover from its second-mover disadvantage. This case focuses on the consumer business, and ignores corporate intranets, servers, web-authoring tools, or tools to build Web storefronts[21] since these products' sales are corelated with the browser's success.

Netscape was a special category of ISV; the Navigator browser is middleware, both an application and a platform from which other applications can be launched.[22] Netscape also embraced open standards, adopting those set by vendor-neutral bodies,[23] albeit embedding proprietary elements into their products. Therefore, Navigator challenged Windows' hold over the PC industry, since applications launched from the browser would be OS-neutral. The rise of web-based computing that Netscape embodied challenged the foundation of Microsoft's business model, which was based on establishing a proprietary standard in a linchpin technology, capturing the bulk of the value, and reaping the benefits of being able to set the pace of technological change.

If browser makers were to displace Windows, they needed to dominate the market in order to set new standards. To do so, they needed a network of distributors and complementary products. As Netscape founder Marc Andreesen observed, Microsoft taught that, '"If you get ubiquity, you have a lot of options.... You can get paid by the product that you are ubiquitous on... [and] on products that benefit as a result.... market share now equals revenue later...."'[24] The most efficient means of achieving this was to pre-install the product on a PC, preferably as the default browser.

Thus, Navigator and IE sit at the centre of a constellation of partners with whom their relationships are primarily distributional, although there is also a technical element through their use of authoring tools. There is no overarching alliance-specific goal, except a desire on the Netscape coalition's part to prevent Microsoft from setting proprietary standards for the Internet.[25] Netscape and Microsoft sought to maximize their distributors in order to gain market share.

Power

Although the browser developer provides technology, in the race to set new standards, power resides in those who bring market share.

The browser developer brings a critical technological contribution its partners. OEMs, for example, needed to introduce Internet-ready products. It was also a critical resource for ISPs and ICPs, whose businesses are Internet-based. Online services such as AOL, Compuserve, and even Microsoft's MSN, recognized that proprietary networks no longer sufficed, and became ISPs instead. For them, a browser is part of the package they need in order to deliver their services. For ICPs, the browser is the platform on which their technology or services are based, and the developer supplies the tools they need to create content and applications that work with the browser, although open standards made this less of a challenge. But, the browser is not limited to providing a technological resource: the developer's website also acts as a marketing/distribution channel.

The OEMs, ISVs, ISPs and ICPs' contributions lie primarily in distribution and marketing: including the software on a disk; adding the browser to an application's installation; providing a link through 'download now' buttons; making it a default browser which loads when the user connects to the Internet; or pre-installing it on a PC with its icon on the desktop. In addition, ICPs could push users toward certain browsers if their websites have features that are only available for these. A partner's value to the browser developer, therefore, varies according to its market share: for example, the top 15 ISPs in the US accounted for 91 per cent of all subscribers, and AOL alone accounted for nearly 50 per cent.[26] When AOL switched to IE, it took market share directly from Navigator's installed base, and may have blocked it from setting a standard.

OSs developers also play a role, since the browser connects through APIs, like other software. Netscape's browser development proceeded on three parallel tracks: UNIX, Macintosh and Windows platforms. Microsoft's IE was originally developed for Windows 95, and later ported to Macintosh, UNIX and Windows NT.

Thus, Netscape's unique and valuable contribution to its partners, in conjunction with Sun's Java technologies, was an opportunity to break free from the need to port applications to different platforms. Moreover, Netscape offered them the potential of a software environment based on open standards, issuing an *Open Standards Guarantee* (June 1997),[27] and publishing its innovations and extensions to existing standards. However, Netscape's challenge was blunted by the fact that it had a technical relationship with Microsoft. Moreover, despite treating the browser as a separate business, Microsoft's presence as an OS provider cannot be ignored since the browser's partners also depended on Microsoft's APIs.

Interdependence

The ISPs, ISVs, ICPs, OEMs and the OSs are interdependent because they provide resources which enhance each others' competitiveness. While the use of open standards theoretically eliminates asset specificity, it has not prevented browser developers from building-in proprietary elements, since they also sell software tools to build websites or develop applications. Thus, at some level, there is asset specificity if web pages or plug-ins are optimized for a specific browser. In the background, however, there is a second layer of relationships, technical dependencies between the ISPs, ISVs, OEMs and Microsoft in their non-Internet applications.

Because Netscape and Microsoft provide technology resources, on paper, they should be less dependent. But, in a two-party competition for market share, their partners have an alternative. So, partners with market share, an efficient distribution model, and access to the end user are more valuable. Moreover, if we look beyond the browser, Netscape and Microsoft can leverage their position in the browser market into their other lines of business, making them even more dependent on their partners. This was critical for Netscape, whose other businesses were all web-dependent, and revenue-generating. However, it is also extremely important for Microsoft, as IE became the tool through which it protected its core asset, Windows.

Browser developers are sensitive and vulnerable to their partners' actions; in a winner-take-all industry, defections may tip the market toward their competitor. Although the browser was free for the end user, the inter-firm relationships have revenue implications, arising from licensing, or renting out prominent positions on the desktop. Sensitivity is a function of both the type of distribution (i.e. the method's efficacy) and the partner's market share. They are more sensitive to partners who guarantee additional users, such as ISPs which set a default browser.

An ISV or ISP may be sensitive to a browser developer's actions if they have developed a closer technical relationship, as AOL did with IE, which created asset specificity. Finally, there may also be revenue-based relationships between browsers and ICPs and ISPs, which link their homepages to the content or service providers' websites.

Although sensitivity interdependence may not be significant, it is fair to say that there is a greater degree of vulnerability, particularly for the browser developers whose non-browser revenues are a function of their market share. For example, Netscape's *Netcenter* and other ICPs link users to affiliated retailers, search engines, and information sources, generating revenues from 'click throughs'. In this advertising model, the greater the viewership, the more the channel provider can charge for its space. Moreover, the browser's success or failure affects other parts of its business, such as the web server and corporate intranet markets, and its ability to set standards. For example, when Netscape was the only choice, it could introduce extensions to existing standards which the other firms would adapt. However, with the rise of IE, and Microsoft's challenge to Sun's Java language, other firms have been faced with the dilemma of choosing which browser to optimize their web pages for.

ICPs can become dependent on the browser providers. For example, Intuit wanted Microsoft and Netscape to develop customized versions of their browsers for its Quicken software.[28] There is also some asset specificity on the ISVs, ICPs and ISPs' parts where they have invested in learning to use the developer tools. Additionally, as the browser becomes the platform for web-based applications, they depend on the browser developers (and other ISVs) to build in greater functionality. However, the extent of dependence is not nearly as great as in their comparable relationship with the OS.

Behaviour

If we compare Navigator and IE's positions, we find that they faced the same challenges. But, looking beyond the browser's partners, we find a key difference deriving from Microsoft's latent power, which comes from three sources. The first is financial resources. Once Bill Gates set his sights on the Internet, Microsoft established an *Internet Platform and Tools* division with 2,500 staff, and caught up to Netscape within months. Microsoft could afford to give away IE and the web server, and granted royalty-free distribution rights to IE.[29] AOL executive David Colburn testified that Microsoft had 'no limitations on what it could spend to gain market share for Internet Explorer'.[30] In contrast, Netscape's web servers and browsers were supposed to be sources of revenue.

Microsoft's latent power also comes from the technical and commercial relationship that OEMS, ISVs, and ISPs have with its OS business. Microsoft could exert pressure on firms in the browser market, particularly as the OEMs *must* have an OS to sell PCs, and ISVs also needed its APIs. Microsoft could assert ownership over the desktop to block the OEMs' relationships with Netscape. Moreover, even Netscape depended on Microsoft to provide APIs so that Navigator would work on Windows platforms. Indeed, the DoJ alleged that Microsoft withheld Windows 95 APIs from Netscape for three months in an attempt to coerce it into dividing the market.[31]

If the most efficient means of distributing any software is pre-installation, then the most direct route is through the OS, instead of negotiating with OEMs, ISVs, ICPs or ISPs. Thus, Microsoft has a built-

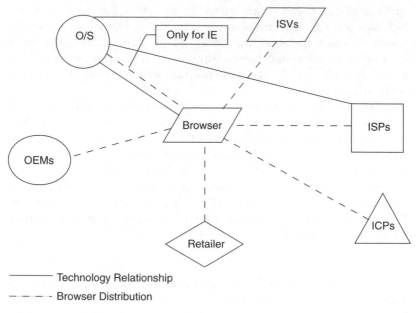

——————— Technology Relationship

— — — - Browser Distribution

Figure 4.2   Internet Browser Relationships

in advantage; Netscape had to adopt more expensive and inefficient distribution methods. In addition, distribution is a two-way street: once Microsoft asserted ownership over the desktop's 'look and feel', it could offer to be the distribution channel for the ISVs, ISPs, and ICPs, a valuable commodity that no other firm in the industry could provide.[32] It blocked OEMs from disadvantaging IE's position on the desktop through licensing restrictions. Moreover, it added features which disadvantaged Navigator. For example, the *Active Desktop* let users access the Internet directly, or link to a website from the Desktop without opening the browser separately. Microsoft promoted its partners by placing their icons onto a channel bar, which had categories such as news, technology, and entertainment, leaving one sub-channel for the OEMs' customer service links.

Therefore, Microsoft's latent power derives from size, its position on the value chain, and the nature of its OS business' relationship with the browser partners, all resources Netscape did not possess. This latent power changed the measures of power and interdependence between IE and the other parties in Microsoft's favour because it could use the OS as leverage. Moreover, it still had the ability to punish and to acquire, and more significantly, impel its partners to behave opportunistically or defect on third parties.

- Compaq Computers.[33] The DoJ investigation was sparked when Netscape's President & Chief Executive Officer (CEO), Jim Barksdale, alleged that Microsoft threatened to cancel Compaq's Windows 95 license over its use of Netscape. Compaq had pre-existing agreements with Netscape and AOL which generated millions in revenues: it placed Netscape's icon on the desktop and removed IE, and promoted AOL, removing MSN from the desktop. In 1996, Microsoft threatened to cancel Compaq's Windows 95 license unless it restored the MSN and IE icons within 30 days. Despite concerns within Compaq that compliance would violate the other contracts, it acquiesced, partly since Microsoft started placing greater emphasis on its relationships with HP and DEC, and downplaying its Frontline partnership with Compaq.
- Intuit.[34] In 1996, Intuit replaced Navigator with IE. Although Microsoft claimed that this was because it developed a customized browser for Intuit's Quicken product, Intuit's President & CEO testified that they preferred Netscape, who did not produce competing products (Microsoft had *Microsoft Money*). Intuit adopted IE because Microsoft would place its Internet-based products on the Windows Active Desktop, and distribute 1 MB of code for its software products. These terms were conditioned on Intuit foregoing business relationships with Netscape, and abrogating its pre-existing promotion and distribution agreement. Intuit agreed so as to keep up with competing financial websites. The *Active Desktop Agreement* prohibited Intuit from promoting Netscape on its own website, from allowing its web site customers to access Netscape's products or services, and from distributing any other browser. Moreover, Intuit had to use Microsoft's proprietary web tools, which developed content that could only be viewed with IE. Microsoft waived some these exclusivity provisions in April 1998, due in part to the DoJ's investigation.
- AOL.[35] AOL's case clearly illustrates how ownership of Windows became a weapon in the battle over Internet technologies. As an ISP, AOL developed Internet connection software for both the Windows and Macintosh platforms and needed a cross-platform browser. AOL determined that its internal browser development efforts were not economically feasible, and signed an agreement with Netscape in 1996 for it to develop a componentized browser that would be integrated into AOL's software.

One day later, AOL signed a browser agreement with Microsoft, making IE its default browser. Microsoft would distribute AOL's software with Windows 95, placing it in a new *Online Services* folder on the desktop. This folder placed Microsoft's MSN service's competitors within its customers' reach, sacrificing its advantage. AOL won this concession because its share of the ISP market gave it the potential to hinder IE's growth.

AOL allowed itself to be bound because it believed that it needed to be on the desktop to compete with MSN. AOL agreed that: it would not ship any other browser; IE had to represent at least 85 per cent of the browsers distributed; and AOL would not distribute, promote or advertise Netscape, even after Netscape became a distributor for AOL's instant messenger service.[36] Under a second agreement, Microsoft paid AOL $0.25 for every customer converted to IE, along with a $600,000 bonus if a certain percentage were switched by an agreed date. In 1997, AOL agreed to further restrictions on its ability to promote or distribute other browsers in return for a place on Microsoft's new *Channel Bar*, which devalued the Online Services folder. Microsoft later added an *Internet Connection Wizard*, a feature which would launch until the user chose an ISP from Microsoft's *Internet Referral Server*.[37] As this feature devalued the Online Services folder further, AOL signed up again so as not to be left behind. AOL abided by the exclusivity provisions even after the 1996 agreement expired to guarantee its place on the Windows desktop. As a result, IE became so entrenched that AOL continued to distribute IE even after it acquired Netscape in 1998.

- Apple.[38] Apple and Microsoft have been long-time rivals, with Apple pioneering many of the innovations found in Windows, such as the graphical user interface and mouse. Unlike the other firms in this analysis, Apple is not tied to Windows. In order to co-opt it in its Internet battle, Microsoft used another source of latent power: ownership of the most popular Mac-based productivity application, the Mac Office Suite, and the fact that Microsoft was the largest software applications developer for the Mac environment. In 1996, Apple shipped its Mac OS with IE, but Navigator was the default browser. In MacOS 8.0, IE's position was upgraded; both IE and Navigator were placed in a folder on the desktop, although Navigator was the default browser. Apple testified that Gates was angry that IE was not the default browser, and in May 1997, Microsoft threatened to stop developing Mac Office 97, even though a beta version had already been completed, unless the browser dispute was resolved to its satisfaction. As Apple was in not in a strong financial position, losing its major productivity application would have had dire consequences. Apple agreed to bundle IE on all Macintosh computers and the Mac OS's for five years, and make IE the default browser; other browsers could only be put in a folder, not the desktop. In return, Microsoft promised to support Mac Office, provide a royalty-free browser for five years, and work with Apple on Java technologies.

• ICPs.[39] Microsoft recognized that ICPs could provide key resources in the battle to set Internet standards if they supported proprietary technologies such as ActiveX , instead of Java, and that, as the premier distribution channel, the Windows desktop was a source of leverage. Microsoft populated its Channel Bar, which OEMs could not remove, with several categories of partners: *Top Tier* partners were placed on the channel bar, and their icons linked users to their websites, while *Platinum* partners were placed under categories such as News & Technology, Business, or Sports. Microsoft promoted channel partners through the Internet link, in its public relations materials, at computer industry events, on its web site, and in some cases, allowed the ICP to include introductory material. The ICPs did not pay Microsoft for this marketing support, but had to distribute only IE, promote IE as their browser of choice, remove any links to Netscape's sites, and could not enter into agreements with rival browser developers where they paid money or other compensation to the developer to promote its content. The ICPs were also required to use Microsoft's Dynamic hyper-text mark-up language (HTML) and ActiveX technologies to build their websites, which hampered the industry's attempts to develop open standards. In some cases, they had to create differentiated content that could only be viewed with IE. Given the importance of being on the channel bar, when Microsoft demanded that Disney remove its brand from Netscape's user interface, Disney acceded even though it believed that this was beyond the scope of its agreement.

The analysis shows that the difference between IE and Navigator's positions lay in Microsoft's latent power. Although financial strength allowed Microsoft to recover from ignoring the Internet, this capability is not unique to it. What is unique is its other source of latent power: a proprietary OS standard that serves as the foundation for the hardware and software industries, and which allows Microsoft to reward firms that cooperate and punish those that do not. Partners placed on the desktop reaped significant savings on marketing and distribution, giving them an advantage over their competitors. Microsoft could also alter the OS' licensing terms to help its other businesses. Thus, the OS gave Microsoft a tool to compel its partners to take actions which benefited it, and a weapon to deter them from defecting.

In Microsoft's threats not to give IBM a license for Windows 95, to revoke Compaq's Windows license, and to cancel Mac Office 97, the negotiating environments were akin to a game of chicken between vastly uneven parties. But, in these cases, Microsoft was operating in an environment it dominated. As the Internet extends to communications and other new media technology, these other firms are not dependent on Microsoft's OS. Although it has financial resources at its disposal, the size differential between Microsoft and some of its new partners is much reduced. Moreover, its new partners learned lessons from the PC industry, and are determined not to let Microsoft develop the same position in their markets.

Microsoft and technology convergence: the limits of power

Once Microsoft recognized the Internet's potential impact on its business model, it acted to steer the direction of the change, but more importantly, looked beyond to embrace the next paradigm shift. It had a new mission statement, '"Empower people through great software, any place, any time, and on any device,"'[40] and a new goal: to be anywhere a user connects to the Internet. Gates' vision is make Windows the platform for these technologies, becoming the interface between different types of hardware, and, potentially, the channel through which consumers conduct online transactions. Microsoft introduced a .NET Platform of programming tools to create, deploy, manage and aggregate extensible markup language (XML)-based[41] web services.

The .NET strategy encompasses a wide range of technologies used to access the Internet, some of which could become the basis for networked homes. To pursue this strategy, Microsoft had to move beyond its traditional partners, and reach out to the communications, consumer product, entertainment and media, and even automobile industries, establishing alliances in a number of key markets. It has also invested in several key areas: video games, enhanced television, and wireless devices and services. Part of this strategy is defensive. If technologies such as Java could threaten Windows in a PC environment, then they are a bigger threat in the development of connected, cross-platform technologies where Microsoft does not have a presence. However, these devices need standards to be interoperable. Microsoft, with its push into higher-end computing with Windows NT and server technologies, and on the other end, into hand-held devices, could bring all these strands together under its umbrella.

Microsoft's alliances in these new areas are traditional resource-based alliances, entailing risk-sharing to develop novel products or services, or finding new ways to achieve existing goals. In many cases, Microsoft is partnering with firms who may compete with it post-commercialization, or who are already competitors. In fact, some partners may become strategic threats as networked products spread beyond communications and IT to other consumer goods. Microsoft has recognized that there is little natural interdependence with these firms, and has constructed interdependence through formal alliances, and the use of equity.

Games

Microsoft's highest profile new product is the Xbox video-game console, its challenge to Sony's PlayStation and Nintendo's Gamecube in the $14B video-game market.[42] Xbox is essentially a powerful graphics-focussed computer with online capability, broadband capability for Internet gaming, and a hard drive so that users can download upgrades to existing games, and ultimately purchase new games.

However, the real significance of such systems are their potential to be a platform for smart appliances in networked homes. Since 2001, Microsoft has invested billions to develop Xbox. Such is the importance of this market, that Microsoft is willing to absorb significant short-term losses; its *2003 Annual Report* indicated that the Home & Entertainment divisions (which also includes consumer software and hardware, PC games, and its TV platform), lost almost $1.8B over two years. Losses from Xbox are estimated to be some $2.4B over two years.[43] Microsoft is not the only firm to recognize the console's potential. Sony, which had established a partnership with Microsoft to develop hardware and software for multimedia devices, rebuffed its offer to develop the OS for PlayStation. Instead, it partnered with AOL, RealNetworks, and Macromedia for e-mail and other online services, and with Cisco Systems, Sun Microsystems and IBM to set open standards for Internet gaming.[44]

Although the Xbox has three times the processing power as the PlayStation 2 or GameCube, content is the determining factor in this market, giving established players with significant games catalogues and established games franchises an advantage. Microsoft also faces the problems of economies of scale in games development, given its smaller user base. Just as ISVs are reluctant to write software for non-Windows environments, it will be more costly for developers to produce Xbox games unless it develops a large market very quickly.

Although Microsoft develops games internally, it also relies on partners in the entertainment and gaming industries. These include a joint venture with film-studio DreamWorks SKG to develop interactive games and other entertainment products, giving Microsoft exclusive rights to some games. Other key partners include veteran games-maker, Sega, which will develop games for it, and work with it on broadband online gaming. Interestingly, gaming giant Electronic Arts refuses to work with Microsoft on online games, due to Xbox Live's licensing model,[45] although it does produce packaged games for it. Thus, Microsoft's primary contribution is the hardware and OS while its partners bring valuable content. While a technologically advanced console gives games developers more scope for their imaginations, Microsoft's resource is not unique, and could be matched by its competitors. But, if the trend is toward connectivity, it may have an advantage over its rivals, as it already has internal capabilities in online services, and multimedia software for audio and video files downloaded off the Internet.

In measuring power and interdependence, size is not a critical factor, since creativity, along with a good sense of what the audience wants, is the key. Microsoft is sensitive to its partners' actions, since Xbox's popularity depends on the availability of hit games and available titles, but not very vulnerable, because of its financial strength. Games-developers are likely to be less dependent on Microsoft because many of them are industry leaders whose products are in demand. Microsoft can reduce its dependence on its partners only if it is able to develop a stable of hits internally, and thereby rely on its partners to broaden its portfolio instead of relying on them to provide the major pull. The movie industry has demonstrated that even 'sure hits' fail at the box office, affecting the popularity of related licensed products. Microsoft's sources of firm power are not as instrumental in the games industry. Absent buying a major games developer, latent power cannot buy market share. Gamers simply want cool products.

Interactive TV

Interactive TV is a much hyped technology that has yet to achieve its commercial potential. Broadly defined, interactive TV lets viewers 'influence, control, and communicate the form and content of their entertainment', and access the Internet. Technologies include: digital video records, integrated TVs, cable set-top TVs, retail set-top netTVs, and satellite/direct broadcast satellite net TVs.[46] Interactive TV encompasses a range of activities including: content; technologies to convert data; a communications layer; and a device layer requiring hardware and an OS. It is driven by two value chains: one for formatting content and the broadcast infrastructure, including developer tools, middleware, and server software; a second for consumer hardware and software. Then, there is the content delivery channel, such as cable or satellite TV providers. Given the number of industries involved in delivering these capabilities, alliances are key.

As with video-game consoles, interactive TV set-top boxes could become hubs for networked homes, particularly as TVs are ubiquitous. Microsoft, therefore, embarked on two sets of complementary alliances – in hardware, to promote a Windows platform, and in CATV, since operators choose the set-top technology and features for their customers and need server technologies to deliver and manage the content.

In this arena, Microsoft saw its primary contribution as the OS for the box and server technologies for the network operators, as well as a channel for these and other devices to interoperate. Hardware companies would take on the PC-makers' role in systems-integration of the set-top box, and cable firms would contribute the customers.

Set-top boxes

Microsoft partnered with a number of set-top box offerings. WebTV, later bought by Microsoft, adopted Windows CE, using hardware initially manufactured by Sony and Philips. Microsoft also partnered with Hughes' DirecTV broadcast-satellite distribution system (partly-owned by AOL), Thomson Multimedia and Sony to develop *Ultimate TV*, a set-top box that could record two programmes simultaneously, and store up to 35-hours of programming on its hard drive. Microsoft's Ultimate TV unit was dismantled less than year later, with the hardware taken over by the Xbox and software by the MSN business units. Microsoft also tried to use formal power to pursue its goals. It bought 7.5 per cent of Thomson Multimedia in 1999 and established a joint venture to develop Windows CE-based e-TVs. Thomson would sell WebTV boxes.

In these set-top box and interactive TV partnerships, it is evident that there were already potential conflicts of interest and tensions between partners. Although Sony partnered with Microsoft on Ultimate TV, and uses Windows in its PCs, Sony's President believes that Microsoft is its biggest competitor, and that they are currently engaged in a number of 'regional wars' in software for set-top boxes, e-commerce, Internet portals, and games.[47] Moreover, Sony adopted the PalmOS for its PDAs and rebuffed Microsoft on the PlayStation.

In Microsoft's alliances in these areas each party contributes a resource needed to compete against other groups. Although Microsoft tried to broaden its activities into hardware, it has since retreated to a more traditional role. Its partners tend to supply the hardware, and the means to reach the customer. Unlike the PC, where customers buy a computer, then find an ISP or decide which browser to use, the cable or satellite TV service provider defines the hardware and software its customers uses, in addition to the line-up of content. This gives the cable companies significant power, since Microsoft cannot bypass them to reach the end user.

Cable

The second strand of Microsoft's strategy focussed on content delivery. Since interactive TV is an upgrade of current cable offerings, Microsoft's position is similar to Ballard's in that it must convince the firms who own the customer to adopt its technology. Microsoft hoped that formal power would provide it with leverage, and invested over $11B in CATV providers in the US, Asia, Europe, Australia and South America.[48] For example, if the CATV operator adopted its server software or interactive TV middleware, it would likely have its hardware supplier adopt a Windows OS as well to achieve greater interoperability. Microsoft found that it bought a seat at the table, but could not translate its formal power into an effective voice.

This was partly due to a strategic blunder. At a 1997 summit meeting with leading CATV providers, Bill Gates announced that he envisioned Windows as the sole OS on the set-top, with Microsoft being paid a per-box fee for the software as well as a per-transaction fee for e-commerce.[49] This convinced an already wary cable industry that he wanted to become the gatekeeper to their customer. Even John Malone, a traditional ally, and part-owner of the Gemstar International Group, which has a direct broadcast satellite service, refused to adopt Windows for its digital cable box.[50] Although Microsoft invested $5B in AT&T to develop advanced interactive TV software, AT&T stated that it would never allow Microsoft to become an exclusive vendor;[51] when Microsoft was late in delivering its set-top box software, AT&T tested Liberate Technologies' software instead, and later dropped Microsoft. Similarly, UPC abandoned trials of Microsoft's software and adopted

Liberate Technologies' in Austria, Norway, Sweden and the Netherlands. Liberate also won contracts to upgrade interactive TV services for Telewest and NTL in the UK, firms that Microsoft held a stake in. As the firms did not depend on Microsoft, they did not hesitate in defecting. However, Microsoft may have reached a turning point. In November 2004, Comcast began deploying Microsoft software on its set-top boxes to a million customers in Washington state, potentially replacing the Gemstar software it currently uses.[52]

In contrast to the PC industry, Microsoft does not have significant power in enhanced TV alliances. In terms of resource contribution, Microsoft brings a key technology – developer tools, middleware and server-software for the CATV operator's server and broadcast infrastructure, and OS software for the set-top box. But, these resources are not unique, as there are competing providers. Unlike software in a PC, set-top boxes do not need to interoperate with each other, but with the content distributor, and their Internet functionality is based on established standards. Moreover, as the definitions of interactive TV and set-top boxes evolve, Microsoft does not have a single point to apply pressure on.

Also, unlike the PC industry, where Microsoft and the OEMs developed a market together, some of the hardware makers are already established in this arena, and have relations with other software suppliers or have internal capabilities. More importantly, they may already have relationships with the CATV operators.

Microsoft is not sensitive to hardware providers' actions, given its financial strength. But, it is vulnerable because of the strategic implications, as enhanced TV is a key prong in Microsoft's drive to introduce proprietary standards to the Internet. Even though Microsoft had the financial resources to invest in hardware makers, and even develop in-house capabilities, it found the market unreceptive. The hardware makers, on the other hand, were not concerned that Microsoft would defect on them since it needed them to support its standard-setting goals.

Power and interdependence

The key resource contributor in this grouping is the cable and satellite TV industry. The operators provide a distribution channel and own the end users; in jurisdictions where cable firms are regulated monopolies, the customer becomes a unique resource. Perhaps even more importantly, the operators determine what hardware its customers use, and what services to provide, and therefore are the software and set-top box vendors' primary customers. They also contribute important knowledge of the market and can provide feedback on what content and services customers want. The CATV operators' prime position helps explain why Microsoft's relationships in this industry often had an equity component – as an attempt to use formal power to substitute for the lack of informal power.

Microsoft possessed latent power, both in its financial resources and in its potential to add value in the future because it owned web portals, services, and content, and to set standards in a number of sectors in the digital media sphere. However, the CATV providers may also aspire to dominate these areas. Its latent power was also diminished since the size differentials between it and its partners were narrower than in some of the other markets it operates in. Moreover, it does not control the technology's OS, which is the foundation of its power in the PC arena. Finally, Microsoft is not able to reach beyond the box to the end customer, who is more concerned with the content than the software running the box.

Microsoft appears to be both sensitive and vulnerable to CATV operators' actions. Microsoft's revenue stream is sensitive to a cable company's decision to use its software or not, although the impact on its finances is likely to be minor. It is vulnerable because these partners are key to its attempts to redefine Internet standards; since operators are resisting it, its existing partners become even more important because they are hard to replace.

How dependent a cable provider is on Microsoft depends on whether it is an established firm, or a new entrant in a liberalized market which sees a partnership with Microsoft as a source of competitive advantage or differentiation against an incumbent. Microsoft's importance to the firm overall will also depend on whether it is hedging its bets through relationships with other technology providers. The operators are not sensitive, because it is highly unlikely that Microsoft would defect, but they could be vulnerable, for example, if Microsoft's technology fails to perform. Operators are also vulnerable if Microsoft succeeds in setting the OS standard; then Microsoft would be in a position to behave opportunistically and reduce cable providers to dumb bandwidth providers, just as OEMs have become dumb PC hardware providers.

Microsoft's foray into the cable business was not one of its wisest investment decisions; not only has it not succeeded in setting standards in set-top boxes, it took significant write-downs in several investments. For example, the $2.6B investment in Telewest Communications was sold after three years for $5M.[53] Today, it has taken a new approach, shifting away from interactive TV, which is heavily Internet focussed, to 'on-demand' services, providing channel guides based on 'Microsoft TV Foundation Edition' software for digital set-top boxes.[54]

Mobile devices

Mobile handheld devices, which include mobile phones, PDAs, and wireless communications devices are becoming alternate means to access the Internet, and thus a key market for Microsoft's goal to place Windows at the heart of the Internet. In this multi-segmented market, Microsoft is playing catch-up against incumbents, and new challengers. There is significant technology and market uncertainty as customer demands change. Since firms need to bundle technologies and services from multiple market segments, competition in the mobile arena is often between alliances. As with alliances in other convergence markets, there is significant room for conflicts of interest and therefore opportunistic behaviour and defection; partners in one segment of the industry back different technologies or solutions in another segment, and may compete with each other in a third.

PDAs were originally electronic versions of organizer/address books, with extra memory for memos, that could be backed up on a PC. The devices became more sophisticated as hardware makers added handwriting recognition, mini productivity programmes, infrared communications between devices, e-mail and wireless communications capabilities. At the other end of the spectrum, mobile phone makers and network operators added functionality to handsets, including calendars, reminders, games, and eventually, text messaging and Internet access. Today, these industries are converging, as PDAs add voice capabilities and smart phones have integrated many of the PDA's functions. At the same time, customer requirements are changing, and users will demand greater interoperability between PC applications and the devices that they carry.

PDA

The PDA market is comprised of hardware makers from both the consumer electronics industry and the computer industry, as well as OSs suppliers, and in some cases, with network operators to provide wireless services. With its beginnings in the consumer electronics, OS providers often produce their own devices, or license. The market leader is PalmSource, the software subsidiary of the Palm device maker, which has licensed the PalmOS widely, primarily to PDA-makers, but also for smart-phones. The PalmOS allows users to view Microsoft Office and Adobe Acrobat files. The firm with the most momentum, and buzz, is Research in Motion, which produces the Blackberry family of wireless communications devices on its proprietary OS, and is partnered with a number of wireless communications providers. Microsoft's contribution to the field is the Windows Mobile platform, which is tailored for PowerPC (PDA), PowerPC phone (PDAs with voice capabilities) and Smartphone (mobile phones with data capabilities), and includes mini versions the Office Suite, as well as IE and its Media Player. For developers, it offers a .NET Compact Framework programming infrastructure to create web-services software; the value of this framework is that it allows developers to re-use code written for PCs or servers.

Although PDAs using the same platform could communicate by 'beaming' data between devices, increasingly communications is via wireless standards, and interoperability is between PC and device. This has made the role of the OS provider even more important, and benefits Microsoft, as it provides a clear rationale for device makers to adopt Windows, since it can offer smoother interoperability between devices. While the PalmOS has primarily been adopted by consumer electronics firms, it is significant that Windows Mobile has been taken up by Dell, HP, and Toshiba – all PC makers. This focus may be paying off. According to Gartner, Microsoft's Windows Mobile overtook Palm OS in sales for the first time in the third quarter of 2004.[55]

Mobile phones

Alliance strategies are critical in the mobile phone arena: to deliver a product to the consumer requires cooperation between handset makers, OS and applications software providers, and network operators. The network operator is critical as it decides what types of services to provide, which then determines what functionality the handset needs. On the other hand, many handset makers have proprietary OSs, and push new innovations for the network operators to adopt. This dynamic is particularly important for Microsoft, which does not produce handsets, and does not have historical relationships with service providers. As in the other areas, Microsoft's goal is to use Windows to drive the technology.

Although industry giant, Nokia, has a leading position in handsets, the market for smart-phones, which allow users to connect to the Internet and have PDA functions, is nascent, made possible by the tremendous investments in 3G networks during the 1990s. As a result, the battle to bring greater functionality to the mobile phone has just begun. The leading smart-phone software offerings come from: Symbian, owned by Nokia, Ericsson, Sony Ericsson, Panasonic, Siemens, and Samsung; Microsoft's Windows Mobile for Smart-phones; and Palm, which is attacking via the PDA market. But, in addition, handset makers have not stopped pursuing internal initiatives.

Microsoft has found that the major handset makers have been reluctant to work with it, and those who do hedge their bets by also developing phones with the other software providers as well. It provides a resource that is not unique and which has not been tested in a demanding telecommunications market, where reliability is critical, and which the major handset makers also have skills in. More importantly, they do not want to give Microsoft room to replicate its success in the PC industry, and grab all the value from new innovations. As a result, Microsoft's strategy has been to initially work with contract handset manufacturers, and partner with network operators who could be convinced to try new functionalities. By 2003, Microsoft had signed 22 network operators. But these are not exclusive relationships; the operators maintained their links to their traditional partners, thereby limiting Microsoft's influence, and since Microsoft needed the access to the operators' customers, it was not in a position to demand stricter terms.

Despite its multitude of relationships, Microsoft has yet to take a significant toehold in the market; launches of its products with Germany's T-mobile and AT&T were delayed, and Orange, which launched Microsoft's SPV phone found that the OS was unstable and often crashed, a problem compounded by the discovery of security flaws. Microsoft has also suffered significant defections in relationships with handset makers. In 2002, Sendo, one of its four handset suppliers, ended a two-year relationship days before it was supposed to deliver handsets to six network operators, announcing that it would adopt Nokia's Series 60 software, and later partnered with Symbian. Sendo defected, despite the fact that Microsoft owned 5 per cent of it. It then sued Microsoft, accusing it of passing Sendo's intellectual property to its Taiwanese handset partner, and won. More damaging was Samsung's defection and criticism of the OS; the fourth-largest handset-maker in the world, Samsung was Microsoft's largest licensee. Samsung subsequently took a 5 per cent stake in Symbian.

However, in this fast-changing environment, the other partnerships have also suffered defections. Motorola exited Symbian in 2003, moving to work with Microsoft and AT&T instead. However, Motorola still pursues Linux/Java-based internal initiatives, and is also working with Oracle. Even though Samsung joined Symbian, it produces handsets with Microsoft, Palm, and Linux technologies. And, despite Ericsson's stake in Symbian, it established a joint venture, *Ericsson Microsoft Mobile Ventures AB*, to provide mobile e-mail solutions to operators. Microsoft would bring server platforms, and Ericsson infrastructure and mobile Internet technologies.[56]

In the handheld computer device arena, the market may have changed enough to give Microsoft a stronger position since using Windows-based platforms will allow users to move between PCs and handheld devices more smoothly than PDAs with a competing OS. As PC OEMs enter this market, Microsoft can leverage off their dependence on it in the PC market, whereas competing OS providers do not have these ties. On the other hand, its power over device makers will not be as strong as in the PC arena because there are alternatives; these OS providers are building functionalities to translate Microsoft applications, and Microsoft will be vulnerable to defections as it seeks to set a new standard.

Conclusions

In the PC-related industries, Microsoft is powerful and independent. Its power comes from owning a proprietary standard that anchors the value chain. Because the rest of the industry's technologies depended on it, it did not need to form alliances. As a result, a resource which conferred power in a specific context became the catalyst for a much more instrumental source of power, financial strength. This latent power insulates Microsoft from its partners' actions, and allows it to recover from strategic blunders.

In the non-PC world, the power differentials between Microsoft and its partners vary significantly, and in some cases, are relatively evenly balanced. Microsoft is interdependent, and in some instances, even dependent on its partners. As a result, Microsoft suffered a number of setbacks and open defections. Microsoft also needed to construct interdependence through formal alliances and through the use of formal power. However, even equity could not bind its partners because they did not depend on its resources.

In these new markets, Microsoft is not in a position to demand that partners use its technology. Even though the firms in these new markets may agree that a single standard would ease the interaction between PCs, internet appliances, handheld computing devices and communications technologies, the preference is for open standards, rather than interoperability based on a Microsoft standard.

Setting the standard for the range of devices which access the Internet will not be easy. Unlike the beginnings of the PC era, where Microsoft and the OEMs grew the market together, these new markets are already populated with incumbents who have pre-existing relationships with other firms. While technological and market uncertainty still exists, this is a process of upgrading existing customers and existing networks. Instead of targeting individual customers, it is targeting the firms who determine which products their customers choose from, such as network operators. But, these firms own critical resources that allow them to balance Microsoft's latent power, and since Microsoft does not control a bottleneck technology, it does not have significant leverage.

5
Ballard Power: Shifting Dependence, Changing Structures[1]

The multi-billion dollar commercial potential of fuel cell technology has generated much excitement in the investment community over the past decade, an enthusiasm shared by those in energy and environment circles. Fuel cells have no moving parts, and generate electricity from an electrochemical reaction between hydrogen and an oxidant, such as oxygen: the only by-products are water and heat, making it the ultimate clean technology. Although there are many potential markets, from electric generation to power for mobile phones, the idea of fuel cell vehicles has captured the public's imagination. Its champions speak of the dawning of a 'hydrogen age' and the beginning of the end of the internal combustion engine (ICE).

Surprisingly, fuel cells are an old technology. They provided onboard electricity for the Gemini and Apollo space programmes, and water for the crew. In fact, the scientific principle underlying fuel cells,[2] reverse electrolysis, was discovered by Sir William Grove in 1839. Although this preceded the development of the petroleum-fuelled ICE by some forty years,[3] the technology's adoption has been stymied by a combination of cost and technological challenges, particularly low power densities compared to the ICE.[4] Many of these challenges remain.

Technologies and markets[5]

There are five major types of fuel cell technologies, based on the electrolyte used. They have very different properties, particularly with respect to operating temperatures, fuelling options, and catalysts (ranging from platinum and gold to advanced ceramics). These properties limit the types of applications each technology can be used in, and have a significant impact on materials costs. They also

Table 5.1   Major Types of Fuel Cell

Type	Operating Temperature	Fuel	Application
Alkaline	70–100 °C	H_2	space, military
Proton Exchange Membrane (or Solid Polymer)	50–100 °C	H_2/reformed H_2	stationary, transport
Phosphoric Acid	160–210 °C	H_2 reformed from natural gas	mid-large scale stationary, rail
Molten Carbonate	650 °C	H_2, CO – reforms natural/coal gas internally	stationary power & vapour, utility
Solid Oxide	800–1000 °C	H_2, CO – reforms natural/coal gas internally	large/very large stationary
Direct Methanol	80–200 °C	methanol	transport

raise technological challenges: some are zero emission only if they are fed pure hydrogen. If hydrogen is derived from other products, such as petroleum, methanol, ethanol, diesel, or natural gas, this process will require energy and generates pollutants. Additionally, since hydrogen is combustible, storage is an issue, particularly in automotive applications.

The general consensus is that the Proton Exchange Membrane Fuel Cell (PEMFC), developed by General Electric in the 1950s, is the most appropriate technology for automotive applications.[6] Uniquely, its electrolyte is a layer of solid polymer which acts as a membrane that allows protons to move through. Commercialization has been held back by cost and technical considerations: PEMFCs use expensive and easily contaminated platinum catalysts, which degrade performance unless they are replaced. As a result, they work best when fed pure hydrogen.

Markets and drivers

Fuel cells can be used in a wide range of applications in three major markets: small-, medium-, or large-scale stationary power generation; transportation, including buses, commercial vehicles, and passenger vehicles; and portable applications, ranging from generators for campsites to mini fuel cells for personal electronics. As a result, the competitive dynamic is not only between traditional technologies, fuel cells and other alternative energy sources, but in some market segments, amongst different types of fuel cells.

Stationary

The market for fuel cell-based stationary power plants is driven by deregulation, increased energy requirements, the need for 'quality' power with a stable voltage, and 'not-in-my-backyard' attitudes which have prevented new capacity from being built near populated areas. In California, for example, competition and environmental health and safety concerns has resulted in no large power plant being built in over a decade; instead, it has adopted a distributed generation model, locating small plants closer to the customer.

In the stationary market, fuel cells compete with existing diesel and natural gas ICE technology, as well as new smaller gas turbines. However, supporters argue that the trend toward micropower favours fuel cells because they are more efficient at smaller sizes than thermal, nuclear or hydro-electric generators,[7] and thus have lower economies of scale.

Transportation

Motor vehicles are a major source of pollution, and various governments, notably the State of California, have mandated more stringent emissions standards, such as a requirement to sell a certain percentage of ZEVs by a given date. California is important because it is the largest component of the world's largest automotive market, and technologies developed to meet its requirements would diffuse to other developed markets as automakers seek economies of scale. Despite significant phase-in periods, now 2007 in California's case, the intent is clear: to transition from ICE vehicles to LEVs and, ultimately, ZEVs.[8] Although the passenger market is the most high profile, there is also a significant market in transit buses and fleet vehicles, which do not face the same technological challenges and fuelling considerations.

Thus, stringent environmental regulations have sparked intensive research in alternative propulsion technologies, including cleaner diesel, electric cars, and hybrid vehicles, which combine an ICE with battery power. Today, a number of automakers, including Toyota, Honda, and Ford, offer hybrid vehicles. However, if governments stand by the ZEV standard, the only possible technologies are fuel cells and electric (battery-powered) vehicles, which are not practical for general use due to their limited range and lengthy recharging times.[9]

While conventional wisdom says that environmental regulation is the catalyst for research in transportation applications, another view is that the automotive industry is pursuing alternative propulsion because they are finding it increasingly difficult to differentiate themselves in terms of scale, range of products, or geographic markets.[10] Technology is one of the few areas where a firm can gain a competitive advantage. The ICE can be improved, but it is a mature technology with decreasing returns on investment, whether defined as technological improvement or cost savings potential. On the other hand, significant improvements in design, performance and cost can be gained from the same investment in disruptive technologies. Given the steepness of the learning curve, the first mover could gain significant cost and performance advantages. GM's *Hy-Wire* prototype is the most revolutionary fuel cell vehicle to date; instead of just replacing the ICE with a fuel cell under the hood, GM has completely redesigned the vehicle so that the fuel cell engine is encased in an 11-inch thick chassis, on top of which different types of bodies can rest. By completely reconceptualizing the vehicle, GM has likely changed the cost allocation amongst the various subsystems and vehicles types, which may compensate for higher fuel cell engine costs.[11]

These two drivers have implications for the extent to which automakers' and fuel cell developers' interests are aligned. If environmental regulation is the driver, then automakers are being pulled into adopting the technology by government and fuel cell makers, and would be expected to try to delay implementation as long as possible. But, if the automakers see PEMFC vehicles as a strategic advantage, they will work with the fuel cell developers to bring this technology to the market first.

Regardless of the rationale, fuel cell companies want to push the technology. With some 55 million vehicles produced annually, the market opportunity for the fuel cell industry is estimated to be around $190B, based on current engine costs of about $3,500 per unit.[12] As a result, fuel cell makers are competing to set the technological standard for the rest of the market. As with Intel, whose success rested on developing faster processors than its competitors, in fuel cells, the race is about developing the most powerful fuel cell with the smallest footprint at the lowest cost, and becoming the supplier of choice. However, the race is not only between fuel cell developers, but between alliances of fuel cell developers and automakers, and between fuel cell makers and automakers' internal development programmes.

Portable 'Off-Grid' and other applications

Portable generation and marine applications have had a relatively low profile. In the portable market, fuel cells compete against traditional small ICE generators, new ICE technologies transferred from the automobile industry, batteries, and advanced battery technologies. Potential markets include emergency residential power, construction, leisure, and auxiliary power for recreational vehicles and boats,[13] as well as miniature fuel cells for use in portable electronics such as mobile phones or laptop computers. The defence establishment, which originally funded fuel cell research, continues to do so: the National Aeronautics and Space Administration uses alkaline fuel cells, and a number of firms are testing fuel cells to power surface naval vessels and submarines.

Commercializing fuel cell vehicles

Despite tremendous technological advances over the last decade, fuel cell vehicles are not expected to be commercialized prior to 2010, and ICE vehicles will likely remain in service for another generation. Even for today's fuel cell industry leaders, there are still tremendous market and technology risks: the market is populated by a wide range of firms, from start-ups to subsidiaries of some of the largest industrial firms in the world. As a result, there are significant differences in the resources that they can devote to R&D.

In automotive applications, fuel cell developers face formidable challenges in introducing a disruptive technology. Incumbent technologies have economies of scale and cost advantages on their side, as well as an established fuel infrastructure. Fuel cell makers cannot bring the technology directly to the end user since they provide a component in one of an automobile's major subsystems, and must work with automakers, most of whom are also conducting research on fuel cells or alternative technologies, in order to commercialize their products. This brings even greater uncertainty to the market. For individual fuel cell firms, success is a function of both technology and partnership strategies.

There is also a question of technical complexity. A fuel cell engine has multiple subsystems, combining the fuel cell stack with fuel, air supply, cooling, and control sub-systems, which is then incorporated with the automobile's drive train and peripheral systems. It may also require an inverter, and/or power conditioner to convert the direct current the PEMFC produces to an alternating current for electrical equipment and transmission systems.

Then, there is the issue of complementary resources, such as fuel and the fuel infrastructure. Fuel choice is critical.[14] Hydrogen and its alternatives vary on a number of properties, including emissions, storage density, impact on human health, safety (particularly combustibility). Using fuels other than hydrogen add to the system's technical complexity and cost. Fuel cell vehicles are also limited by network effects – how long will it take to convert all filling stations? And, how much will it cost? Since incumbents have already made significant investments in the existing infrastructure, they would prefer fuelling options that have the lowest switching costs for them, for example, by deriving hydrogen from petroleum-based products.

The marketplace question is as challenging as the technological considerations, since fuel cell technology development is being driven as much by environmental regulation as by strategic considerations. Fuel cell vehicles must be cost-competitive. How much more would consumers pay to be environmentally-friendly? Despite rising gasoline prices and growing environmental awareness, JD Power and Associates show that trucks (including Sport Utility Vehicles (SUVs)) still account for over 50 per cent of the US market.[15] Moreover, regulation adds an additional layer of uncertainty as to which technologies are appropriate and under what time frame.

Thus, fuel cell developers must create an ecosystem conducive to the mass commercialization of fuel cell vehicles. Fuel cell firms need to ally with automakers, who provide the vehicle (figuratively and literally) which brings their product to market. But, they also need to work with their competitors, automakers, and fuel-providers, whether these are traditional oil and gas players or new entrants, industry associations, environmental groups, academia, government agencies and regulatory organizations to develop the supporting infrastructure, such as the *California Fuel Cell Partnership*, and the *Fuelling a Cleaner Canada* initiative, amongst others.

This web of relationships creates a number of potential conflicts of interest. Fuel cell firms cooperate in order to create a market, but compete to provide the most powerful technologies to automotive partners, and to be first to market. At another level, although fuel cell firms and automakers work together, the automakers have invested billions of dollars in the ICE and it is in their own interests to prolong its use, particularly if they do not have advanced alternative propulsion capabilities. In December 2004, 11 automakers (Toyota, GM, Ford, Daimler, BMW, Mazda, Mitsubishi, Porsche, Volkswagen, Honda, and Nissan) launched a suit against the State of California to try to block its new greenhouse gas regulations which limit vehicle emissions.[16]

If the fuel cell is the technology of the future, the automakers will not want to cede power over a core system, the engine, to a supplier. Thus, many automakers are also pursuing internal R&D and non-fuel cell LEV options. These conflicts of interest are also present at the infra-structural level, in debates over whether there should be a hydrogen infrastructure or reform other fuels. Here, governments and non-governmental organizations are likely to focus on environmental effects, while the oil and gas industry and even automakers are likely to favour less stringent environmental standards, and allow the use of carbon-based fuels. The less stringent the standards, the more likely that the ICE's main beneficiaries can meet these without ceding value to a new industry.

Even if fuel cell vehicles are commercialized, fuel cell firms face significant challenges ensuring that they retain a substantial role and capture a large share of the value. Just as consumers today do not tell automakers whose components to put into a vehicle, tomorrow's con-sumers are unlikely to determine which fuel cell the automakers use. The fuel cell firm cannot access the large transportation market without the support of an automaker, or more likely, automakers, as economies of scale will determine if its product can be built at an acceptable cost. There is also a question of lock-in; once an automaker has chosen a supplier and designed its vehicles around a certain fuel cell's characteristics, asset specificity may mean that competing fuel cells are locked out until a class of vehicles or their engines are redesigned. Currently, there are a number of joint efforts amongst fuel cell developers and automakers: Renault-Peugeot Citroen-Fiat-Nuvera, United Technologies Corporation with Hyundai, Nissan, and BMW, respectively, and Ballard-Daimler-Ford. However, if fuel cell vehicles are not commercialized soon, memberships may change.

Influences on fuel cell vehicle alliances

Two of the most important influences on fuel cell vehicle alliances are regulation and technology. Governments set emissions standards and the dates when these targets must be met, as well as fund research ini-tiatives in energy efficiency or pollution control, which indirectly determines which technologies can be adopted. Fuel choice and the supporting infrastructure also influence which technologies are feasible, and government plays a role in these decisions, as well. For fuel cell vehicles, if emissions regulations are more stringent or if non-PEMFC technologies are unreliable, then automakers have greater incentives to cooperate. But if governments allow LEVs instead of adhering to a zero emission standard, or PEMFCs cannot meet required performance criteria, then its partners would want to manage their risk by investigating other technology options.

In technology-based alliances, technological innovation plays a key role in an alliance's desirability. For example, the introduction of hybrid vehicle may further delay the commercialization of fuel cell vehicles, by taking some of the pressure off the need to achieve zero-emissions. Additionally, the auto OEMs also want time to reap a return on their investments. Even within fuel-cell technology, there is no guarantee that any firm can retain a technology lead.

At the inter-alliance level, a major factor which influences a partner's desired action is how successfully the alliance competes against other PEMFC vehicle developers, and sometimes versus an OEM's internal R&D efforts. Fuel cell firms cannot be sure of non-equity partners; many automakers test fuel cells from multiple providers, while conducting independent R&D, and can still switch partners relatively costlessly at this point in time. Honda is a case in point; it is working with Ballard, but also developed a fuel cell which it claims is smaller, more efficient and less costly than current offerings.[17]

At the alliance level, the partners' positional interests are not aligned, resulting in a tension between the group- and firm-level goals. This tension may be ameliorated through contractual terms, or by structuring an alliance so that different firms control different elements important to the group's success. Despite these types of structures, and even if the partners agree on the ultimate goal, they may still disagree over the technology's design, the materials or the inputs used, and commercialization strategies. The extent of co-specialization of technologies also plays a key role determining whether the partners are able or likely to cooperate or defect. The more complex the final product and the greater the co-specialization within the system, the harder it is for the firms to defect and switch to alternative providers.

Ballard Power Systems

Ballard Power Systems was founded in 1979 by physicist Geoffrey Ballard as a contract research house focussing on high energy lithium batteries. In 1983, Canada's Department of National Defence and National Research Council contracted it to develop a low-cost PEMFC that would use less platinum, and find an alternative to DuPont's patented Nafion membrane. Their progress exceeded expectations, leading to two subsequent contracts.

In 1989, Ballard decided to bet its future on the fuel cell, bringing in a professional management team and raising millions in venture capital funding. It also delivered its first fuel cell to Daimler for testing. Since then, Ballard has become one of the most respected names in PEMFC development. On the technology front, it has reduced the use of platinum, increased the power of the fuel cell stack, increased the cell's power density, reduced the stack's footprint, and found more cost effective membranes and catalysts. One of its biggest early break-throughs was a prototype transit bus; this was a vital marketing boost, helping outsiders understand the company's ultimate purpose. It led to funding for more advanced test vehicles, resulting in commercial demonstration projects for the transit authorities in Vancouver and Chicago by 1998. Ballard has continued to demonstrate its technology, building prototype generators, and delivering stacks to major automakers, including Daimler, Ford, GM, Honda, and Nissan, for testing and feedback. Currently, it has more test vehicles on the road than other fuel cell firms. Ballard also matured as a company, going public on the Toronto Stock Exchange in 1993, and listing on NASDAQ in 1995.

Although its focus is on automotive applications, Ballard has targeted all three market segments: stationary generators; transit buses and passenger cars; and generators for portable/emergency applications. Ballard's goal is to become the partner of choice to developers of PEMFC systems, OEMs, and their customers by developing brand awareness. It would focuses on R&D in components, systems, and manufacturing processes. On the operations side, Ballard wants to simplify product design, and lower costs through economies of scale and by developing long-term supply relationships, such as its agreement with Johnson Matthey to develop catalysts. Ballard allies with leading firms to gain market knowledge and distribution channels, access complementary technology, develop manufacturing skills, and to access capital.[18]

In the stationary market, Ballard's first alliance was between its subsidiary, Ballard Generation Systems (BGS), and GPU International (GPUI – now FirstEnergy), the international power generation and distribution arm of New Jersey-based GPU, in 1996. GPUI invested $14.9M for part-ownership in BGS. In 1997, BGS added ALSTOM of France as a partner and shareholder. BGS' geographical coverage was extended further in 1998, with the addition of EBARA of Japan as a partner and shareholder. Except in the case of GPUI, these alliances also established joint-venture subsidiaries to pursue specific market segments. In 2000, Ballard added its first partner in the portable market, Coleman Powermate, to develop co-branded PEMFC portable and standby power units, and leverage off Coleman's network of retailers and distributors. Additionally, Ballard and Tokyo Gas began developing a 1-kW natural gas-powered fuel cell power generator for Japan's residential market.

On the automotive side, in 1992, Ballard deepened its relationship Daimler into a collaborative (non-equity) partnership to jointly develop fuel cells. This evolved into a formal alliance in 1997, and expanded a year later when the Ford Motor Company joined.

Ballard's vehicular alliance

Since its establishment in 1997, Ballard's vehicular alliance has undergone several structural changes, which attest to the robustness of the relationships and the partners' recognition that flexibility is a key ingredient in alliance success. The alliance's restructuring reflect changes in power relationships, shifts in responsibilities, and variations in the extent of interdependence. It also demonstrates both natural and constructed interdependence, and shows how constructed interdependence in technology relationships can evolve into natural interdependence.

Ballard lay the foundation for its vehicular alliance by deepening its eight-year relationship with Daimler, which invested C$202M for 25 per cent of Ballard Power and two seats on its eight-member Board; they established two joint ventures, *dbb fuel cell engines* (later renamed *XCELLSIS*)[19] to develop and commercialize PEMFC systems for automotive applications,[20] and *Ballard Automotive*, their sales agent. XCELLSIS became the proxy through which Daimler contributed to the alliance, and Daimler was the majority owner. Daimler's share in Ballard was diluted when Ford joined alliance, investing C$302.7M in cash for 15 per cent of Ballard and 22 per cent of XCELLSIS. They formed a third company, *Ecostar*, which was the vehicle through which Ford, the majority owner, made its contribution; Ecostar develops electric vehicle drive systems, including electric motors and electronic control systems. Ecostar then acquired 1/3 interest in Ballard Automotive. Structurally, Ballard anchored the alliance; Ford and Daimler do not have direct working relationships with it, only indirect ones through their investments, their commitments to purchase, and through their proxy companies.

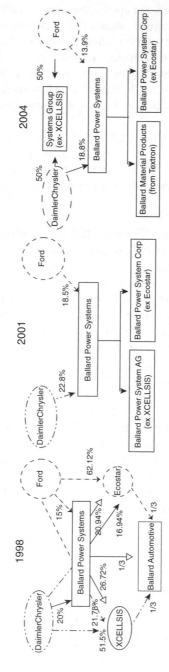

Figure 5.1 Ballard–Daimler–Ford: Alliance Evolution

As Ballard broadened its range of products, for example, purchasing the carbon products division of Textron, it reorganized and stream-lined its corporate structure. EBARA's and GPUI's, and later ALSTOM's, investments in Ballard were shifted to the company level instead of in BGS. The bigger change came with the *Third Vehicular Alliance Agreement* in October 2001. Ballard acquired XCELLSIS and Ecostar (renaming them *Ballard Power Systems AG* and *Ballard Power Systems Corporation*) with shares, raising Daimler's and Ford's owner-ship stakes to 24 per cent and 20 per cent, respectively. Daimler and Ford agreed to invest another C$110M through a private place-ment, half at the closing of the transaction, and the other half within three years if Ballard undertook any secondary offerings in that time, and were prohibited from selling their stakes for six years. Daimler and Ford would purchase PEMFC engines exclusively from Ballard and could not develop or sell PEMFC engines. Daimler and Ford could not license Ballard's PEMFC technology for at least six years, but would be given privileged information about pre-commercial technologies six-to-nine months ahead of their competitors.

The acquisitions brought skills in PEMFC engines, electric drive trains, capability to integrate these, and power electronics for station-ary applications. Ballard would become a fuel cell systems provider, with capabilities in several segments of the automobile value chain, and be responsible for all R&D efforts. Technologically, it left Daimler and Ford more dependent on Ballard's ability to deliver of PEMFCs and their peripheral systems. But, they also had greater control since they owned almost 45 per cent of the company, and could act together to block corporate actions requiring $2/3$ votes. They could also remove officers and had veto power over some decisions.

The alliance was restructured again in July 2004, in a move intended to reverse some of the changes made in 2001. In the proposed changes, Daimler and Ford would repurchase the former XCELLSIS, reducing their stakes in Ballard to 18.8 per cent and 13.9 per cent respectively. Part of the rationale may be that the 'balance of plant' is key to the automakers' competitive advantage, and engine system development is not Ballard's core competence. Moreover, given the importance of this subsystem, third-party automakers were not likely to purchase one partly-owned by their competitors. In return, Ballard would be released from provisions giving Ford and Daimler lead time before a technology could be sold to other automakers, and has the right of first-refusal to work on electric drive-trains for Daimler, mirroring an existing agreement with Ford.

The three partners share a goal of developing fuel cell vehicles at a price consumers accept, and staying ahead of competitors in their respective industries, but beyond these, they have divergent interests. Ballard, for example, envisions a future as the Intel of the fuel cell industry, stating that it wants to be the fuel cell and fuel cell systems supplier of choice for the auto industry, although the latter goal appears to have been stymied by its partners. It retains the right to sell to Ford and Daimler's competitors, although it cannot establish other vehicular alliances; accordingly, it would prefer that the fuel cells and systems set standards, so that automakers can easily switch to its technology, rather than seeing fuel cell developers build according to the automakers' specifications. Ballard bears the most risk if this disruptive technology does not succeed; having identified transportation applications as its major market, Ballard's *raison d'être* may come into question if the PEMFC automobile market does not materialize. While Ford and Daimler operate in the automobile or low-emissions vehicle markets, Ballard is confined to the market for PEMFC vehicles.

Ford's and Daimler's primary businesses are designing, manufacturing and marketing cars, and they want to be at the forefront of the automotive market regardless of the engine technology. In PEMFC vehicles, Ford and Daimler have bet that Ballard gives them the best chance to commercialize this technology and gain a competitive edge. The alliance is also a means for them to share risk and reduce their own R&D costs – as a public company, Ballard's other investors have made significant contributions to the group's efforts. While they want to advance Ballard's technology, this does not mean that they want other firms to benefit from their input – which led to the restrictions on Ballard's ability to sell new products to other automakers. It is in their interests to make Ballard's fuel cell systems more asset specific, so that they perform best with their vehicles, or to ensure that a vehicle's performance depends less on the fuel cell's characteristics than on proprietary technologies in other segments of the value chain, such as XCELLSIS' engine systems. If PEMFC vehicles fail, or if emissions standards are lax enough to support other technologies, they may not remain committed to the alliance. Although Daimler and Ford have made large investments in the Ballard alliance and in PEMFC vehicle development, these are small compared to their annual revenues of over \$150B each. While Daimler-Ford-Ballard are trying to create a market for fuel cell powered vehicles, their alliance does not preclude Daimler or Ford from conducting independent research on PEMFC technology, or developing and commercializing competing technologies.

Thus, Ballard's vehicular alliance illustrates the potential conflicts of interest between the different stakeholders along the PEMFC vehicle value chain. In addition to the tensions which arise due to their positional interests, two of the three partners are direct competitors. The structure of the alliance and its subsidiary companies, as well as each party's commitments and limitations on their actions illustrate that the members recognize the tensions inherent in their working relationship, and are attempting to mitigate them by constructing interdependence. Moreover, encouraging the sale of fuel cells, and electric drive trains outside of the alliance tempers Daimler's and Ford's interest in increasing asset specificity.

Behaviours

In this alliance, Ford and Daimler's relationship is inherently competitive, and became more so after Daimler acquired Chrysler. Initially, they cooperated indirectly through XCELLSIS and Ecostar, and only to develop fuel cell vehicles, but will be co-owners of the *Systems Group*, formerly XCELLSIS. Once fuel cell vehicles are commercialized, Ford and Daimler will also compete in the PEMFC markets. Ballard also competes with Ford and Daimler, albeit indirectly, since its fuel cells may power other automakers' vehicles. Currently, Ford also appears to compete with the alliance through sales of hybrid vehicles, such as the Prodigy and the Escape SUV. While hybrids may be an intermediate step to eliminating ICE-vehicles, they are potentially a compromise technology which satisfies regulators enough to delay fuel cell vehicles further.

Despite the competitive dynamic, Ballard-Daimler-Ford have managed their relationship successfully, achieving numerous technology breakthroughs and bringing the technology to the cusp of commercialization. The alliance's success, particularly in the ability to restructure their roles, implies that cooperation has dominated the relationship thus far. Without their respective resource contributions, they cannot meet their goal to commercialize PEMFC vehicles: Ballard cannot reach the automotive market except through automobile OEMs; Daimler and Ford need Ballard's skills in fuel cell development. Thus, Ballard is a vehicle through which they can learn, stay ahead of their competitors, reduce their technology risk, and save on R&D. They also limit intra-alliance competition through non-compete agreements to Ballard, and the subsidiaries, and commitments to purchase. However, these promises may be largely symbolic. For example, the commitments to purchase expire at roughly the same period that mass commercialization is expected to take off.[21]

Although the three firms share an overall goal, this does not mean that they would not be tempted to benefit at the expense of their partners, for example, by engaging in a learning race to reduce their dependence. Ballard, for example, would welcome more automotive partners. The automakers could also work against Ballard's interests by delaying the introduction of fuel cell vehicles, by introducing LEVs or by lobbying for looser environmental standards. These actions, if successful, would have a significant impact on Ballard's cash flow and potentially, on market confidence. Introducing LEVs can hurt partners who do not have LEV capabilities. Additionally, neither Daimler nor Ford are prohibited from conducting independent research in PEMFC technologies and vehicular systems; although they are obliged to share their research, tacit knowledge, for example, in production processes, is not easily transferred.

Ford and Daimler could defect on the alliance or their partners, for example, by selling their stakes in Ballard and exiting to pursue other technologies or develop PEMFC vehicles on their own, or acquire Ballard to change the balance of power in the alliance. Either scenario is unlikely prior to commercialization, since the alliance allows them to share market and technological risk. Ballard has limited ability to defect, since it can only reach the end user via an auto OEM, but, it could dissolve the alliance to focus on non-vehicular markets. In that case, Ballard may not need to buy back Daimler's and Ford's stakes, but if it wishes to partner with different automakers, it will be a necessity.

Although this alliance has shown resilience in managing several structural changes, the 2001 and 2004 realignments can be interpreted as attempts to change the balance of power within the group. The 2001 restructuring brought all of the technologies under Ballard's umbrella, including the engine systems which allow automakers to differentiate their products. In doing so, Ballard would control a greater percentage of the value of a fuel cell vehicle than by being a stack provider.[22] Industry observers believe that the 2004 restructuring was instigated by the automakers, as a means of regaining control over a core element, and potentially, reducing fuel cell developers to the role of a major components supplier.

Power and interdependence

What constitutes power in this alliance? In technology-based alliances, a firm's resource, its substitutability, appropriability, and how vital it is to the group's success, rather than size, are key. However, fuel cell vehicle alliances' goal is to introduce a disruptive technology that changes the way several vital internal systems operate. Since fuel cell makers cannot access the market if an automaker does not design-in their technology, this gives the owners of the host technology leverage in negotiations, particularly if they also have the ability to develop the technology themselves and if they are large enough to help achieve economies of scale.

In the race to develop fuel cell powered vehicles, a number of firm-specific factors contribute to a firm's weight or power within an alliance, the most important being technology. The fuel cell developer who produces the greatest power density, reliably, at the lowest cost is going to be the most attractive partner. The firm's leverage, however, is also dependent on how far ahead of the competition its technologies and processes are, and its ability to protect its intellectual property. At the same time, technological competence and experience in innovation are important attributes in the automaker; the fuel cell firm depends on it to maximize the vehicle's performance. If PEMFC vehicles do not meet consumers' expectations, they will have difficulty being accepted in the market, and may leave the door open for other technologies. A second key contribution is reputation, to help legitimize the fuel cell maker and its technology. A third consideration is related to firm size, namely market share, since the fuel cell firm's revenue and its ability to achieve economies of scale is directly related to the number of vehicles its partners manufacture. Given the number of high-technology start-ups, management expertise is also an important contribution, particularly experience in manufacturing processes, sales and marketing, as well as distribution channels. Finally, size, in terms of market capitalization and revenue base, may also be important, as this gives the larger firms the potential to coerce, and options to try to reduce their dependence.

The relationship-specific factors which contribute to a firm's power and interdependence in an alliance focus on issues such as the nature of the relationship, the respective firms' commitments, the scope of the relationship, and the extent of co-specialization and integration required. In this alliance, the equity relationships are one-way and confer formal power to Daimler and Ford. The contract terms and the firms' respective commitments also add to our assessment; these include commitments to license, to purchase, to not compete, and the exclusivity of these arrangements. The scope of the relationship looks to how much of a partner's operations are affected by the alliance activity, and how important the alliance is to the firm's overall operations. Ballard, for example, has bet its future on fuel cell vehicles. For Daimler, automobiles are one aspect of its operations, albeit an extremely important one. The firms' positions on the value chain can also give one leverage over another as resources can be contributed sequentially. The extent of technological or operational integration also impacts the respective firms' power and interdependence. The greater the degree of integration, the less able the alliance members are to extricate themselves from the group without incurring significant exit costs.

Contribution to the Alliance

Ballard

In the beginning, Ballard's contribution to the alliance was solely technology, and one of uncertain commercial potential. Over time, it could lend its name and credibility to its partners' efforts since its technology is considered to be amongst the most advanced in its field. As the alliance evolved, Ballard's technology contribution also broadened. After the acquisitions in 2001, Ballard contributed: PEMFCs, fuel processors, balance-of-plant elements which integrate fuel cells into an automobile's systems, and electric drive trains. Ballard and its associated companies have been awarded over 1,700 patents.

The principles which underlie fuel cell technology are taught in high school science classes; where Ballard adds value is in making the fuel cell more powerful, finding substitutes for costly materials, and engineering the interaction between the fuel cells in a stack, and between the stack and the systems it powers. Ballard's R&D has focussed on developing cheaper polymers for its membranes, reducing its dependence on suppliers, and on reducing the amount of platinum required in the membrane electrode assembly. This is critical to lowering component costs. At the same time, Ballard has increased the electrodes' tolerance to contaminants, prolonging their useful life, and which is vital if fuelling options lead to reforming hydrogen from impure fuels. Ballard also conducts R&D into the interactions between the fuel cells within a stack, since its architecture and the materials used define the system's efficiency, power density, and cost. Aside from its automotive partners, it is collaborating with materials suppliers, such as Johnson

Matthey and UCAR International Inc. to find lower cost inputs. However, Ballard's most important work today may be in developing lean manufacturing processes.

Daimler

Daimler's commitment to developing fuel cell vehicles has been reiterated at the highest levels. For example, even when announcing a quarterly loss of over $1B in a February 2001 conference call with analysts, Chairman Jürgen Schrempp spoke of its investment in Ballard as a strategic initiative.[23]

Ballard and Daimler's association stretches back to 1989. Although the early relationship was primarily transactional, it has deepened into knowledge-sharing, and has allowed Ballard to hone its skills in automotive applications. Daimler provided Ballard with early insight into the auto industry's requirements, as well as credibility as it began to target the auto market. Even better, since Daimler produces transit buses, it provided Ballard with testbeds that had less stringent size and weight constraints than autos. According to Ballard, its learnings from early field trials allowed them to reduce the next generation engine's weight by some 50 per cent.

Daimler brought a number of assets to the alliance. The equity investment was a much needed cash injection, and was seen as a sign of confidence in Ballard's technologies and strategy. It also assured Ballard of a customer, and strengthened PEMFC vehicles' chances of entering the market against hybrids and improved ICE vehicles. Daimler also brought its experience in designing and operating manufacturing systems, since Ballard had been an R&D house. Lastly, Daimler also brought together several more segments of the fuel cell vehicle's value chain, including marketing, distribution and service functions, and balance of plant technology.

Daimler's contributions, via XCELLSIS, focussed on integrating Ballard's fuel cell stack and systems with fuel processors (if necessary), and within the larger electric-engine systems. XCELLSIS was also responsible for R&D, commercialization, manufacturing, marketing, and sales and service of PEMFC systems for automotive applications. Another key role is to integrate the engine system with the drive train. Although Daimler sold XCELLSIS to Ballard in 2001, it and Ford bought Ballard out in 2004.

While Daimler made a significant contribution to the goal of commercializing PEMFC vehicles, it could not guarantee the alliance's success against other automakers or other technologies. The one resource that it could not provide was a significant market share and thus the ability to help Ballard achieve economies of scale and scope and hopefully set a standard. Daimler is one of the oldest and most respected names in the automobile industry, but a niche player focussed on the luxury vehicle market. Even after its merger with Chrysler in 1998, the new company still only accounts for some 5.2 per cent of global production.[24]

Ford

Ford entered the vehicular alliance in 1998, bringing additional capital, and adding credibility to its goal of commercializing PEMFC vehicles. Ford provided Ballard with an second channel to the market, instead of having to rely solely on Daimler. Ford contributes to many of Ballard's and the alliance's goals due to its sheer size and weight in the automobile industry. It produces around 12 per cent of the world's cars, and has a global presence; more significantly, Ford and its subsidiary marques account for some 21 per cent of new car sales in the US, the key market.[25] Ford's participation would potentially allow Ballard to achieve the economies of scale needed to bring PEMFC costs in line to compete with ICE technology. As with Daimler, Ford also brought its expertise in designing and operating manufacturing systems and processes, and engineering skills, along with a sales and marketing organization, a network of distributors, an automotive finance operation, and a service and parts organization.

On the technology side, Ford, through its majority-owned subsidiary, Ecostar, was originally responsible for developing the electric drive train components and systems. At the same time, its technology has broader application than just the PEMFC vehicle market; electric drive systems can be used in hybrid and battery-powered vehicles, and have stationary generation applications as well, and is therefore less dependent on the success or failure the alliance's PEMFC vehicle development. Since this unit has now been absorbed into Ballard's operations, Ford's primarily role is a conduit to the automotive market.

Weight of contribution to alliance

In Ballard's vehicular alliance, the question of which party is the most powerful centres around the relative importance of Ballard's technology, and Ford and Daimler's contributions of capital, their roles as a conduit to the automotive market, and their work in adapting existing systems to work with a new power source. Ballard's contribution is arguably the most important piece of the puzzle. If Ballard fails to

Table 5.2   Contribution to the Alliance

	Ballard	Daimler	Ford
Type of Contribution	Fuel cell stacks & systems Monitoring & control Power systems Patent portfolio Drive train	Fuel cell engine systems Engineering, design & operation of manufacturing systems & processes Capital Legitimacy Distribution Transit vehicle market	Fuel cell engine systems (with Daimler) Engineering, design & operation of manufacturing systems & processes Capital Legitimacy Distribution
Substitutability of Contribution	Not substitutable as long as Ballard technology is ahead Some asset specificity; fuel cells are not completely 'plug and play'	Other automobile OEMs available ... but few with the same history of working with fuel cells Strong commitment to FC vehicles. Has been working with Ballard since 1989	No auto OEMs available with the same market share; GM pursuing internal development
Qualitative/ Ability to add value in the future	Provides access to new technology developments. But, no guarantee that Ballard can stay ahead indefinitely. Ability to manufacture at reasonable cost key	Ability to design engine systems and concept vehicles that maximize the fuel cell's potential and compensate for changing vehicle cost structure	Ability to design engine systems and concept vehicles that maximize the fuel cell's potential and compensate for changing vehicle cost structure

develop fuel cells with adequate power and a small enough footprint to fit inside a passenger car, and at a reasonable cost, Daimler's and Ford's efforts in engine and drive train technology will not produce a vehicle which meets consumer expectations. The automakers' importance to Ballard lies in providing an experimental platform, complementary technology, and ultimately, a conduit to the consumer.

In terms of formal power, Daimler and Ford will own 34 per cent of Ballard (once the restructuring has been approved), and hold seats on its Board. They have informal power through their ownership of critical complementary technologies, and latent power, deriving from their relative sizes. However, this is blunted by the alliance structure: neither Ford nor Daimler could take over Ballard without the other's acquiescence.

The three firms' relative importance to the alliance will change; as the technology moves toward commercialization, different skills and resources will be required. At the alliance's inception, Daimler and Ford's contribution of capital and legitimacy, and direct feedback in implementing fuel cells in automobiles were critical to Ballard. Today, these assets carry less weight since Ballard can fund the next stage of development, and has the legitimacy to go directly to the market. However, as it moves into the production phase, Daimler and Ford's experience in manufacturing become more vital. But, these skills are more substitutable. Daimler's and Ford's importance will grow again in the future; as launch customers, they will account for a significant percentage of Ballard's revenues, and will be vital to Ballard's ability to achieve economies of scale, particularly if Ballard's other customers, such as Honda, pursue internal development.

Interdependence

The relationships amongst Ballard, Daimler, Ford and their subsidiary and joint venture companies are characterized by natural and constructed interdependence. Their natural interdependence is a function of their respective positions on the value chain, the nature of the of their contributions, and the extent of asset-specificity. The extent of interdependence is mitigated by the availability of substitutes, their options outside of the alliance, and whether the automakers regard the alliance as a real option, leaving Ballard to bear most of the risk.

However, Ballard, Daimler and Ford also introduced terms which constructed interdependence where none existed according to firm-specific variables, such as commitments to purchase PEMFCs and electric drive train components from Ballard, and PEMFC systems from XCELLSIS. Although the commitments are neither symmetrical nor unlimited, they increase interdependence. These linkages become exit barriers over time, as they increase asset specificity and co-specialization, creating natural interdependence, and because they involve joint ownership of intellectual property. Moreover, as the alliance evolves, it becomes increasingly difficult to bring in additional automotive partners, beyond an arms-length relationship, because of the complex commitments involved.

Ballard and Daimler

The relationship between Ballard and Daimler has evolved significantly since 1989. At the outset Ballard was an unknown research house, and Daimler was one of the most respected automakers in the world. Today, Ballard is generally believed to be the leader in PEMFC technology. The balance of power in their relationship has shifted, and they have become increasingly interdependent as they move toward commercialization. However, given the fact that Ballard was dependent on Daimler, why did it construct interdependence when the alliance was formed? Daimler likely recognized that Ballard needed another automotive partner, and therefore, equity became the tool that guaranteed that it would have a voice over who that future partner would be.

Ballard is both sensitive and vulnerable to Daimler's actions. From a financial perspective, it is sensitive to Daimler's funding for R&D, and its purchase of fuel cells and engineering services, even though Daimler is one of a number of automotive and stationary power customers testing its products. However, its sensitivity will increase at commercialization, since Daimler will be one of two major customers for its fuel cells and electric drive trains, unless it can attract more auto customers. Should Daimler defect, Ballard would see an immediate and large impact on its revenues.

Ballard is vulnerable to Daimler on both technological and market grounds. Ballard depends on Daimler's integration of its fuel cells in the balance of plant to demonstrate the technology's viability. It is also vulnerable to Daimler's continued purchase of its fuel cells and drive train technology. Should Daimler defect, it would have a financial impact, but even more importantly, would be seen as a no-confidence vote in Ballard's technology. Additionally, since Ballard had to forgo opportunities to work closely with other automakers, it will find it difficult to develop the same type of relationship with other automakers, assuming that there are any who still lack a PEMFC partner.

Daimler is less sensitive to Ballard, who only represents one, albeit important, input in its product, but it is vulnerable since power cannot protect it from technology risk. Though its commitment to purchase exclusively from Ballard is limited by the technology's performance, this may still entail significant search and switching costs. For example, there are few fuel cell firms not allied to automakers, who would likely constrain the fuel cell firm from giving third parties their most advanced technologies, as Daimler did with Ballard.

Table 5.3   Ballard–Daimler Relationship

	Effect on Ballard	*More dependent*	*Effect on Daimler*
Sensitivity	Defection would have immediate impact on revenues, stock price.	B	Today, Ballard has no immediate revenue effects on Daimler. Daimler will be more sensitive post-commercialization.
Vulnerability Firm-Specific	Skills in engine systems development critical, and not unique. But, increasingly hard to replace as fuel cell vehicles get closer to commercialization. Daimler makes significant contributions to R&D; may be hard to replace if an exit signals no-confidence.	=	Vulnerable to PEMFC's performance. Ballard's resource is critical, but not unique. But, hard to replace if it is the technology leader and if other FC developers are constrained by their automotive partners. Daimler large enough to absorb financial costs of switching providers, but may impact strategic positioning especially closer to commercialization.
Relationship-Specific	Not much asset specificity or operational integration on Ballard's part.	D	Some asset specificity as engine system and vehicle is designed around the Ballard stack's footprint/performance Will have some operational dependencies at commercialization.
Symmetry	Automakers are Ballard's only route to the market. Daimler is an owner and has control over some strategic decisions. Ballard's entire operations affected by vehicular alliance.	B	Fuel cells potentially affect a large portion of Daimler's operations, if technologies can be leveraged into their other businesses.

Ballard represents a key resource which is unique so long as its technology is more advanced than others'. Daimler's vulnerability to Ballard has increased over time due to relationship-specific factors: in the beginning, Daimler could easily switch fuel cell providers, but today, there is greater technological and operational integration. The XCELLSIS engine systems are designed around the Ballard stack's characteristics, which in turn, impacts its manufacturing operations. Thus, unless Daimler can replicate Ballard's stack internally, replacing Ballard could result in a not insignificant re-design of its propulsion and drive train systems. Moreover, if the fuel cell is key to the vehicle's performance, then Daimler is vulnerable to the performance of Ballard's technology, as its reliability has an affect on its vehicles' reputations. Daimler's vulnerability is also greater than Ford's since it had foregone hybrid vehicles, and is now trying to catch up to the industry leaders in this area.

The relationship is asymmetrical in Daimler's favour based on relationship-specific factors. Daimler owns over 18 per cent of Ballard and has two seats on its Board. Ballard cannot establish alliances with other automakers or explore marine applications without giving Daimler an opportunity to participate. The scope of the relationship is also much wider for Ballard. Far more of its operations and revenue streams are tied to the success or failure of this alliance than Daimler's. If fuel cell vehicles are not commercialized, or commercialized with another firm's technology, Ballard will not have a viable business. On the other hand, if the alliance fails, Daimler will still produce cars, and it has other revenue streams in aerospace and power generation. Ultimately, Daimler's contribution is more important to Ballard's ability to achieve its goals than vice versa.

Ballard and Ford

Ballard and Ford's relationship provides a counterweight to the Ballard-Daimler axis. Ford owns some 14 per cent of Ballard and has two seats on the Board. However, Ford's electric drive train contribution, which has been transferred to Ballard, was farther removed from fuel cell and engine system development, and is not specific to PEMFC vehicles. Unlike Daimler, which has placed its bet on the fuel cell vehicle, Ford has hedged, taking a more evolutionary approach and introducing hybrid vehicles.

Ballard is sensitive and vulnerable to Ford, although less vulnerable from technology risk than with Daimler. Ballard is sensitive to Ford's commitment to continued funding, and purchase of engineering services for the next two generations of fuel cells. Post-commercialization,

Table 5.4   **Ballard–Ford Relationship**

	Effect on Ballard	More dependent	Effect on Ford
Sensitivity	Defection would have immediate impact on revenues, stock price.	B	Today, Ballard has no immediate revenue effects on Ford. Ford will be more sensitive post-commercialization.
Vulnerability Firm-Specific	Ford's manufacturing skills not unique. Ford's purchase of fuel cells may be critical to Ballard's ability to manufacture cost-effectively. Drive-train technology has been transferred to Ballard. Ford makes significant contributions to R&D; may be hard to replace if an exit signals no-confidence.	B	Vulnerable to PEMFC's performance. Ballard's resource is critical, but not unique. But, hard to replace if it is the technology leader and if other FC developers are constrained by their automotive partners. Ford large enough to absorb financial costs of switching providers, but positioning especially closer to commercialization.
Relationship-Specific	Not much asset specificity or operational integration on Ballard's part.	F	Some asset specificity as engine system and vehicle is designed around the Ballard stack's footprint/performance. Will have some operational dependencies at commercialization.
Symmetry	Automakers are Ballard's only route to the market. Ford is an owner and has control over some strategic decisions. Ballard's entire operations affected by vehicular alliance.	B	Ford has options in hybrid vehicles.

Ballard will become even more sensitive to Ford; given its commitment to purchase Ballard's PEMFCs, non-cooperation would have an immediate and large impact on Ballard's revenues. Ford's participation likely allows Ballard to achieve economies of scale in production, and potentially economies of scope across a range of vehicle sizes, so losing Ford will have an impact on its production cost.

Currently, Ford is not sensitive to Ballard's actions, but it may be more sensitive and vulnerable in the future. Ford's sensitivity would increase if Ballard were its sole supplier of PEMFCs and drive trains, but would still be a limited by how widespread its production of PEMFC vehicles is. Ford is also more sensitive than Daimler in that it is a pure play automaker.

Ford is also more vulnerable on the technology front, particularly as it has transferred its electric drive train technology to Ballard. In terms of firm-specific resources, Ballard provides the anchor technology in a PEMFC vehicle, and Ford designs the vehicle around Ballard's and XCELLSIS' technologies. This raises the switching costs for Ford, both in terms of redesigning its vehicles and manufacturing platforms if it chooses to exit. However, Ford's vulnerability is limited insofar as its size gives it more leeway to absorb switching costs. Given that Ford's strategy is to use hybrids as an intermediate step to PEMFC vehicles, it is also less vulnerable than Ballard and Daimler if the market is not defined as zero emissions. In this case, Ballard's resource is not as unique and can be substituted by technologies that Ford already owns. If Ballard defects, or if its technologies fail, Ford is still a viable company. However, Ballard would find it much more difficult to replace Ford, and is far more vulnerable.

Given the structure of the vehicular alliance, the relationship is asymmetric in Ford's favour. Ford has formal power over Ballard, and can influence its strategic direction and is privy to its management's decisions, making it harder for Ballard to engage in opportunistic behaviour. Additionally, Ford can prevent Ballard from working closely with other automakers. The scope of the relationship is narrower for Ford; fuel cell vehicles are a tiny element in Ford's operations, and the prospect of Ford's entire automobile production being affected by Ballard's actions is not in the immediate future.

The relative importance of the firm's resource contributions may favour Ballard. Ford's primary contribution today is market access and know-how in engineering, design and manufacturing processes. Ballard, on the other hand, allows Ford to stay ahead of the competition, and also takes most of the risk if fuel cell vehicles fail. Given that the bulk of the work on fuel cells and systems is being done by Ballard and Daimler (despite the fact that Ford now plays a much larger role in XCELLSIS); this frees up resources that Ford can use to strengthen its position in hybrid vehicles.

In terms of how important the partner's contribution is to the firm's ability to achieve its goals, Ford's contribution is more critical to Ballard than vice versa. Ballard needs Ford to be one of its customers when fuel cell vehicles are commercialized given its importance as a leading automaker. This is particularly important if other automakers are closed off to it – the only comparable target is GM, which has chosen internal development. If Ford's goal is to develop a PEMFC vehicle, Ballard currently provides it with the most advanced technology; but if Ballard loses this position, other fuel cell makers would covet a relationship with it.

Daimler and Ford

While Daimler and Ford work with Ballard and through the former XCELLSIS to develop PEMFC vehicles, their relationship is inherently competitive. At the inception of the alliance, Ford and Daimler competed in a limited number of market segments, but since Daimler's acquisition of Chrysler, the two firms compete in virtually every segment of the automobile market. Their stakes in Ballard are also large enough that they can ensure that Ballard's actions will not benefit the other disproportionately. Within the alliance, Daimler and Ford interact as members of Ballard's Board of Directors. They are also indirectly related through commitments to purchase PEMFC systems and electric drive train components and systems from the subsidiary companies.

With their joint ownership of the former XCELLSIS, Ford and Daimler have become more sensitive to the others' actions and vulnerable to their joint venture's ability to deliver the balance-of-plant system on time and on cost, since these play a large role in determining the vehicle's performance, and therefore account for a significant element of the vehicle's competitive advantage. Additionally, as PEMFC vehicles are designed around the performance characteristics of these assets, there are significant switching costs, assuming that there are alternatives available. Ford is more vulnerable to defection, since its original contribution to the alliance, the electric drive train technology, is less directly related to the vehicle's performance. It is unclear how much capability it has in engine system technology,

Table 5.5   Daimler–Ford Relationship

	Effect on Daimler	*More dependent*	*Effect on Ford*
Sensitivity	No revenue effects. But, Ford's defection may lead to Ballard requiring more funds from Daimler.	=	No revenue effects. But, Daimler's defection may lead to Ballard requiring more funds from Ford.
Vulnerability Firm-Specific	Indirect impact; Ford's defection will impact the Ballard stack's unit costs.	F	Partnered in former XCELLSIS, but technology contribution came from Daimler. May not be able to match its skills in FC engine systems.
Relationship-Specific	Some asset specificity as vehicle is designed around the former XCELLSIS' systems.	=	Some asset specificity as vehicle is designed around the former XCELLSIS' systems.
Symmetry	Daimler is focussed on fuel cell vehicles.	D	Ford has more flexibility to deal with regulatory environment; already has hybrid vehicles.

since XCELLSIS was originally part of Daimler. However, Daimler is more vulnerable than Ford at the strategic level: if Ford decides to pursue hybrid vehicles as its technological solution to environmental regulations, this would change the environment in which Daimler launches fuel cell vehicles, and may delay introduction.

How symmetrical is Daimler's and Ford's relationship in fuel cell vehicles? In terms of firm-specific factors, Ford is more dependent on Daimler's contributions based on how closely related to fuel cells their technologies are. At a higher level, however, Daimler, like Ballard, depends on Ford's weight in the industry to create a PEMFC vehicle market. From a relationship-based perspective, much of Ford and Daimler's interdependence is constructed from the equity investments in, commitments to purchase from, and non-compete provisions with, the subsidiary companies. Ford, for example, is obliged to buy

XCELLSIS engines so long as it owns shares in it. It is also obliged to buy drive trains exclusively from Ecostar. Daimler, on the other hand, was obliged to purchase fuel cell systems from XCELLSIS so long as Ballard and Ford own shares in the subsidiary, and up to five years after it ceases to own shares.

Summary

As the analysis illustrates, measuring interdependence is complex, and the extent of interdependence varies between partners and between each firm and its alliance. Interdependence also varies according to the parameters being set, for example, whether we define the relevant market as PEMFC vehicles or LEVs.

At the bilateral level, Ballard and Daimler have the most interdependent relationship, as XCELLSIS and Ballard provide complementary technologies to enhance the fuel cell's capabilities for automotive applications. Each is affected by the other's actions, even if the effects are not symmetrical. Ballard's relationship with Ford is less close today because it is based on market access and manufacturing processes, without a direct technology linkage. But, although Ballard is likely to be more concerned by Daimler's action in terms of the impact on technology development, Ford's actions have a larger impact on its position in the PEMFC vehicle market. Despite their co-ownership of XCELLSIS, Ford and Daimler have the least interdependent relationship.

When we consider the alliance as a whole, Ballard is dependent on both Ford and Daimler for strategic reasons. The two automakers act as counterweights. Absent one, Ballard would be much more dependent on the other, as it would provide the only channel to the market. Ford and Daimler guarantee Ballard's independence as a company but not its freedom of action. At the alliance level, the two automakers are also more dependent on each other than in their bilateral relationship: their combined production requirements are needed to ensure that Ballard and their subsidiary companies are able to achieve the economies of scale necessary to make fuel cell vehicles cost-competitive.

Constructing interdependence

To date, non-cooperation has been constrained by a number of factors, the key one being the fact that Ballard appears to have maintained its R&D lead in PEMFCs. Additionally, since the market is still a decade away from mass commercialization, the competitive tensions between the auto OEMs have yet to come to the fore, and the automakers may still consider the alliance a real option, a means of managing risk in the face of uncertainty. Moreover, the partners have built interdependence into the structure of the alliance, including a complex framework of equity exchanges, and commitments to purchase, and to license. However, the latest restructuring of the alliance has kicked away some of these measures, and it remains to be seen whether non-cooperation could enter into the equation absent these constraints.

The alliance's structure, particularly the division of labour along the fuel cell vehicle system value chain, increases interdependence, as some technologies become co-specialized over time. And, although Ecostar was initially a separate unit that focussed on electric drive trains, Ford has become more tied now that this subsidiary has been absorbed by Ballard. Additionally, although Ford was largely isolated from the active research on PEMFC and system technology, it has now been brought in on engine development, which increases the knowledge transfer from its participation.

Early on, the alliance's complex ownership structure played an important role in increasing the interdependence. Daimler and Ford hold significant equity stakes in Ballard and have seats on its Board, giving them a unique perspective on its operations and strategic goals. The subsidiary companies were also jointly-owned, but each dominated by one party, allowing the automakers to direct the commercialization of technologies vital to them. To ensure that the firms did not provide second-tier technology to the joint companies, the firms also made commitments to purchase that remained in place so long as the other partners co-owned the subsidiaries. The cross-shareholdings made the subsidiaries' and Ballard's activities more transparent.

The alliance also created interdependence by including commitments to purchase from Ballard, XCELLSIS and Ecostar, subject to certain limitations, particularly post-commercialization. These discouraged the partners from duplicating R&D in these areas. It also created interdependence as offtake provisions, particularly where the buyer is a launch customer, account for a large percentage of the seller's sales. In addition to the commitments to purchase, Ford and Daimler's dependence on Ballard increased because they were prohibited from competing in the development, production, distribution, sale or service of PEMFCs.

Constraining defection

As the alliance evolved, the firms have built in a number of provisions to constrain defection, either through the takeover of Ballard by one of the auto companies, by Ballard allowing itself to be taken over by a third party, or by Ford or Daimler exiting the alliance and disposing of Ballard's shares. These included commitments not to dispose of shares before a certain date, to grant the others the right of first refusal before disposing of shares. Exits were also complicated by the fact that ramifications could include unwinding activities in the subsidiary companies. For example, if Daimler disposed of its Ballard shares, the other two could have forced Daimler to buy out their stakes in XCELLSIS. This response to exits also takes place at the subsidiary level. One of the reasons for the tit-for-tat approach is that many of the commitments to purchase fuel cells, fuel cell systems, and electric drive trains were contingent on ownership in Ballard or the subsidiary companies.

The alliance agreements also raised the cost of acquiring Ballard. If Ford were the acquirer, Daimler could force the others to divest their interests in XCELLSIS. Arguably, constructed interdependence gave each firm a competitive advantage in an important component of the value chain, thus reducing the value of pursuing PEMFC vehicles independently. If Ballard defects by allowing itself to be taken over by a third party, Ford and Daimler are less vulnerable because they own the engine systems, and could replace Ballard, even if it is costly. But, Ballard would have the right to licence XCELLSIS' vehicular fuel cell systems technology and Ford's fuel tank system technology.

Constraining opportunistic behaviour

The vehicular alliance agreement incorporated a number of measures to limit the partners' ability to behave opportunistically. In Ballard's case, anti-dilution measures give Daimler and Ford the right to purchase shares to maintain their ownership stake at certain levels. Ballard and the subsidiaries were also shielded from opportunistic behaviour through non-compete measures, and requirements to share R&D.

On the flip side, the alliance also makes room for competition in PEMFC technology, perhaps as a concession in order to bring the parties together in the alliance, but this also gives the other parties the tools to retaliate against opportunistic behaviour. For example, Daimler, Ford and Ballard are allowed to compete with XCELLSIS on fuel cell systems technology and with the former Ecostar in drive train technology.

There are also provisions giving the partners the right to license each other's technologies on a non-exclusive, non-transferable and royalty-bearing basis. This right protects the other parties from opportunistic behaviour by the technology holder. In a sense, it also protects the other parties by giving them the ability to punish the technology holder by manufacturing their own components. The automakers may license Ballard's PEMFC technology, and future improvements for their own branded cars, buses and trucks.

Conclusions

To date, the story of Ballard's vehicular alliance has been one of non-defection, although it is difficult to determine whether the partners have behaved opportunistically given the lack of transparency in technology-based alliances. Non-defection may be explained by two different sets of factors. The first revolves around the fact that the environment-level, alliance competitive, intra-alliance, and firm-level factors, have all favoured cooperation. Even when Daimler's financial stresses could have cast doubt on its commitment, senior management has remained publicly committed to fuel cell vehicles.

The second set of factors focuses on power and interdependence, and the constraining role it would play even if one of the parties wanted to exit. In contrast to most of the other alliances in this book, it is clear that power is relatively evenly distributed in this alliance. Ford and Daimler's formal power and context-specific sources of power are balanced by Ballard's technology, which is its source of power. However, it also shows the limitations of context-specific sources of power; if the market were defined as low-emissions vehicles instead, then Ballard would clearly be less powerful than its two partners. Additionally, the partners are interdependent based on resources contributed to the overall goal, and on their respective positions on the value chain – they deliberately constructed interdependence via contractual terms to bind each other further.

Measures of power and interdependence are just snapshots in time, and the temporal element must be brought back into play. Not only does alliance restructuring shift the parties' relative dependence, interdependence changes because where there are no viable substitutes today, there may be in the future. What happens post-commercialization, after a number of the conditions of constructed interdependence expire? Additionally, all three of the parties will be competing explicitly in the automobile market, particularly via Ballard's sales of fuel cell stacks to other automakers. In that case, will the alliance's cross-shareholdings and the penalties associated with exiting be enough to hold a partner in?

Much also depends on whether Ballard can maintain its technology lead, and whether the value-added in PEMFC vehicles comes from providing the most powerful stack, or in the OEMs' implementations of the technology. Given that the automakers have taken this function back, we may surmise that the engine system is the critical element. The answer to this question could be the difference in whether Ballard is the Intel of the automotive industry, or whether it becomes a producer of PEMFCs according to an OEMs' specifications.

6
Global Airline Alliances: Constructing Interdependence

The rise of strategic alliances has been associated with technology industries, but aviation has been a leader in adopting cooperative competition, and continues to pioneer new approaches to alliance structure and governance. Although passenger alliances are the most high profile, airlines cooperate on a range of activities along the value chain, and many partners in one venture compete in another. Airline alliances also have a significant history of non-cooperation, and importantly for this book, non-cooperation is relatively transparent compared to other industries.

Airline alliances provide a counterpoint to the technology-based cases elsewhere in this book because the nature of the resources contributed is very different. Technology firms generally bring firm-specific knowledge or capabilities that derive from their innate innovativeness. Airlines' firm-specific resources include competencies in IT, reputation, sales networks and capital, but many of the most important resources are granted or inherited: geographic location, route authorities, slots at airports, customer base. Airline alliances are less about breaking new ground than improving competitiveness through service enhancements, although efficiency and cost-savings are becoming increasingly important, and require changes in the way the firms cooperate. Structurally, airline alliances are horizontal; members are tied together through a base level of reciprocal commitments, although some partners have closer bilateral ties.

The characteristic which most differentiates international aviation is the shadow of regulation. In spite of increasing liberalization, the industry sits on the nexus of international (traffic) and economic (competition law) regulation. Regulation has created an environment conducive to alliances, but often defines the type of resources the firms can contribute and the extent of operational integration allowed. These determinations can destabilize alliances as carriers seek partners with whom they can derive greater value, dropping those with whom they face regulatory constraints. Thus, a carrier's most vital resource, antitrust immunity, which permits it to coordinate schedules, fares, and pool revenues and costs, is a government-specific resource, and as BA and American have found to their detriment, one that can be held hostage to larger political considerations.

Industry environment

Regulation

International civil aviation is a '*global industry*, but one served by national firms.'[1] Beginning with Britain's claim to absolute sovereignty over its airspace and right to non-national treatment of foreign aircraft,[2] to the establishment of government-owned – and subsidized – flag carriers, aviation has been treated differently than other industries. Even the US, which has no state-owned carriers, has not been able to resist propping up bankrupt airlines, and establishing nationality clauses to limit foreign ownership and control.

The *Convention on International Civil Aviation* (*Chicago Convention, 1944*) established the rules and institutions governing international aviation, and defined international traffic rights (*Freedoms of the Air*).[3] But, the US and Britain's failure to agree on commercial issues created a regime where traffic rights would be negotiated bilaterally.

Since the late 1970s, the US has pushed for greater liberalization through bilateral Open Skies treaties. Their scope can vary significantly, but generally lift restrictions on the numbers of carriers allowed to fly between two countries, letting the market determine capacity and pricing; competition law became the primary regulatory instrument. However, foreign ownership restrictions remain in place. Open Skies treaties are almost a precondition for antitrust immunity to be granted to international alliances. The Netherlands was one of the first signatories; this agreement paved the way for Northwest Airlines and KLM's comprehensive alliance.

The EU has made the most radical changes, and has succeeded in deregulating the intra-EU market: in 1973, Member States were granted 5th and 7th freedom rights; in 1993, foreign ownership restrictions were eliminated;[4] and cabotage was introduced in 1997. Today, all intra-EU traffic is considered domestic. Until recently, the Chicago regime still applied to traffic between Member and non-Member

Table 6.1   Freedoms of the Air

Freedoms of the Air	
1st Freedom	The right of overflight.
2nd Freedom	The right to land for technical or non-traffic reasons, such as maintenance or to refuel, *en route* to a third country.
3rd Freedom	The right to carry traffic from a carrier's home country to another country.
4th Freedom	The right to carry traffic from another country to a carrier's home country.
5th Freedom	The right to carry traffic between two countries outside of the carrier's home country, so long as the flight originates or terminates in its home country. E.g. Cathay Pacific Flight CX888 originates in Hong Kong, disembarks and takes on passengers in Vancouver, before terminating in New York City. 5th freedom rights are sometimes segmented further: intermediate-point; beyond-point; and behind-point.
	Added Later
6th Freedom	The right of an airline to carry traffic between two foreign states, with a stop in its home country.
7th Freedom	The right to operate stand-alone services between two foreign states.
8th Freedom	The right to operate within a foreign state's domestic market ('cabotage').

states, limiting the effect of scrapping foreign ownership restrictions. It also meant that EU-rest of world traffic rights were still negotiated bilaterally. However, a 2002 European Court of Justice decision determined that the Member States' bilateral deals were in breach of laws established to create a single European market. This has opened the door for negotiations on a US-EU open skies agreement .

Economics

Since the September 11th terrorist attacks, the airline industry's financial troubles have never been far from the news. Yet, the years of economic crises, liquidations and bankruptcy protection filings that followed were only the latest in a history of boom and bust. The airline industry is extremely sensitive to its environment and financial volatility is endemic: losses in lean years outstrip the profits in good years, and historically, the industry has failed to return the cost of capital.

The challenge for airline executives is how to maximize the number of seats sold at the highest possible price while minimizing costs. Revenue per seat varies significantly between classes of service, but also within classes, according to when a ticket is bought, who sold it, and how flexible it is. Product differentiation is largely based on flying experience, such as levels of service and amenities that make travel smoother, but even these are becoming commoditized in coach class. More dangerous for traditional carriers is the low fare carrier model, which originated in the US, and has spread to Europe and Asia. These carriers have made customers even more price sensitive, forced down yields across product classes, and have contributed to breaking the traditional carrier's business model.

The industry is capital intensive with significant fixed and variable costs, and is driven by economies of scale, scope and density[5] so that size of airline and size of market play important roles in determining profitability. Capital investments in aircraft and infrastructure have long lead-times, often resulting in airlines investing during the peaks of economic cycles, but taking delivery in the downturn.

Since demand for air travel is income-elastic, macroeconomic factors such as recessions can have a large negative impact on load factors. It also affects the types of tickets purchased: high-yield business customers may downgrade their class of service or trade-off flexibility for lower prices, and carriers may need steeper discounts to attract price-sensitive travellers. Then, there are political shocks. The Persian Gulf War (1990–1), for example, led to the first ever decline in world air passenger traffic.[6] The September 11th attacks resulted in North American airspace being closed for two days; in the aftermath, North American and European carriers reduced their flights by up to 25 per cent, and laid off over 70,000 staff.[7]

Alliance rationales and activities

Cooperation has been part of the aviation industry since its inception. Cooperative competition, however, is a relatively recent phenomenon. Alliances are a means to circumvent foreign ownership rules and restrictions on traffic rights. It is also a means to increase revenues, achieve economies of scale and scope, access resources, enter new markets cheaply, improve competitive positioning and share risk. Partners bring new destinations, allowing allow carriers to develop a global network faster and with less investment, and bring transfer traffic to their domestic networks. Ideally, alliances enhance an airline's financial position in good economic times and act as a cushion during downturns.

Alliances can improve a carrier's position *vis-à-vis* domestic competitors, providing '"market share gain without balance sheet pain."'[8] Allied carriers increase market share at the expense of non-aligned carriers, affecting their high-yield traffic disproportionately, because of customer-service-oriented advantages, including more flexible schedules and flight frequencies, wider accrual and redemption opportunities for loyalty programmes, and lower fares for transfers onto partners' flights. As a result, there is a multiplier effect beyond the routes that carriers cooperate on, enhancing system-wide total factor productivity, and improving a carrier's performance across a number of economic measures, including pricing, profitability, and share price.[9] The caveat, however, is that these benefits depend on the scope of the partnership and degree of integration. To date, code-share agreements have provided most of the substance in airline alliances.[10]

Even if the incremental revenue a partnership brings is not significant in terms of an airline's overall operations, it can mean the difference between profit and loss on a route. This is crucial because carriers' flight frequencies provide a competitive advantage: if A has 65 per cent of the daily flights and B has 35 per cent, B's market share will be less than 35 per cent since customers will prefer A's more robust schedule. If B's route becomes unprofitable and it reduces frequencies, it will be even less uncompetitive and may be forced to exit the market.

The industry magazine, *Airline Business'* annual alliance surveys highlight several trends. First, only a limited number of carriers adopted alliances in the 1980s, but alliances have spread rapidly since the mid-1990s, in terms of alliances per carrier, and the number of carriers in alliances. Second, the use of equity is falling as a proportion of alliances. Third, there has been a significant amount of turbulence, as carriers drop partners from regions where there is insufficient traffic or as they search for stronger partners in various markets. However, perhaps the most salient point is the change in alliance structure, from bilateral relationships to global alliances.

Airline alliances can be segmented according to the scope of activities covered.[11] Focussed alliances cover specific activities, for example, route-specific code-share agreements, established for tactical reasons, such as increasing feed from key markets. For example, prior to joining Star Alliance, bmi British Midland (bmi) took a 'promiscuous' approach,[12] partnering with a number of direct competitors, including American, United and Continental in the US and Austrian, Lufthansa, and Air France in Western Europe.

Comprehensive alliances often widen the scope of code-sharing across the networks, and include activities which require greater operational integration, such as ground handling services and facilities, loyalty programmes, schedule coordination, crew exchanges, joint development of systems or systems software, joint marketing, joint maintenance, and joint purchasing. One of the longest-standing comprehensive alliances is Northwest-KLM, which includes revenue and cost pooling in parts of their networks.

Comprehensive alliances differ as to the level of integration, as the joint activities often become difficult to reverse over time. For example, if one party provides IT support, or they develop joint IT systems, these can create significant exit barriers. Austrian Airlines claimed that switching from Qualiflyer to Star cost about 600M schillings ($42M), of which 40 per cent could be attributed to IT, primarily because it had relied on Swissair for these capabilities.[13]

Equity plays an ambiguous role. It is seen as a sign of commitment, but it has neither prevented investors or recipients from defecting, nor stopped investors from competing with the recipient. For example, BA owned almost 25 per cent of US Air when it announced a comprehensive alliance with American, and Austrian defected from Qualiflyer to Star, despite the fact that Swissair held a significant stake in it. It has also led to conflict, notably a court case between Northwest and KLM, when it was feared that KLM was becoming too influential. Equity may be an inadequate glue: while the recipient welcomes the investment at times of financial strain, once it has recovered, it seeks to reduce the investor's role.[14] Over the years, the number of equity alliances has remained relatively constant despite a dramatic increase in the numbers of alliances. Swissair accounted for almost 20 per cent of these, while other airlines, such as Cathay Pacific, have argued that good partnerships should stand on their own, and not need equity to cement the relationship.

Global airline alliances

There is a qualitative difference between bilateral and global alliances. Arguably, bilateral relationships are not strategic, but tactical, focussing on the economics of specific markets. The decision to join a global alliance *is* strategic. In choosing an alliance, a carrier commits to a path for future growth, particularly as the groups are becoming increasingly structured and require greater operational integration. The decision to join an alliance can also result in severing long-established relationships that conflict with new partners' interests.

Global alliances change the nature of the game, particularly on the customer interface. The most obvious difference lies in branding: the carrier's advertisements, livery, stationery, loyalty programme cards, lounges carry the alliance's and its own logos. They also widen the benefits carriers can provide – easing transfers amongst member carriers' flights, making loyalty more valuable, increasing the number of lounges available, and providing ticketing assistance regardless of which partner issued the ticket.

Global alliances are also strategic in that they dictate the carrier's set of partners. Although carriers had developed bilateral networks in the past, there was little or no expectation of exclusive dealing since these relationships were mainly tactical. A global alliance creates the expectation that a carrier would work with 'family members' first. However, this expectation is not always realized.

Today's global alliances operate on two levels of commitments: alliance and partner. All members promise reciprocity on a number of customer-service issues, such as loyalty programmes, lounge access, or through check-in, although compensation is negotiated on a bilateral basis. The list of reciprocal commitments may grow as the groups evolve and have a larger impact on operations. Passenger Name Record servicing, which SkyTeam advertises, allows passengers to change tickets with any SkyTeam carrier's agents; this requires a greater degree of access and interoperability with each others' IT systems. Star Alliance has gone farther, announcing plans to develop a common IT platform which increases the level of commitment needed at the alliance-level.

Much of the alliance's value, however, resides at the bilateral level, specifically, in flight operations. Within an alliance, most carriers only have significant ties to a few partners, focussing on specific markets; the other partners' markets are simply inconsequential. Equity investments, or sales, maintenance or revenue-management support relationships, are also largely a bilateral concern. Thus, there is significant variation in the carriers' interdependence.

The ramifications of exiting from a global alliance are more significant than exiting bilateral relationships, which only impacts a segment of a carrier's customer base. Exiting an alliance affects a large percentage of customers who fly internationally, as well the carrier's domestic operations because of transfer traffic. In addition, global alliances often have significant switching costs where alliance-wide projects create operational linkages amongst partners. In contrast, a constellation of bilateral alliances allows carriers to isolate their relationships and to exit one without affecting another. They can also replace a partner with its rival. In a global alliance, even if an airline ends a bilateral relationship, it cannot renege on its base level commitments. Additionally, it may be constrained from replacing that bilateral relationship because of the alliance's exclusivity rules, or because the potential partners are in competing alliances.

Influences on the firm's attitude

The conventional wisdom is that there is little downside to airline alliances – at worst, they are revenue neutral. However, defections have been rife.[15] What then, influences a carrier's desire to stay or go?

Environment

Regulation is the defining characteristic of international civil aviation, a catalyst for alliance formation; alliances are often viewed as substitutes for the mergers and acquisitions which take place in other industries. This implies that alliances are temporary structures, and airlines will be committed so long as regulations bar industry consolidation. The KLM-Air France merger in 2004, the first between two major flag carriers, may be a first step in breaking the group-vs-group dynamic.

Regulation also impacts an alliance's competitiveness and may lead partners to defect, if competition law requirements hamper meaningful cooperation. For example, the US DoJ and the European Commission's refusal to grant American and BA antitrust immunity, absent concessions neither will accept, prevents them from competing on a level playing field against SkyTeam and Star, who have trans-Atlantic antitrust immunity. This has led American and BA to explore alternatives, threatening Oneworld's stability.

Industry structure impacts a firm's choice of behaviour; in aviation, the momentum has clearly been toward global alliances. This created a bandwagon effect, as non-aligned carriers sought to join an alliance quickly, for fear of being locked out. Today, the industry has reached strategic gridlock, since all of the major US carriers have chosen sides, and the major carriers who remain outside choose to do so. So, airlines unhappy with their alliances may be forced to stay because there is nowhere to go, or because the cost of being non-aligned outweighs the downside in its current alliance. But, if a major carrier collapses, this could open the door for an industry-wide re-alignment.

Alliance-competitive environment

At the alliance-competitive level, all things being equal, the more successful the alliance, the more likely it is able to forestall non-cooperation. According to United Airlines, during the late 1990s, Star's traffic growth stretched its members' ability to keep up with demand[16] – if the absolute gains are large and returns exceed the firm's expectations, it is unlikely to be as concerned with relative gains. The opposite is true if the alliance is failing to meet expectations.

With group-based competition, alliance-level metrics become important, as the 'more destinations, lounges, flights' message is simple to convey to customers and members. So, alliances compete for members to cover gaps in their networks and try to poach desirable carriers from other groups. The Star Alliance has stressed alliance-level metrics, living up to its motto, 'the airline network for earth' in a relentless membership drive. On the other hand, Oneworld stresses the 'quality' of its membership,[17] and SkyTeam carriers have indicated that there should be limits to alliance size.[18] The reality, however, is that what defines success is not clear-cut if alliances are a tool of strategy, rather than a strategy. It is not a pure large numbers game, but a question of coverage in the world's most lucrative markets, and members' financial performance.

Intra-alliance environment

The intra-alliance factors influencing firm behaviour focus on the conflicts that can arise between the carrier and its alliance, or with partners over an alliance's direction, the nature of alliance initiatives pursued, and the group's composition.

Global airline alliances have a distinct corporate identity, and therefore alliance philosophy can become a source of tension – does it compete on a reputation for customer service or network coverage? Do they want a Star, Oneworld or SkyTeam entity or 'one partner serving all alliance customers' – a question of alliance versus carrier pre-eminence? Star and Oneworld have alliance organizations staffed by secondees and independent hires, creating a risk that these organizations will develop independent views, even if they are accountable to the members.

Alliance expansion can be a source of conflict, as members may want to bring in third parties with whom they have historical ties, but which conflict with other partners' favoured carriers. Additionally, although new members strengthen the group's competitiveness, they may compete with an incumbent, and the larger the alliance, the greater the risk of conflict. Each expansion impacts an airline's returns and its influence within the group. For example, under an alliance's exclusivity rules, new entrants may force incumbents to sever existing relationships which compete with it. Even if the new entrant serves the same market, the incumbent may not reap the same benefits due to their networks' fit, customer bases or reputation.[19]

The question of exclusivity also affects non-cooperation. The more stringent the rule, the more likely it is that the alliance cannot meet some of its members' idiosyncratic needs, and the more likely it is that new entrants will disrupt the incumbents' existing bilateral relationships. But, a relaxed approach increases the possibility that a member's bilateral partners conflict with its alliance partners. Some alliances are more pragmatic, recognizing that their members have strategic interests and that there are questions of fit between partners; however, they agree that a carrier can only be in one global alliance, and that ideally, members would phase out relationships with airlines in competing groups.

A carrier's decision to cooperate or defect may also depend on the structure of its bilateral ties in the alliance, which may result in tightly woven subgroups. For example, BA's joint operations with Qantas allows them to dominate the 'Kangaroo Route' between Australia and the UK, and allowed BA to divert three 747s to other parts of its network, making this relationship more valuable to BA than the rest of Oneworld.[20] If the reverse were also true, this dynamic implies that if one member exited, others may follow. If entire subgroups defect, these could trigger alliance collapses.

Since naturally-occurring interdependence may not be strong enough to bind members, alliances have constructed formal and informal exit barriers. For example, Star has introduced financial penalties for exit.[21] Less formal measures include exclusivity provisions, which raise the cost of rebuilding a network. Capital intensive alliance-wide projects become exit barriers if members are reluctant to walk away from investments. Likewise, joint operations, such as using a partner's staff for sales, ticketing, and check-in at international destinations, also increase switching costs.

An alliance's skill at managing conflict can play an important role in ameliorating non-cooperative behaviour. The general consensus is that Thai was sidelined as Star's Southeast Asian hub after Singapore's entry. To forestall a defection, Star has tried to find ways for Thai to derive greater benefits from its participation.

Firm internal

An airline's product is not fungible, so it has an incentive to sell the space, even at a deep discount, if only to cover its fixed costs. Absent shared costs and revenues, partners will compete for the very price-sensitive customer with special classes of fares and last-minute deals. They may be even more tempted to compete in the case of block-space agreements, where the code-share partner pays for a certain number of seats, regardless of whether they are sold.

There is also a question of whether the alliance provides all the resources that the airline needs, such as the right customer mix, partners with strong brands, or other assets necessary for it to compete effectively in its domestic market. If not, can the missing pieces be brought in through a bilateral partnership, or is there another alliance which meets the firm's needs more closely? Moreover, domestic considerations may hold a carrier back from signing on to some alliance-level customer service initiatives: a carrier in a very competitive market would want to provide its customers with more service enhancements, whereas a monopolist has little reason to be generous.

Today, after global economic downturn, vigorous new competitors, and decline in traffic after terrorism, war, and disease, airlines are in the midst of a financial crisis and face a dilemma. Most have reduced flight frequencies or eliminated destinations, relying on their alliance partners to help fill these gaps. But given the huge financial losses many are facing, they will be more tempted to behave opportunistically, in order to improve their own bottom lines.

Behaviours

Competition

In airline alliances, cooperation is a façade over operational realities; it takes place primarily in customer service, since this is easiest to achieve and relatively easy to exit from, and in more integrated alliances, in some back office functions and joint purchasing. Unlike technology partnerships, competition is an integral part of the alliance environment. The majority of the airline executives interviewed expect their partners to compete on price, flight frequencies, available connections, and on quality of service and flying experience. But, having these expectations does not mean that competition does not strain relationships.

With the exception of routes where they pool all revenues and costs, carriers compete for traffic on other routes and to third-country destinations, even on code-shared flights. Alliance partners have separate seat sales and special offers, and to date, most still have individual sales forces. They also compete by purchasing unused routes or airport slots from other airlines, even where these compete directly with a partner's spheres of influence or key markets, as United did with Pan American's German routes or American's purchase of Eastern's Latin American routes. These purchases also serve to reduce their dependence on their partners. For example, United's and BA's relationship ended when United began its own service to London.

Interestingly, United's executives have claimed that it does not compete with Lufthansa, the other large carrier in the Star Alliance, arguing that they draw customers from the hinterlands (behind-point) of their own hubs, Chicago and Frankfurt, rather than target their partners' core customers. But, industry observers have disputed this benign view, arguing that during the Asian financial crisis (1997–8), United moved aircraft from trans-Pacific to trans-Atlantic routes, a move Lufthansa matched flight-for-flight.[22] United has also offered Boston-Frankfurt return, for about one-fifth Lufthansa's price, even though one journey would be operated by its partner;[23] Lufthansa later matched United's prices.

Opportunistic behaviour

The extent of competition in airline alliances narrows the scope for opportunistic behaviour. Since there are no standard alliance agreements, few categories of behaviour can be labelled opportunistic. Each group permits a greater or lesser degree of competition and has different expectations of exclusivity. Nevertheless, opportunistic behaviour does occur at both strategic and operational levels.

For example, if partners expect that future expansions into each other's market would be done in cooperation, it would be considered opportunistic if the partner cooperated with a third partner instead. Opportunism also takes place at the alliance level, on the issue of membership, since new entrants who strengthen the group's position can hurt incumbents.

Operationally, as alliances expand their cooperative activities, this opens the door to greater opportunism. Even if firms agree on a goal, members have competing interests since many airline groups also have maintenance, IT, ground handling, or catering subsidiaries that they want to protect. Members could also compel others to support their vision of how a project proceeds, which may not be the best or the most cost-effective solution, through delay or by hurting its partners' interests in other areas.

Defection

Exits are the most easily observed behaviour in airline alliances. The 275 exits (as of 2001) in a database created from a subset of the *Airline Business* alliance surveys identifies seven categories.[24] The simplest is when parties end a relationship which is not replaced. In these cases, the alliance may have been a tool to test the market, followed by the carrier's entry or withdrawal. Defections occur when a partner is replaced by its competitor, such as BA's game of musical chairs with different US partners before settling for American. Exits may result from changes in strategy, such as joining a global alliance. In a few cases, a carrier moved from one multiparty alliance to another. Just as rare, and counterintuitive, are exits from multiparty relationships to bilateral ones, such as Mexicana's exit from Star in late 2003. However, this supports the contention that if most carriers are tied primarily to one or two partners in a alliance, it could replicate most of the value with a small number of new partners and no alliance-overhead cost. Finally, there are involuntary exits, where a carrier has become insolvent or has been acquired by another.

Power and interdependence

Power in global airline alliances comes from owning or controlling resources, many of which are related to firm size. Although we can identify the generic sources of power, which resources are the most important are also a function of the specific alliance, and its philosophy and market focus.

4.1 Power

In airline alliances, a firm's power is a function of firm-specific resources, the size of alliance and size distribution of membership, and any additional rights conferred by the group's governance rules. All things being equal, the larger the airline, the bigger the network, the larger percentage of traffic carried, the greater its power in the alliance. Objective measures of power such as market capitalization and financial strength are less important since financial stability is not a hallmark of the industry, and because regulatory constraints limit their usefulness. Thus, a carrier's informal power comes from the size of its customer base and the quality of its revenues, its contribution to the network, and its market's importance, and can be enhanced by resources conferred by regulators, including route authorities, landing slots at congested hub airports, and most importantly, the prospect of antitrust immunity. These regulation-based resources, such as bmi's ownership of valuable slots at London's

Heathrow airport, can give smaller carriers more power than they would otherwise merit.

The alliance's governance structure may change the power distribution. Majority voting allows smaller carriers to gang up on larger ones, while consensus gives each party veto power, and weighted voting reinforces the power of the larger carriers. However, these formal measures may not reflect how the alliance actually operates.

Interdependence

In the airline industry, natural interdependence is generally not sufficient to bind partners, particularly as many partnerships exist only because of artificial barriers created by regulators. There is little natural interdependence at the group level. As a result, carriers have had to construct interdependence, in some cases by establishing a formal alliance infrastructure.

Carrier and alliance

How sensitive is a carrier to its alliance and vice versa? A carrier's sensitivity is a function of the value of transfer traffic, and other partner revenue from loyalty programmes and lounge access. But, while they are equally sensitive in terms of the immediacy of the impact of an alliance's actions, the magnitude varies. Major US carriers such as American and United derive about 70 per cent of their revenues from domestic traffic, and while alliance traffic is important, it remains incremental to the domestic activities.[25]

The alliance and carriers are vulnerable to each other's actions. An airline's vulnerability depends on how critical an alliance is to its business strategy, the importance of international traffic to its revenue base, the alliance's contribution to its global reach, the value of transfer traffic from its partners, and its options outside of the alliance. In the past, a strong carrier from the US, Asia and Europe would have options as it is a desirable partner, but given strategic gridlock, even these carriers will have difficulty finding alternatives.

Vulnerability is also a function of temporal factors; carriers have bargaining power when negotiating their entry but lose it as they adjust their schedules, discard conflicting bilateral relationships, and as options outside of the alliance disappear. Members become more dependent as other carriers join alliances, and if its alliance has strong exclusivity rules. Operational integration also increases as alliances pursue more initiatives together, which raises exit costs, particularly for smaller members, as they may have outsourced key functions to the group. In other words, alliance rules which construct interdependence create relationships that may evolve into natural interdependence.

The extent of a carrier's dependence on the alliance is also a function of network density (the numbers of linkages between partners), such as extensive code-share or operational support agreements, or multiple cross-shareholdings amongst the partners. This effectively closes off a small carrier's threat of exit: the smaller the airline, the less able it will be to afford the switching costs, and, the smaller its geographic network, the less it is able to handle the volume of international traffic without an alliance.

The alliance's vulnerability depends how unique and important a member's resources are: the carrier's reputation, the importance of a carrier's market, how much high-yield traffic is generated to/from it, as well as the value of its domestic destinations. The anchor carriers from Europe, Asia, but especially the US, are critical to the alliance's functioning, but even the loss of a smaller carrier would impact the group's high-yield traffic from the region. The Swissair case in this chapter shows that alliances are vulnerable to the financial stability of its most important members. Today, if one of the US anchor carriers were liquidated, their respective alliance's value to its members would decrease significantly, and would potentially cause it to implode.

Beyond the anchor carriers, the alliance is not vulnerable to its members' actions. Since there are fewer viable global alliances than available carriers, non-core members can be substituted by others in their regions. Moreover, these carriers contribute only a fraction of the alliance's competitive resources, and become even less significant as the membership grows.

As the industry structure solidifies into three alliances, asymmetries in dependence will tilt further in the alliance's favour. In the major international markets, an alliance is a critical resource – not being in one is a competitive disadvantage. An alliance is not easily substituted, given the array of resources it brings, and the scope of the carrier's operations affected. Aside from Japan Airlines, few major international carriers from the three anchor regions have remained outside an alliance.

Between alliance partners

The significant commitments occur between individual carriers. These ties create *de facto* subgroups, such as SkyTeam's Northwest-Continental-Delta or Star's Lufthansa-Austrian-LOT Polish Airlines (LOT)-bmi-Scandinavian Airlines (SAS), which often derive greater value from each other than the rest of the alliance. These present a more credible threat to the alliance's survival, as a mass exodus could result in the alliance's collapse.

A firm is sensitive to its partners' actions with respect to the impact on its revenues or cash flow, the magnitude of the effect, and its affect on its ability to deliver its products. In an airline alliance, this depends on whether cooperation is in flight operations or operations support. Since contractual obligations mean that exits lag the announcement, often by several months, there is no immediate impact on revenues. And, where two carriers have no bilateral ties, for example, Star's Singapore and LOT, if one exited, the impact will be negligible, coming primarily from the loyalty programme, and transfer traffic.

Airlines, however, are very sensitive to disruptions to operations. This was clearly demonstrated in the post-September 11th shutdown of North American airspace: it took the better part of a week to get passengers to their final destinations, move aircraft from one point to another, and normalize operations. Where there is significant operational integration, such as code-sharing, coordinating flight schedules to maximize connections, handling each other's ticketing, or baggage handling and ground support, then purely internal issues, such as labour strife, have knock-on effects throughout the alliance.

Vulnerability asks how well a firm is able to cope with its partner's actions. Losing a partner affects a carrier's competitiveness in the foreign market, since allied airlines are able to offer their customers lower fares for connecting traffic beyond the international gateway, and the partner helps sell the carrier's inventory in its market. It is also more vulnerable to those partners with which it has established deeper relationships, such as code-shares, or operations and IT support. The effect is not only a matter of lost revenues, but also the cost to replace the resource. For example, if a code-share breaks up, the parties must exit the route or invest in services; in Qantas and Canadian Airlines' case, each flew one leg of the Vancouver-Hawaii-Sydney route. After Canadian was acquired by Air Canada, Qantas had to extend its service all the way to Vancouver, an effort Air Canada had to match. The effects are magnified in a comprehensive alliance.

What does a partner bring? How important is this resource to the carrier? How much will it cost to replace it? Some resources, such as traffic rights or slots at an overcrowded airport, are unique, and cannot be replaced. Carriers are also vulnerable in that there is a relatively limited pool of appropriate partners per relevant market, given the monopolistic history of the industry. For example, Oneworld cannot replace Canadian, since Star's Air Canada is the only major Canadian carrier left.

Vulnerability interdependence also increases with operational integration or co-specialization. For example, antitrust immunity allows KLM-Northwest to coordinate schedules, and pool revenues and costs across the Atlantic. Since neither carrier has sales and ticketing functions in the foreign market, the cost of rebuilding this infrastructure would be high, particularly with respect to market knowledge. Where one partner provides the other's yield management system and services, as American did for Canadian, then the relationship can become very dependent. On the other hand, although Austrian was dependent on Swissair's IT capability, and was part-owned by Swissair, it defected to join Star, illustrating that dependence is not an infallible means of predicting cooperation. But, it is fair to say that in Austrian's case, extenuating circumstances, namely Swissair's attempted hostile takeover, made high switching costs acceptable.

Symmetry focuses on the partners' relative importance to each other, taking into account strategic level issues. The key question is how important is the partner's market, the carrier's own operations in that market, and whether the partner's resource can be substituted. Symmetry is also a function of each carrier's relative size; the larger the carrier the smaller the impact.

According to airline executives, bilateral alliances between large and small carriers benefit the smaller disproportionately. The larger carrier, with a bigger customer base, feeds more traffic to the smaller on both an absolute and percentage basis. To illustrate, in the Canadian-BA relationship, BA flew to all the largest Canadian business markets. Even though it brought high-yield traffic, Canadian could not add significant value to BA's Canadian interests. On the other hand, Canadian's customers gained access to BA's global network, and it benefited from BA's transfer traffic.[26] This gives the larger carrier bargaining power as they negotiate the division of the benefits: it is in the smaller carrier's interests to split the incremental revenue in a manner that recognizes that the larger partner's contribution, so it is unlikely to gain its theoretical maximum.

Historical alliances: Swissair[27]

Swissair was the first carrier to pursue a multiparty alliance strategy. These alliances had their own brand identity, but were less sophisticated in terms of standardising base levels of commitment than today's. Swissair pursued a complex two-alliance strategy – one group of long-haul or transcontinental carriers for global reach, and a second group of regional carriers from the European market. However, each of its alliances collapsed after repeated defections. As a result, Swissair overcompensated when structuring its last alliance, Qualiflyer.

Power, interdependence and behaviour in Swissair's early alliances

Throughout the 1990s, Swissair pursued a dual alliance strategy – one to access the Asian and US markets, and a European one for regional traffic feed. Swissair's early alliances varied in terms of the parties' contributions and the scope of cooperation, generally focussing on customer service. Attempts to pursue deeper integration failed.

In *Global Excellence* (1989–97), Swissair, Delta and Singapore made symbolic equity exchanges. Delta was the most powerful, based on resource contributions, accounting for the largest share of traffic, revenues, destinations, market and able to transfer more traffic to its partners than vice versa. However, after eight years, the carriers did not pursue enough initiatives to generate value from the relationship or to form natural exit barriers, leading Singapore to exit for a relationship with Lufthansa. Absent an Asian partner, Swissair formed *Atlantic Excellence* (1997–9), using equity to a greater extent. Swissair owned half of Sabena, and 10 per cent of Austrian, giving it more power over these carriers and a larger voice at the alliance level. But, Delta was still by far the most powerful and least dependent. Again, partners defected to relationships that could bring greater value.

Power differentials in the *European Quality Alliance* (1989–95) were far less significant. The group had two larger and two smaller carriers, whose contributions largely complemented each other. Despite cross-shareholdings, formal power was not significant. As the largest carrier, Swissair was the most influential member, and appeared to be the driving force, for example, pushing for greater integration. The anecdotal evidence indicates that Swissair sought greater power, which it could not achieve in its global group, but even so, interdependence was not strong enough to hold its partners in. Finnair and SAS exited because they were not tied to European Quality, but also because they an exit option in Lufthansa.

One of the recurring themes in Swissair's early alliances is that they collapsed after a series of defections. While the reasons behind the exits vary, in all of the cases, it is evident that interdependence within the alliance was not strong enough to hold them in when alternative options became available.

Qualiflyer: creating dependence

In 1998, Swissair and a subset of the Atlantic Excellence members founded yet another European alliance, *Qualiflyer*. For the first time, Swissair did not have a complementary long-haul alliance, at a time when other carriers were moving toward a global alliance model. Had Swissair abandoned its global aspirations or was it waiting for an opportunity where it could 'punch above its weight' in terms of influence? Austrian, Sabena, AOM France, Crossair, Lauda Air, TAP Portugal, and THY Turkish Airlines were joined in 1999 by Air Europe and LOT, and in 2000 by Air Littoral, Portugalia and Volare Air. The small carriers brought a diverse range of assets, including access to the Italian regional market, the French domestic markets and overseas territories, as well as the Portuguese market and connections to South America. The alliance level goal was to code-share where possible and cooperate on IT, baggage handling, sales, training, cargo, and maintenance and to establish a common loyalty programme.

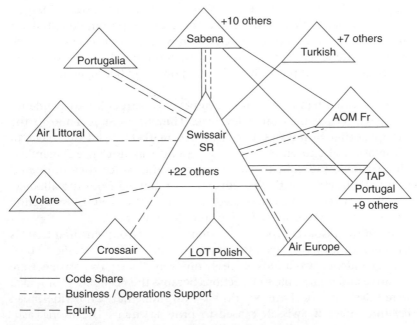

————— Code Share
————— Business / Operations Support
— — — Equity

Figure 6.1 Qualiflyer Members and their External Partners

Structurally, Qualiflyer differed from the earlier alliances in that it was a constellation. As Figure 6.1 shows, Swissair anchored the group: each member has a direct relationship with it, but generally, not with each other.

Since Swissair's previous alliances had disintegrated after a series of exits, it learned from experience to forestall defections by constructing dependence or through the use of equity. Qualiflyer members had to patronize Swissair Group-owned companies for aviation services, a requirement driven in part by its business model: it was mainly a non-passenger traffic business that needed a large captive market to feed the other units.[28] Additionally, it used equity liberally. By May 2000, the Swissair Group had taken or promised to take equity stakes of between 30–50 per cent in all but one of its partners. It increased its stake in Crossair to 70 per cent and agreed to increase its stake in Sabena to 85 per cent.

Power and interdependence

In Qualiflyer, Swissair created an alliance in which it was clearly the most powerful partner on both informal and formal terms; it was by far the largest, accounting for some 30 per cent of revenue passenger traffic, and its revenues were over four times that of the second-largest carrier, Sabena. Thus, it would be the most important conduit for transfer traffic. It also contributed the most important resources, such as IT, maintenance, operations support, and reputation. Swissair supported its informal power with formal power, by taking equity stakes in its partners.

On the other hand, Swissair's attempts to construct interdependence also gave its partners more leverage. They brought revenue to the Group's other businesses, and access to markets it did not have an automatic right to enter since Switzerland was not an EU member. The partners, individually, were not powerful, since they only contributed a fraction of the benefits Swissair derived from the alliance. Swissair's partners also detracted from it as the bevy of struggling regional carriers took away from its premium image.

Given the resources that it contributed, the Group ensured that its partner airlines were dependent on it. In terms of firm-specific factors, the dependence was almost entirely one-way. Swissair's partners were sensitive and vulnerable to its actions because the resources it provided were mission critical and would have an immediate and widespread revenue effect if Swissair ceased to provide them. The more cash-strapped carriers were also sensitive because Swissair provided needed capital and its service contributions affected flight operations. Furthermore, since Swissair's resources permeated its partners' operations, switching and exit costs would be relatively high. The extreme case is Sabena, which was being managed by a Swissair-owned company in addition to cooperating on sales, reservations, ground handling, IT, cargo operations, and code-shares.

Conversely, Swissair was not dependent on a specific partner's resources. Swissair's airline operations were only somewhat sensitive to the smaller carriers in terms of revenues from transfer traffic, or code-shares, since European traffic only accounted for half of its revenues and Qualiflyer's contributions a fraction of that. Its partners' actions could affect its other businesses, but again, Qualiflyer carriers were not their primary customers. Given the scale and scope of the Group's operations, a single partner's actions would not have a significant impact on it.

Given the nature of its resource contributions, and its partners commitments to utilize its services, Swissair clearly had power over its partners and they were clearly dependent on it. Swissair did not have to take such large equity stakes. Aside from LOT, where Swissair outbid BA and Lufthansa for its stake, it is not evident that the other European carriers had many options outside of Qualiflyer.

In spite of the fact that Swissair was clearly the most powerful party, and its partners depended on its resources, when it constructed interdependence, it not only bound its partners, but also itself. Swissair's commitments to increase its equity holdings, guarantee its partners' debts or serve as a lender of last resort, increased its exposure to its partners' financial performance. Swissair, therefore, weakened its own position by creating a situation of mutual dependence: even though its partners depended on Swissair for operational support, this was balanced by their potential impact on Swissair's profit and loss and cash flow. Moreover, the structure of the alliance commitments meant that Swissair faced significant exit costs.

The environment, the alliance, and the fall of Swissair

Given the airline's stellar reputation, the Swissair Group was assumed to be a profitable operation. The reality was that although the Group's operations were profitable, financial management and investment strategies brought losses – between 1989–2000, average net margins were lower than average operating margins by almost 5.5%. Additionally, between 1995–2000, data from *Airline Business'* annual surveys show that the Group's operating margins underperformed the industry average every year, and underperformed on a net margins basis in all but two years. This is in spite of the fact that the volatile passenger transport business only accounted for about half of its operations, and that it had diversified in order to smooth out its earnings.

Although external factors, including a changing competitive environment with the new global airline alliances, played a role in weakening its financial position, the majority of its problems are the direct result of its use of equity to bind its partners. This was evident in the Group's balance sheet and cash flow statements. From 1997–2000, liabilities doubled due to bank loans, and provisions to cover expected liabilities from its airline investments. The effects on cash flow were just as severe: between 1997–2000, free cash flow was negative CHF 1347M. By 2000, Swissair was also propping up its French partners by an estimated CHF 80M per month, while Sabena had to be restructured and recapitalized.

By 2000, the Group stated that it no longer had the ability to finance its strategy, particularly as its associated companies were resisting calls to restructure. Therefore, its only choice was to restructure the Group itself: stem cash outflow by exiting loss-making investments and focus on the airline business. Thus, while Swissair succeeded in preventing its partners from defecting from the alliance, it now had to defect. But, constructed interdependence raised its exit costs as some of its commitments could not be abrogated without financial compensation. Sabena proved to be the stickiest investment as it teetered on the brink of bankruptcy in 2001. This required further capital injections from its owners, Swissair and the Belgian government.

Extricating itself from its alliance commitments was just one element of the restructuring plan; the Group began disposing of assets, including core businesses, such as its Nuance retail stores, and stakes in Swissport ground handling operations. Whether these measures could stave off bankruptcy became moot after the terrorist attacks in the US fundamentally altered the industry's operating environment.

Ultimately, the Swissair Group's bankruptcy was the result of failures in partner choice and structuring its alliance. The resource-based analysis showed that the relationships were asymmetrical in Swissair's favour: it contributed mission-critical resources which required operational integration on its partners' parts, and which had high switching costs. It did not need to use equity to hold its partners; equity, along with promises to guarantee loans, or act as a lender of last resort made the Group sensitive, and ultimately, vulnerable to its partners' financial crises. Moreover, these investments undermined its diversification strategy by increasing its exposure to the volatile airline business. Finally, its partner choice was questionable – investing in weak carriers from the same geographic region increased its exposure to the same macroeconomic environment. In constructing a cage to prevent its partners from exiting, Swissair locked itself in as well, weakening, rather than strengthening the Group.

Modern era of global alliances[29]

The modern era of global alliances began in 1997, and has rapidly changed the nature of competition in the industry. But, these new institutions already face serious challenges. The alliances, established at the peak of an economic cycle and on top of a stock market bubble, sought to increase revenues by pursuing high-yield international business travellers. But, political shocks, changes in the macroeconomic environment, increasingly price-sensitive business travellers, and the rise of aggressive new competitors have combined to break the traditional carriers' business model. With yields falling, the 'revenue up' mentality has been replaced by 'revenue retention' and cost control.

What this means is that the alliances' original *raison d'être* is being undermined. In their original incarnation, the carriers' promises to each other were primarily customer-service oriented, and not very sticky. While they still pursue revenues, increasingly sophisticated customer-service promises need to be supported by infrastructures, requiring greater commitment. At the same time, alliances are trying to remain relevant in the new environment by adding cost initiatives, such as joint purchasing, or outsourcing within the group. But, from a resource contribution perspective, is a pool of partners chosen to increase revenue appropriate for these goals? Would a carrier achieve more with other airlines, or with firms outside of the industry? And, if alliances are substitutes for mergers, does it want to pursue the level of integration and commitment these initiatives represent? This hybridization of the alliance's purpose could lead to defections, and perhaps more worrisome, continuous tension within a group as members resist different aspects of proposed changes.

The alliances have taken different approaches to constructing interdependence, and in reacting to the changing environment. Star has been the most focussed on constructing interdependence at the alliance-level, pursuing a wide range of initiatives on both the revenue and cost sides. Oneworld's carriers construct interdependence at the bilateral level, encouraging network density. It has retained its focus on revenue generation, giving its members room to take radical approaches to restructuring their businesses. SkyTeam's constructed interdependence appears to be at a regional subgroup level, although the ultimate direction remains unclear given its rapid growth.

Star Alliance

The Star Alliance, founded by five airlines in 1997, is the first truly global alliance, and has been the most successful at attracting new members. Currently, its 15 members (Air Canada, Air New Zealand, All Nippon, Asiana, Austrian Airlines, bmi, LOT, Lufthansa, SAS, Singapore, Spanair, Thai, United, US Airways, Varig) serve over 770 destinations, and accounted for 21 per cent of the world's passenger traffic (by revenue passenger kilometres) in 2003.

From an alliance development perspective, Star has reached further than the others in pursuing alliance-wide initiatives in revenue generation (for example the *Star Alliance Enhanced Benefits Package* joint loyalty programme attack on BA in 2004), and in developing common infrastructures. Its members have shown loyalty, supporting Air Canada's takeover of Canadian Airlines. But, Star also has a history of opportunistic behaviour, particularly with respect to alliance growth, and it has the distinction of being the only group to have suffered a defection. Symptomatic of the airline industry, few of its carriers are consistently profitable, but it has more members facing financial crises. Since 2001, Ansett Australia collapsed, Air New Zealand was re-nationalized, and until recently, Air Canada, United, and US Airways were under bankruptcy protection. Continued financial instability may threaten Star's ability to deliver alliance-level projects, from both a financial and personnel availability perspective.

Star has moved the furthest in terms of institutional development; its Frankfurt-based headquarters has over 65 staff to pursue joint efforts in IT, Sales and Network, Marketing and Loyalty, and Products and Services. While this has allowed it to develop more alliance-level initiatives than its competitors, a strong alliance bureaucracy does raise questions of whether the institution reflects the interests of the members, and may be a source of tension if the carriers view the bureaucracy as telling them what to do, or if the management team is not perceived to be impartial.

Power

Given Star's focus on network breadth, the most important resource contribution, and therefore source of influence, would appear to be the carrier's network size and passenger traffic. By these informal measures,

143

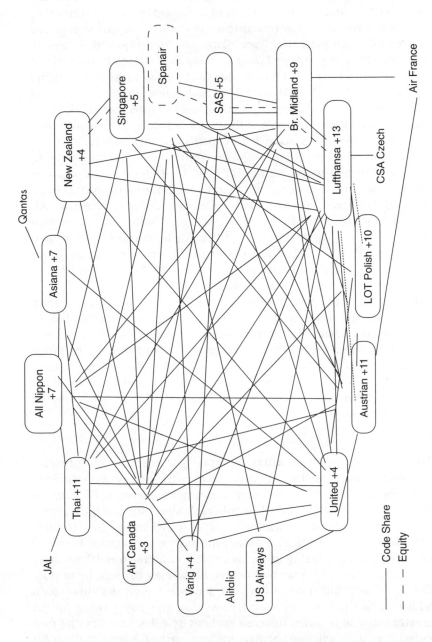

Figure 6.2   Star Alliance Members and their External Partners

the most powerful members of the group must be United and Lufthansa, which were second and ninth largest in the world by passenger traffic in 2003, and have trans-Atlantic antitrust immunity. They are well placed to exert influence, since they have bilateral relationships with 12 and 14 other members, respectively. Power accruing to size is reinforced by both the number of members and the size distribution of its membership: after United, six rank between 9–17, another five between 27–45, and the rest between 92–112. Star's pursuit of alliance-level projects also conspires to magnify the influence of the larger members, since smaller ones may have neither the personnel nor expertise to participate fully.

The value of other carriers' resource contributions has been demonstrated in other ways. Lufthansa and United invited Singapore Airlines, one of the most reputable in its region, to join, even though its rival Thai was one of Star's founding members. Likewise, Air Canada's value was proven in its merger battle with Canadian Airlines. United's value is enhanced because it is one of two US carriers permitted to fly to London Heathrow. By the same token, bmi's primary value to the alliance is its large share of slots at Heathrow, which enhances Star's position there.

The governance rules give the members formal power, and a voice over the group's direction on issues such as membership and alliance-level projects. Theoretically, this gives incumbents a veto over new entrants; but the reality is that other members may exercise their own informal power and 'lean on a holdout'.[30] Equity does not play a large role, with the exception of bmi, where Lufthansa and SAS own 30 per cent and 20 per cent respectively, and Spanair, which is SAS's wholly-owned subsidiary.

Interdependence

More so than the other alliances, Star is attempting to construct interdependence at the alliance level with sticky investments. A prime example is its recently-announced *Common IT Platform Project*,[31] which will allow all members to share software, databases and technical platforms, and may make it difficult to link to non-members. Star also places greater emphasis on a 'master brand',[32] with Star level marketing initiatives that could take mindshare away from its carriers. This may be positive for weaker carriers, by providing legitimacy, but it creates greater dependence on the alliance. In addition to these alliance-level measures, the governance fosters greater bilateral linkages through exclusivity rules, encouraging new entrants to drop existing partners for Star carriers. Surprisingly, most members still have code-share relationships with outside carriers, including those in competing alliances.

Although alliances are not sensitive to individual carriers in general, Star may be both sensitive and vulnerable to its members' financial instability because of the extent of alliance-level projects. If customers are concerned about a carrier's survivability, bookings will fall, reducing traffic feed to the rest of the alliance. Anecdotal evidence suggests that this is already happening to US Airways, and to a lesser extent, United after it failed to win approval for a government loan guarantee.[33] In the worst-case scenario, the sudden loss of a large carrier has a significant financial impact on the group, and will threaten the viability of Star-level projects.

Interdependence varies considerably at the bilateral level. Some carriers have deep bilateral ties: Lufthansa and United operate with a trans-Atlantic revenue sharing agreement; United and Air Canada's code-share agreement covers both their networks; and SAS has an extensive code-share, harmonized pricing, and sales and marketing relationship with Lufthansa. More interesting, however, is Lufthansa's relationships with Austrian and LOT; both have subsumed their loyalty programmes under Lufthansa's *Miles & More*, giving up their primary interface with their best customers, to depend on a partner-competitor instead. In contrast, Swiss International Air Lines, the successor company to Swissair, withdrew its commitment to Oneworld after it reportedly clashed with BA over loyalty programme issues.

Within these clusters, carriers become both more sensitive and vulnerable to their partners' actions, since these tend to be regionally focussed, and represent each other's most important markets. They also become more vulnerable over time as their operational integration increases, particularly where one carrier maintains IT systems for the other partner.

Behaviour

United's recent behaviour illustrates how a firm's financial requirements may cause them to take actions not in their partners' interests. In October 2003, it sold two pairs of slots at London Heathrow to BA, raising some $20M in cash, and making further savings by cutting loss-making routes.

While Star has been the most successful at bringing in new carriers, growth has also been a vehicle for opportunism. While additional members may be positive in terms of traffic and destinations, in a large alliance, it increases the likelihood of network overlap, which can create tension amongst members, although it also provides opportunities to reduce costs through code-sharing. This is already the case in Central Europe. However, new members also bring diminishing returns, particularly if a new member's market is not important to the majority of the incumbents.

The first major instance of opportunism was against founding member Thai. Lufthansa established an alliance with Singapore Airlines, making Singapore its primary hub in the region. This placed a third party's interests above a Star member's. This act of opportunism was compounded by the alliance when Singapore was welcomed into Star. Singapore draws traffic away from Bangkok, and Thai claimed that Lufthansa's actions costs it some $16M per year;[34] additionally, Singapore's entry reduced the weight of Thai's contribution. Star has responded to Thai's reported disaffection by identifying ways to make 'side payments', for example, maintaining a small business centre in Bangkok, and exploring the use of Thai-made airline service products.[35] Thai's marginalization clearly demonstrated its lack of power, although it may have options outside of Star.

Austrian, whose primary focus is Central and Eastern Europe, faces a similar situation with respect to new entrants in its regional markets, although the carriers involved do not have the same brand recognition as Singapore. Over the past several years, Star has brought in LOT, and intends to add Croatia Airlines and Adria of Slovenia as regional carriers. More interestingly, while Star and Lufthansa had been non-committal about whether they would consider a Swiss entry, Austrian publicly declared its opposition.[36] However, in March 2005, Lufthansa appeared to settle the question by acquiring Swiss.

Star also has the distinction of being the only alliance today to have suffered a defection, with Mexicana's exit in 2003 over differences with United. This has weakened Star's competitive position further in Latin America, particularly as Mexicana then teamed up with American. More recently, a New Zealand High Court decision, which blocked Qantas's proposed alliance and investment in Air New Zealand, may have prevented another carrier from being pulled from Star; however, this may still happen as the Australian authorities have approved the partnership.

Oneworld

The Oneworld alliance was established by American, BA, Canadian Airlines, Cathay Pacific, and Qantas in 1998, as a formalization of a number of pre-existing bilateral relationships, and in response to the new approaches triggered by Star. Since then, it has grown to

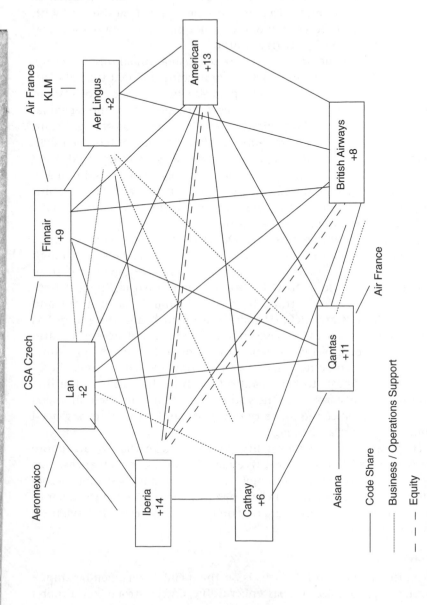

Figure 6.3 Oneworld Members and their External Partners

include Finnair, Iberia, Aer Lingus and Lan (formerly LanChile), but lost Canadian after it was acquired by Air Canada. It has also suffered other setbacks, most notably BA and American's inability to acquire antitrust immunity, and in the failed negotiations with Swiss. Even so, it serves over 570 destinations and accounts for over 15 per cent of global passenger traffic.

Oneworld was the first alliance to establish a formal infrastructure, but its philosophy and approach is significantly different than Star's.[37] Unlike Star, which aggressively pursues alliance-wide projects, including cost-savings initiatives,[38] Oneworld appears to be more facilitator and coordinator than initiator, and does not absorb significant resources from its members. Additionally, the alliance has been deliberately low-key in the recent crisis-filled years, so as not to distract the carriers from focussing on restructuring their businesses, implicitly acknowledging that the airlines can get a better and faster return on investment and human resource utilization with firm-specific initiatives than through alliance-wide initiatives.

In terms of alliance philosophy, Oneworld claims to be unconcerned with falling behind in the race to capture new members,[39] although American, Iberia and Lan took advantage of Mexicana's exit from Star to bring it closer to Oneworld's sphere. Instead, its goal is to develop a network of strong brands with sound management and finances in a clearly defined market segment,[40] and the group has passed up applicants who have ended up in other alliances.[41] It is also clear that if there ever was a debate over Oneworld-vs-carrier branding, the alliance has been relegated to a supporting role. This partner choice philosophy appears to have paid off, both in the number of airline industry awards won by Oneworld carriers, and in their financial performance: since the industry downturn, only American has faced continued financial challenges.

However, focussing on quality does not mean that it can ignore network breadth as a competitive factor against other alliances, particularly as 'quality' is an intangible. Moreover, having strong competitors may make it more of a challenge to achieve things at the alliance level, since these competitors rely on the alliance less, and have their own ambitions.

Power

Even though Oneworld's focus is on the quality of its membership, a carrier's network size and passenger traffic, and control of key airports are still important components of firm power and influence in the alliance. By these informal measures, the most powerful members are American and BA. However, given the small numbers of members, and relatively narrow size differentials – five are in the top 19, and the other three are between 58–72 – their dominance is not as pronounced as in Star's case, and even less so given the strong brands in the group. Moreover, the membership is small enough that in spatial terms, each member forms a vital link in a chain of connections around the globe: duplication is minimal.

American and BA's informal power is reinforced by the fact that they were two of four carriers allowed to fly from the US to London Heathrow, although Cathay has also recently received permission to fly London–New York. Unfortunately, their strong position at Heathrow, and resulting market share in the world's richest business market, has been the major obstacle to them being granted trans-Atlantic antitrust immunity.

There are also elements of formal power at both the alliance and carrier levels. Decision-making is based on consensus, and carriers have exercised their right to block initiatives.[42] Equity primarily plays a symbolic role within the alliance. Together, BA and American own 10 per cent of Iberia, and in September 2004, BA sold its 18 per cent stake in Qantas after it became clear that the Australian government was not going to lift foreign ownership restrictions, and because their relationship had matured to the point where equity was not needed to cement it.

Interdependence

Oneworld's membership and operational philosophy limits its ability to increase its members' dependence on the alliance, although it is exploring areas to jointly achieve greater cost-savings, for example engine maintenance. The exception is in sales, where it has developed large portfolio of fare products that target clearly defined market segments and third markets, and where the group can clearly offer more customer benefits than any carrier on its own. Additionally, this area provides an opportunity for the alliance to take the lead in non-home markets. How dependent is Oneworld on its members? Clearly with a smaller membership and less network overlap than Star, each member plays a larger role in the group's competitiveness – for example when it lost Canadian airlines, it lost most of its Canadian-origin high-yield traffic to Star, even though it still served the key business destinations; those members who faced Star partners in their home markets also lost out since Star-Air Canada could offer better connections and pricing.[43]

Interdependence rests at the carrier-to-carrier level through code-share agreements, and carrier-initiated back-end projects, which may be facilitated by Oneworld. As Figure 6.2 illustrated, Oneworld has a dense network of bilateral linkages, one of the most important being BA-Qantas, who are tied together by an extensive joint-venture code-share agreement, reciprocal ground handling and catering, joint purchasing, shared airport lounges and sales offices, and cooperation on freight transport worldwide. They are also the only carriers to have antitrust immunity between Australia and Europe. American and Qantas have also developed a strong relationship beyond their flying operations; they initiated a 10-year agreement for joint purchasing, including aircraft, and shared airport facilities. This relationship proved its value in November 2001, when Qantas took up American's aircraft delivery when it was not able to.[44]

Behaviour

In contrast to Star, which has taken a harder line on exclusivity, Oneworld does not have exclusivity provisions, beyond not belonging to more than one global alliance.[45] The members recognize that there are tactical gaps in the network and therefore have to compromise on third-party relationships.[46] This approach is more pragmatic, acknowledging that despite cooperation, carriers must act in their own shareholders' best interests, and in some parts of the world, airlines have interests that must be respected.[47] For example, American is unhappy with BA's code-shares with America West on services to Phoenix, Los Angeles and San Francisco, but accepts it because while it has very little impact on its revenues and operations, it brings a large benefit to BA.[48] But then, it has a relationship with Swiss. This does not mean that actions that harm a partner will not have consequences, but the reaction may depend on whether the route or region are strategic to your partner or the alliance.

Although opportunism has implicitly been defined as working with the competition, even instances of cooperation between two carriers in the same alliance can hurt other members. For example American and Finnair partnered on Helsinki-London, a route BA also flies – a good deal for the partners, but not for BA.[49]

Bringing together a group of strong firms that can survive without the alliance also increases the potential for competition within the group. For example, despite a long-standing and profitable relationship, Qantas took actions that would reduce its dependence on BA, outbidding it to purchase two pairs of slots at Heathrow in January 2004. Additionally, it is inaugurating services to London via Asia that compete directly with BA. Similarly, Cathay is taking advantage of new rights granted by the UK government to fly between London Heathrow and New York, putting it in direct competition with BA and American. Intra-alliance competition is likely to grow, as American has increased capacity on international routes by 17.3 per cent in 2004 to try to escape the overcapacity plaguing the US domestic market.[50]

Since its inception, one of the primary sources of potential instability has been American and BA's lack of antitrust immunity, which has led them to explore alternative scenarios. BA's options included purchasing an immunized European carrier such as KLM, or changing its US partner by joining SkyTeam. In turn, American established relationships with Swissair and Sabena in 1999; when the three were granted antitrust immunity, this raised the possibility that Zurich could challenge London's importance as Oneworld's inter-continental hub.[51] However, this dynamic may no longer be in play – although American and BA still do not have immunity, they have begun code-sharing across the Atlantic. More significantly, with alliance consolidation, there is nowhere for American to go ... unless United or Delta become insolvent.

SkyTeam

SkyTeam, the late mover in the global alliance game, has shown the most momentum, making significant gains in membership since Air France, Delta, Aeromexico and Korean Air founded it in 2000, followed shortly by Alitalia and CSA Czech Airlines (CSA). SkyTeam has taken a 'big bang' approach to growth, bringing in KLM, Northwest and Continental in September 2004, to become the second largest alliance in terms of global traffic share. It has also signed memorandums of understanding with Aeroflot and with China Southern, the first to capture a Chinese carrier. However, as with Oneworld, SkyTeam members believe that there should be limits to growth, and Air France unequivocally rejected the idea of Swiss joining the group.[52] Uniquely amongst the global alliances SkyTeam also has a cargo component, which includes all but Northwest and Continental.

If Star can be characterized as stressing the group, and Oneworld as focussed on bilaterals, SkyTeam could be described as a transatlantic linkage of two strong regional groups bound by extensive bilateral ties: the Northwest-Continental-Delta alliance in the US and Air France-KLM in Europe. Uniquely, SkyTeam does not have a formal infrastructure; Delta sees the group as a 'self-governing' organism.[53]

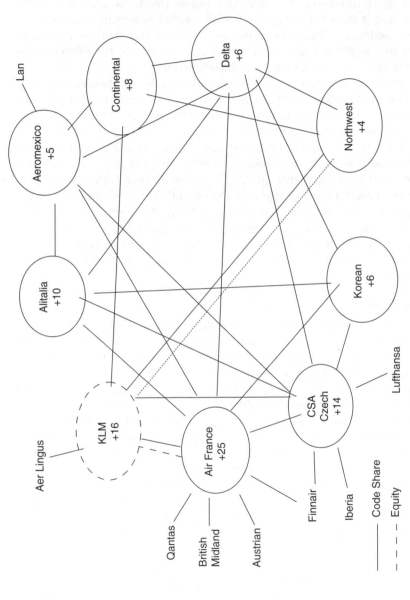

Figure 6.4 SkyTeam Members and their External Partners

This encourages direct communications amongst the members instead of via a central body, and may allow it to be more nimble. While the chief executives hold semi-annual meetings, the work is done through a plethora of working groups. Air France has spoken against creating bureaucracies,[54] but it is questionable whether this non-structure is tenable if the group continues to grow, and with Air France-KLM pre-occupied with post-merger integration, and Delta with financial restructuring.

However, despite the lack of a formal infrastructure, SkyTeam has achieved considerable gains in cooperative activities, particularly on the cargo side, where they have established a sales joint venture in the US with integrated revenue management. In an innovative move, SkyTeam established a marketing alliance with Coca Cola, arguably the world's most valuable brand, and its local bottlers. With antitrust immunity, it has also moved further than the other alliances in terms of the scope of joint-sales activities.

Power

If power and influence accrue from a carrier's network and passenger contribution, SkyTeam has the most balanced composition: with the new Air France-KLM, it will be the only one whose leading European member is as large as the American one. SkyTeam has minimized size differentials within the group: seven members are in the top 25, Aeromexico is in the top 55, and only CSA sits outside of the top 100. Over the past year, Delta's power has been blunted: by Air France's expansion; from the entry of the new carriers, which dilutes its voice in the larger group; and because of its focus on internal restructuring efforts. The new US carriers increases SkyTeam's coverage in the US market, but more importantly, Northwest strengthens its position in Asia, with a hub in the large Japanese market. Although Korean is the group's only Asian carrier, its contribution to the alliance's resources may be diluted because of reputational effects. Although Delta is working with Korean to improve its safety record, Delta, and others have had to suspend partnerships with it in the past.

With its merger, Air France-KLM has become a more powerful voice within the group. Not only is it the leading European carrier, and a source of transfer traffic, it brings a vital resource: airports with room to grow. Amsterdam and Paris-Charles de Gaulle Airport (CDG) have five and four runways, respectively – compared to Heathrow's two, and three in Frankfurt. Both Oneworld's and Star's primary European hubs are already at capacity, whereas CDG already owns the undeveloped land around the airport. This could become a key competitive factor in the future.

Perhaps the most important resource brought to the table is antitrust immunity, which allows for deep cooperation with significant revenue and cost benefits. Air France, Alitalia, CSA and Delta have immunity across the Atlantic, affecting 17 markets. This allows them to share revenues, integrate flight schedules, coordinate aircraft utilization, and harmonize pricing; this in turn results in 'neutral' sales, whereby there is no price differential between different carrier options on the same route. This group, plus Korean, also have immunity across the Pacific, allowing Delta and Korean to coordinate sales. SkyTeam is the only alliance with trans-Atlantic and trans-Pacific immunity, which allows it to compete more effectively for corporate travel contracts. With the entrance of KLM, Northwest and Continental, the number of markets where SkyTeam can cooperate will increase, if regulatory approval is granted.

Formal power, in terms of equity, does not play a role in SkyTeam. Interestingly, it has adopted a weighted voting structure, based on a carrier's size, which reinforces the power of the larger carriers. However, like the other alliances, the preference is to come to a negotiated consensus, rather than resort to voting.

Interdependence

SkyTeam has constructed group-level interdependence in a number of areas, the most important being joint sales, which has been made possible by antitrust immunity. This makes the carriers more sensitive to their partners' actions, and the benefits generated raise exit barriers. This is particularly true for the smaller carriers in the alliance, such as Alitalia and CSA, which do not have the global reach of an Air France-KLM. If these sales account for a large percentage of revenues, they could even become vulnerable to the alliance. Even for Delta, which has a large domestic base to draw from, SkyTeam activities account for some $600M (almost 5 per cent) of annual revenue or 25 per cent of its international revenues.[55] SkyTeam is also trying to construct interdependence and reap cost savings through maintenance 'centres of excellence'. The host-carrier for these operations would be chosen for its product expertise and competitive pricing. Ideally, these centres would do all the work on specific types of engines for the entire alliance, but currently, members may choose to go outside of the alliance for these services.

As with the other alliances, SkyTeam is vulnerable to its largest members' continued membership in the group, and in particular Air

France-KLM, which will now carry 26 per cent of the group's total traffic, and for which there is no substitute without breaking up one of the other two alliances. SkyTeam's sensitivity and vulnerability to the financially troubled Delta, which carries another 26 per cent of its total traffic, has been ameliorated with Northwest and Continental's entries. But, SkyTeam, like Star, remains sensitive to the financial precariousness of Delta, and in particular, Alitalia, which appears to have just staved off liquidation.

Although SkyTeam has constructed alliance-level interdependence, the core relationships are still based on strong bilateral ties. Similarly to Oneworld, it has not adopted extensive exclusivity rules to increase interdependence. Although there are exclusivity provisions, the goal is to remain flexible.[56]

At the bilateral level, SkyTeam does not yet have the same depth of inter-firm linkages as Star and Oneworld, but this is primarily due to the fact that the new entrants have yet to fully exploit the opportunities available. In addition, its members still have extensive ties outside of the alliance – on average 10.4 external partners, with Air France leading with 25 external partners. Interestingly, both Air France and CSA also have code-share relationships with Star and Oneworld carriers. As a result, the extent of interdependence amongst the members varies considerably, although the three US carriers clearly form an interdependent subgroup. But, perhaps the tightest bilateral relationship centres around KLM-Northwest, who have been partnered for over 15 years; their commercial agreements cover code-sharing through large parts of their respective networks, revenue sharing, joint marketing, and pilot training. Neither carrier has any sales or ticketing staff in the other's markets.

Behaviour

SkyTeam's structure has closed the door to some areas for opportunism, but left it open in others. For example, achieving harmonized pricing across the Pacific and Atlantic effectively forecloses competition and opportunistic behaviour in alliance-carrier home markets. But, given the number of external partners, including those from competing alliances, this leaves room for competition with partners and opportunistic behaviour with respect to third markets.

Aside from firm-specific reasons, Air France's merger with KLM was part of a strategy to increase its voice and vote in the alliance. Air France has argued that European carriers need to consolidate in order to balance (or more aptly, counter) their US partners' influence in their alliances.[57] Air France's undisputed preeminence as SkyTeam's European partner has led to Alitalia voicing discontent. It has been the biggest loser in SkyTeam's expansion, now ranking eighth out of nine in size. Alitalia recently speculated that it would be better off partnering with Lufthansa instead, as Air France seemed to want to keep it in a subordinate role. Alitalia had aspired to be part of the Air France-KLM merger, but was rebuffed.

Conclusions

The cases show that more powerful and less dependent carriers are able to act in their own interests. In Star, this has led to some incumbents having to co-exist with rivals. In SkyTeam, Air France acted to re-balance an unbalanced distribution of power. At the same time, Northwest and Continental's entry turned the system into a multipolar, rather than bipolar, one.

The cases also show that in the airline industry, there is not enough natural interdependence to bind carriers to their alliances. As a result, alliances have resorted to constructing interdependence through exclusivity provisions, in flight operations, operations support, and in some cases, with equity. The goal of operational integration is to change the pattern of relationships, to raise exit costs, so that over time, the relationship may evolve into natural interdependence. However, as Swissair clearly illustrated, equity must be used carefully.

The alliances also highlight contrasting approaches to constructing interdependence. Star's governance encourages greater interdependence amongst its partners. In reality, this means that smaller carriers become more dependent on the larger members, given the large number of linkages. Furthermore, its exclusivity rule limits its member's options outside of the alliance. Oneworld accepts that its partners have distinct interests, and focuses on using bilateral ties to construct interdependence. As a result, this dilutes the larger carriers' power by increasing the voice option available to less powerful members.

There are significant implications for smaller carriers. Alliances are vital because they do not have a global reach, and need the transfer traffic their partners provide. While alliances leave room for self-interested behaviour, the exit option may be sealed off since the negative consequences of being outside of an alliance are likely to be greater than accepting a sub-optimal return in the alliance. However, given the uneven distribution of informal power within the existing alliances, smaller carriers are unlikely to have an effective voice on decisions strategic to their larger partners.

Global alliances were formed during a period of economic expansion, but face a radically different environment today. As a result, carriers need their partners more than ever in order to maintain service while reducing capacity, but at the same time, their precarious financial positions may focus their attention on maximising relative and absolute returns. This will likely intensify competition between alliances, but also competition and opportunistic behaviour within the group.

7
Putting the Firm Back Into Alliance

The formal study of alliances has struggled to catch up with developments in the practice of alliance management. Even though competition is almost solely between groups in some industries, we do not fully understand how alliances compete, or how to measure whether or not they are successful. In other areas, despite the fact that increasing numbers of partnerships involve multiple firms, much of the research focus remains on bilateral ties. But, because multiparty alliances have more complex relationships, we cannot simply extrapolate from the existing findings and apply it to the new setting. Management research has yet to come to grips with the fact that multiparty alliances have evolved to the point of creating institutions with permanent staff. The lessons of bureaucratic politics, from political science, suggest that there is a danger that bureaucracies will end up pursuing objectives which perpetuate the organization or lose sight of the fact that the firm's first loyalty is to its shareholders, creating larger fissures between alliance- and firm-level interests. These types of developments have ramifications for intra-alliance dynamics, and may threaten the stability of some groups.

The debate in management theory over whether or not firms should enter into alliances was overtaken by events, spurring a wealth of research into specific issues in alliance management and operations. With the acceptance that alliances are not a fad, alliance research runs the risk of focussing so much on the group that it loses sight of the firm. Alliances challenge the traditional boundaries of the firm. Alliances are changing the structure of the competitive environment. Alliances are critical to many firms' ability to achieve their strategic objectives. *But*, alliances are not profit and loss centres, and changed practices do not mean that the rationale or the purpose of the firm has changed.

Despite its focus on the dark side of alliances, this book does not dispute the value of the work in alliance-operations and management and trust-building, but is meant to complement it and remind managers that measures to promote cooperation and trust cannot eliminate non-cooperative behaviour because of inherent differences in the firms' interests. At the same time, managers must remember that even if a firm is in a position of power and even if its partners are dependent on it, it does not follow that it will take advantage of its position. The rationale behind the analysis of power and interdependence is to see which partners *could* act opportunistically and not *whether* they would. If the alliance has built cooperation and developed trust amongst its members, this should temper inclinations to behave opportunistically or defect.

This book also reminds managers that alliances are a tool of a firm's strategy, and therefore should not be viewed as permanent fixtures. It is perfectly rational for firms to enter into alliances in order to pursue their interests. Strategies that use alliances do not signify that management has eschewed competition in favour of cooperation. Alliances, therefore, do not represent a paradigm shift in the nature of inter-firm relationships: firms remain self-interested actors; firms are profit-maximizers; and firms care about their strategic positioning.

If we accept that alliances are but a tool of strategy, and that alliances have no intrinsic value, then, it is natural to put the focus on the firm and the forces that shape its attitudes toward cooperation. These show that while intra-alliance dynamics and alliance-competitiveness influence how a firm views its alliance, external forces and firm-internal considerations can also play a significant role.

Lessons learned

The cases shed light on a number of questions: power and interdependence's relationship to firm behaviour, the nature of firm power, and the implications for alliance structure and partner choice. However, given the idiosyncrasies in each of the industries represented – Microsoft's dominant position, and the shadow of regulation in the automobile and aviation industries – the lessons learned are meant to provide guidance rather than prescription.

Power, interdependence and non-cooperation

What do the case studies tell us about non-cooperation and the role of power and interdependence in a firm's ability to act? The Microsoft

Table 7.1   Findings

	Microsoft-PC	Microsoft-Non-PC	Ballard	Qualiflyer	Star	Oneworld	SkyTeam
Power/ Influence in Alliance	Powerful and independent. Informal power (from technology) enhanced by size and financial strength. Fragmented and competitive partners.	Power more evenly distributed; Microsoft's partners own the key resources: content, customers.	Power relatively evenly distributed: size, formal power balanced by technology. Balance in Daimler and Ford's favour because of equity.	Large alliance, dominated by Swissair. Large power differentials – both formal and informal.	Large alliance, wide power differentials. Governance structure attempts to balance informal power.	Mid-size alliance, with large power differentials (but not as wide as Star) Governance rules balance informal power.	Mid-size alliance with narrow power differentials, reinforced by governance rules.
Interdependence	Others dependent on Microsoft's technology. Also need Microsoft as a ubiquitous and efficient distribution channel.	Firms interdependent, but many substitutes. Microsoft needs the others to reach the end customer.	Highly interdependent in fuel cell vehicle markets: technology, asset specificity, design, end product's performance. Ballard more dependent because cannot reach market independently.	Partners obliged to use Swissair Group services. Swissair committed financial support.	Little natural interdependence; trying to construct at alliance level. Deeper interdependence between specific carriers. Exclusivity rules.	Little natural interdependence; trying to construct through dense bilateral connections. Pragmatic approach to exclusivity.	Little natural interdependence; constructing interdependence with alliance level projects. Deep interdependence between regional groups.

Table 7.1 Findings – *continued*

	Microsoft-PC	Microsoft-Non-PC	Ballard	Qualiflyer	Star	Oneworld	SkyTeam
Behaviour	Microsoft can defect/behave opportunistically toward hardware, software and service providers. Also able to compel others to defect against their own partners. Microsoft able to punish resistance.	Partners have behaved opportunistically and defected on Microsoft.	No defection; opportunistic behaviour (if any) is not transparent to outsiders.	Swissair reneged on commitments; exit costs too high.	Smaller partners' interests sidelined by large partners, especially in alliance expansion.	American, BA sought alternatives absent antitrust immunity.	Air France using merger with KLM to balance Delta's power.

and Star Alliance cases suggest that powerful and less dependent firms can behave opportunistically or defect from their alliance. In other cases, firms that are equally powerful, in terms of their resource contributions, but not dependent on each other, are also able to be behave opportunistically or defect. This was most evident in the relations between BA and American Airlines. More surprisingly, firms that are not powerful, but not dependent on the alliance – because there is little operational integration, or because they have options outside of the group – are able to exit from their alliances. Although this appears counterintuitive, even firms which contribute the most important resources to the alliance's goal have less leverage over parties which are not dependent on them.

Microsoft, in the PC hardware and software industries, represents one extreme of the power and interdependence spectrum. The firms in the PC hardware and software industries are naturally dependent on Microsoft. Not only does it own the most critical technology resource in the PC value chain, its resource is not substitutable. As a result, Microsoft is both powerful and independent, and can exercise power to protect its position. This was clearly demonstrated in its ability to force changes to licensing terms on the PC makers, particularly with respect to a 'standardized' user experience. In Intel's case, Microsoft punished non-cooperation by threatening not to support future technology innovations. Microsoft was also in the rare position of being able to force other firms to take actions contrary to their own customers' interests, or to defect from third parties.

However, the Microsoft cases also illustrate the limits of power. In the non-PC markets, Microsoft needs its partners' resources, and found that cash and formal power arising from equity investments does not buy loyalty. The CATV and mobile phone operators recognize that they hold the more vital resources, and are willing to take Microsoft's cash, but will act according to their own interests. Since there is no natural interdependence with these parties, Microsoft had to establish formal alliances, and use equity to try to bind its partners.

In contrast, the Ballard alliance is a prototypical technology development alliance between a start-up company and established firms. It provides the clearest illustration of how alliance partners' relative power and interdependence change over time. Daimler and Ford brought legitimacy and cash to Ballard when it was still testing out its technology. Today, Ballard is a desirable partner because it has proved its technology, and as fuel cell vehicles move toward commercialization, its contribution is becoming a more important element in the automakers' design and planning.

The four airline alliances examined differ in terms of their distributions of power and in the extent of interdependence at the group level and between individual members. The airline cases present some expected as well as some counterintuitive findings. They show that firms which are not powerful in their alliance, and depend on their partners' resources, are unlikely to exit, as is the case with Thai Airways. But, carriers that were not powerful also defected – so long as they did not depend on the alliance, for example, Finnair and SAS in the European Quality Alliance. Swissair's early alliances clearly showed that absent significant interdependence, through operational integration, for example, it is relatively easy for firms to leave, even from long-standing relationships. But, Austrian Airlines' split with Swissair also highlighted the limits to interdependence; Austrian could go because it had an option in Lufthansa, but also because it was willing to pay the switching costs involved in dissolving a deep relationship.

Swissair also reminds us why we need to better understand power and interdependence between firms. Swissair did not recognize that its Qualiflyer partners were already dependent on it, and bound them further through service agreements with its subsidiaries. However, Swissair bound itself by taking large and unnecessary equity stakes, by making capital commitments, and by promising to be a lender of last resort. These ties meant that Swissair's own financial health became dependent on its partners', and ultimately led to its liquidation.

These cases suggest that interdependence is a more valuable indicator than power on questions of exit versus no-exit, as it takes into account external factors, and therefore the number of options available to the firm, regardless of its size. On the other hand, the question of a firm's power within its alliance may be better indicator of an ability to behave opportunistically.

The nature of power and interdependence

The cases clearly illustrated that there are multiple potential sources of power, and what constitutes a power resource is context-dependent, and may be of limited benefit beyond the scope of the alliance, or if the alliance's goals change. Interestingly, even financial resources, the most fungible source of firm power, are of limited utility in some environments, and may be constrained by regulation in others.

While the type and importance of a technology resource is key to determining a firm's power in technology alliances, the cases highlighted subtle distinctions. Power may accrue to a technology holder because of the technology's performance, or because the technology sets a standard. This is the difference between Ballard and Intel, and Microsoft: Ballard's and Intel's sources of power come from their ability to stay ahead of the competition. But, power that derives from superior performance may be more ephemeral if competitors catch up, or if the market's requirements change the sources of competitive advantage. In contrast, Microsoft's power derives from owning a standard that sits on *the* key point in the value chain, not from how well Windows performs.

Power is relative. So, a firm's power in an alliance is not a raw measure of its resources, but also depends on who its partners are, the number of firms in the alliance, and the governance rules that are put in place. In Ballard's case, the two counterweights, Daimler and Ford, blunt each other's ability to use their formal or latent power.

The question of interdependence brings together both alliance-internal considerations and factors outside of the alliance. The cases show that firms which rely on others to distribute their product or which need their partners' resources in order for their product to sell are extremely sensitive to others' actions. Just as Ballard needs Ford and Daimler to integrate its fuel cell, AOL recognized that it could not afford to be locked off the Windows desktop. All things being equal, small or pure-play firms are more sensitive because the impact on them is likely to be larger, and because cash flow is directly related to a firm's solvency. On the other hand, the airline industry is unique amongst the cases studied in that both large and small carriers are sensitive to a partner's actions on a route-specific basis, even if the overall effect on a large carrier's operations may be negligible.

However, both large and small firms can be vulnerable to their partners' actions given the impact on strategic-level considerations. A firm's vulnerability is largely a function of the options available outside of the alliance and how critical and unique a firm's contribution is. For example, Daimler's efforts in fuel cell vehicle development would be vulnerable if Ballard's technology failed, particularly as they move toward commercialization.

Both types of interdependence weaken a firm's position *vis-à-vis* its partners, but sensitivity may be even more important than vulnerability, particularly to smaller firms, as it affects working capital. Ultimately, firms collapse even if they are profitable and even if they have strategic options for the future, if they do not have cash.

Power and interdependence are not static, and any assessment only provides a snapshot of a point in time. Relative power shifts, as unique assets become less so, as technologies and operations become more integrated, and as firms relinquish other relationships to focus on alliance partners. Moreover, depending on the alliance's goal, relative power may shift as different parties own key assets as the alliance evolves.

Structuring relationships

While this book began as a study of the role of power and interdependence in allowing firms to act on non-cooperative impulses, the findings led to a broader set of lessons on structuring the relationships and tasks between firms in alliances. The cases suggest that interdependence is the glue that binds the firms in an alliance, and can be 'natural' or 'constructed'. If interdependence is what binds firms to their alliances, this may have ramifications for alliance size and the tools used.

Table 7.2   Findings – Implications for Structure

	Natural vs Constructed Interdependence
Microsoft – PC	Natural dependence. 'Structure' based on contracts.
Microsoft – Non-PC	Little natural interdependence. Constructed interdependence with formal alliances, equity.
Ballard	Natural interdependence. Constructed interdependence in R&D sharing, guarantees to purchase etc… may evolve into natural interdependence with co-specialization.
Qualiflyer	Little natural interdependence. Constructed interdependence tying parties to Swissair.
Star	Little natural interdependence. Formal infrastructure with large bureaucracy. Constructing interdependence at alliance level with group-based activities.
Oneworld	Little natural interdependence. Formal infrastructure clearly in supporting role. Constructing interdependence through extensive and intensive bilateral ties.
SkyTeam	Little natural interdependence. Constructed interdependence through alliance activities.

In the PC hardware and software industries, Microsoft's partners are bound to it by technology requirements. The need for the microprocessor and applications software to interoperate with Microsoft's OS created a naturally-dependent relationship. As a result, Microsoft did not need to establish formal alliances with these firms. In contrast, Microsoft needs formal alliances in the new non-PC industries it is attempting to enter. It recognizes that it does not provide a unique resource, and therefore, must construct interdependence, even going so far as taking equity stakes in its partners.

The Ballard-Daimler-Ford alliance utilized both natural and constructed interdependence. At the alliance's inception, Ballard was dependent on its partners, but the group constructed interdependence by creating technology-based subsidiaries that specialized in different segments of the value chain, and by establishing non-compete, technology sharing, and off-set agreements. This was in addition to the investments Daimler and Ford made in Ballard. These measures tied the two automakers more closely to each other, in addition to their technology relationship with Ballard. Moreover, this alliance suggests that constructed interdependence, such as through technology choice or a division of labour, can evolve into natural interdependence over time.

Unlike technology development alliances, airlines have little natural interdependence; much of their interdependence derives from the constraints placed on the industry by regulators. As a result, airline alliances have gone farther than others in constructing interdependence – although constructed interdependence should not be confused with establishing infrastructures. The three global alliances have taken different approaches: Star, the largest, focuses on identifying ways to bind individual members to the group, since the membership is too dispersed to develop both broad and deep bilateral links; Oneworld and SkyTeam, on the other hand, are still small enough that their members can be bound by the depth and breadth of their individual linkages. While constructed interdependence may have been necessary when the alliances were formed, today, these ties may not be necessary given the strategic gridlock in the industry.

However, although constructed interdependence may allow firms to tie their partners to the alliance, alliance managers need to decide whether or not they want to pursue this course of action. Is it better to have partners who willingly participate or to tie-in partners who want to leave? Malcontents in an alliance can play the 'spoiler', hindering the group's ability to work efficiently or effectively. Moreover, depending on the tools used to bind its partners, a firm may have to bind itself as well, and limit its management's ability to pursue the firm's interests. There is also a practical element: the firms that need constructed interdependence to bind their partners are likely to be the more dependent. If the other firm recognizes the relative power distribution, it is in its own interest to resist attempts to restrict its actions.

Managerial implications

A primary goal in this work is to remind managers to take a realistic view of alliances. Alliances can be an invaluable tool, but despite shared goals, partners have divergent interests and cannot be expected to put the alliance's interests ahead of their own. Firms choose to ally because it is the most appropriate tool under the circumstances at a given time. Should those circumstances change, or the firm does not achieve its expected returns, then it will be less inclined to continue cooperating.

Managers therefore need to understand *why* firms choose to not cooperate, and recognize the factors that influence their partners' attitudes toward cooperation so that they are not surprised by defections or opportunistic behaviour. An early warning could provide the firm with an opportunity to develop strategies to try to pre-empt a key partner's defection. The framework provides managers with a structured approach to examine the *how* in non-cooperation, and allows them to identify which partners they need and evaluate whether those partners rely on them in return.

For those firms establishing partnerships, an analysis of power and interdependence is particularly useful in the alliance formation process as it sheds light on their bargaining power, and can be used to evaluate potential partners. For example, all things being equal, a firm should choose the firm which would be most dependent on it. Power and interdependence can also frame the thinking about alliance size. Given resource contributions, and the extent of natural interdependence, at what point are the natural ties too weak to bind the firms? How should firms structure relationships and tasks within the alliance to minimize their partners' ability to defect? And, since power and interdependence change over time, how does this impact the type and duration of commitments required? Will constructed interdependence evolve into natural interdependence?

However, while firms may try to structure an alliance to balance out their relative dependence, this may not be possible given their bargaining positions at the time of alliance formation. The question therefore becomes how each firm might be able to deter its partners from engaging in non-cooperative behaviours. If the firm is unable to do so on its own, is there the potential for coordinated action within the alliance? Could sanctions be introduced in the alliance-governance?

The book's findings have significant implications for small firms. Despite the fact that technology or knowledge, factors not related to size, are a key contributor to power in resource-based alliances, it appears that small firms will find it hard to escape from the inherent advantages large firms have, such as their greater ability to recover from mistakes or absorb the costs of opportunistic behaviour. Small firms are more likely to be pure-play firms whose entire business is tied to its alliance's prospects, and thus non-cooperative behaviour will have a much larger impact on them. Additionally, large firms have an advantage in industries where there are few constraints on the use of equity. They can punish non-cooperation by acquiring that partner, or that partner's competitor. Moreover, even where the small firm provides a unique resource, its power is muted *vis-à-vis* larger partners who serve as distribution channels, unless it sets a proprietary standard that all in the industry must adhere to. This is the difference between Ballard and Microsoft's positions, even before Microsoft became the pre-eminent power in its industry.

Going forward

This work is just a first step in understanding the implications of power and interdependence as a means of analyzing alliance relations, the drivers of non-cooperation in alliances, and the unique characteristics of multiparty alliances. As such, for each question it begins to answer, a host of others are raised.

We set out to draw attention back on the firm in an alliance, rather than on the alliance. The assumptions present a world view that does not treat cooperation as a radical break from traditional beliefs about firm behaviour, but as a rational choice taken to strengthen a firm's competitive position in the future. Conflict, or the *potential* for conflict, is an enduring condition. This focus on the firm also places the alliance in the context of a firm's overall operations – its interests outside the alliance affect how it views its alliance. So, while we should not ignore operational issues, theories of alliance structure, or trust-building, these cannot fully explain non-cooperation.

The assumptions presented bring together strategic and operational perspectives on alliance. Disaggregating the influences on the firm into their component levels of analysis is an important step in identifying and analyzing the individual factors that affect how a firm views its alliance. Which level of influence is the most important? What is the dynamic between these levels?

The findings raise important questions of whether power in an alliance, and interdependence between alliance partners, have different effects. The findings from this limited number of cases suggest that interdependence is more important in constraining defection. While the focus has been on defection, what do power and interdependence mean for lower levels of non-cooperation, or are these behaviours a function of alliance-structure and governance factors?

The power and interdependence framework also presents a number of practical challenges for future research. One of the most important is refining indicators of relative resource dependence, which requires quantifying what are, in many cases, subjective values. Absent developments in these areas, inter-industry comparison is not possible. Another challenge is the fact that firms are reluctant to admit to non-cooperation, and in many cases, the 'victims' of opportunistic behaviour are not aware that it has ever taken place. Where opportunism is not transparent, is it possible to identify which firms have been hurt by their partners' actions, but are unable to exit?

At a broader level, the literatures that management researchers have borrowed from to study interfirm cooperation confirm that corporate alliances are part of a broader phenomena of partnerships between self-interested actors. Not surprisingly, given the rich history of diplomatic alliances, international relations theory has much to contribute. However, it also suggests that the interdisciplinary approach taken here is just a beginning, and that the international relations and political science literatures can make further contributions to understanding operational issues in alliances. These include the structure of coalitions and how to determine optimal size, issues of organizational structures to enhance voice and reduce exit, approaches to balance of power, functionalist approaches to alliance evolution, as well as bureaucratic politics.

More important, however, are the strategic implications for firms: the body of international relations theory adopted in this work explicitly accepts that members of groups have individual interests and that cooperation is a temporary state. Our analysis of the dark side of alliances shows that there are inherent tensions and conflicts of interest between firms which even operational success will not eliminate. While the literature's focus on 'getting alliance operations right' may dampen some non-cooperative impulses, it is difficult to alter fundamental differences which arise from the firms' respective requirements. These tensions may remain latent if the alliance is successful, but could easily come to the fore if it is not.

* * *

Without cooperation from alliance practitioners, academics and consultants face significant challenges trying to further our understanding of what makes alliances work, and what impedes perfect cooperation. As outsiders, we have to infer the reasons behind observable actions, and may end up drawing the wrong conclusions. I welcome your reactions to this book, and invite alliance managers to share their experiences in the trenches of alliance management at: wilma.suen@strategic alliance.ca.

Notes

Chapter 1   The Dark Side of Strategic Alliances

1. D. O. Faulkner and M. de Rond, 'Introduction: Perspectives on Cooperative Strategy', in *Cooperative Strategies: Economic, Business and Organizational Issues*, (eds) D. O. Faulkner and M. de Rond (Oxford: Oxford University Press, 2000), p. 3.
2. These include: P. R. Varadarajan and M. H. Cunningham, 'Strategic Alliances: A Synthesis of Conceptual Foundations,' *Journal of the Academy of Marketing Science 23* (Fall 1995), (accessed 25 August 1999), available from Academic Search Elite; C. T. C. Compton, 'Cooperation, Collaboration, and Coalition: A Perspective on the Types and Purposes of Technology Joint Ventures', *Antitrust Law Journal* 61 (1993) 864–8; B. M. Gilroy, *Networking in Multinational Enterprises: The Importance of Strategic Alliances* (Columbia, SC: University of South Carolina Press, 1993), p. 34; P. F. Cowhey and J. D. Aronson, *Managing the World Economy: The Consequences of Corporate Alliances* (New York: Council on Foreign Relations Press, 1993), p. 7.
3. The literature has taken a number of approaches to describing multiparty alliances. Among the types are: constellations (Gomes-Casseres); strategic networks and strategic alliances (Child and Faulkner); alliance networks, alliance portfolios, and alliance webs (Doz and Hamel).
4. Gomes-Casseres highlights independence, limited control and incomplete contracts. M. Y. Yoshino and U. S. Rangan, *Strategic Alliances: An Entrepreneurial Approach to Globalization* (Boston: Harvard Business School Press, 1995), pp. 4–5; Gomes-Casseres, *Alliance Revolution*, 34.
5. D. O. Faulkner, *International Strategic Alliances: Co-operating to Compete* (New York: McGraw-Hill Book Company, 1995), p. 17.
6. Yoshino and Rangan, *Strategic Alliances*, 18.
7. The rise of the alliance during the 1990s was driven by mutually-reinforcing environmental and firm-level factors. In the firm's operating environment, key changes included: globalization; management focus on core competencies and outsourcing non-core functions; and increasing product complexity, particularly the need for skills and technologies from diverse industries.

   Changes in the external environment force firms to reassess their competences and determine whether they have the capability to respond. If yes, is the level of risk entailed in making a commitment acceptable? If not, should they acquire the capabilities or partner? Therefore, access to resources, tangible and intangible, is a key driver of alliances. Alliances also allow firms to share the costs of developing products with high minimum efficient scales, and reduce risks by acquiring 'real options' in competing technologies. Thus, alliances allow firms to trade off technology and market risk for relational risk.
8. J. C. Jarillo, 'On Strategic Networks', *Strategic Management Journal*, 9 (1988) 36; O. Williamson, 'Transaction-cost Economics: the Governance of Contractual Relations', *Journal of Law and Economics*, 22 (1979) 234.

Chapter 2   The Challenge of Non-Cooperation

1. H. J. Morgenthau, *Politics Among Nations: the Struggle for Power and Peace*, 5th edn, revised (New York: Alfred A. Knopf, 1978), p. 188.

2. A. Ariño, 'To Do or Not To Do? Noncooperative Behavior by Commission and Omission in Interfirm Ventures', *Group & Organization Management*, 26 (2001) 5–9.

3. F. R. Root, 'Some Taxonomies of International Cooperative Arrangements', in *Cooperative Strategies in International Business*, (ed.) F. J. Contractor and P. Lorange (Lexington, MA: Lexington Books, 1988), p. 75.

4. J. Child and D. Faulkner, *Strategies of Cooperation: Managing Alliances, Networks and Joint Ventures*, (New York: Oxford University Press, 1998), p. 187.

5. A. A. Berle and G. Means, *The Modern Corporation and Private Property* (New York: Macmillan, 1932).

6. J. M. Grieco, 'Anarchy and the Limits of Cooperation: A Realist Critique of the Newest Liberal Institutionalism', in *Controversies in International Relations Theory: Realism and the Neoliberal Challenge*, (ed.) C. W. Kegley, Jr. (New York: St. Martin's Press, 1995), p. 152.

7. W. H. Riker, *The Theory of Political Coalitions*, (New Haven: Yale University Press, 1962), p. 20.

8. R. O. Keohane and J. S. Nye, *Power and Interdependence*, 3rd edn (Boston: Longman, 2001), p. 9.

9. J. B. Tucker, 'Partners and Rivals: A Model of International Collaboration in Advanced Technology', *International Organization*, 45 (1991) 88.

10. Y. L. Doz and G. Hamel, *Alliance Advantage: The Art of Creating Value Through Partnering* (Boston: Harvard Business School Press, 1998), p. 196.

11. M. E. Porter, *Competitive Advantage of Nations* (New York: Free Press, 1990), pp. 612–3.

12. G. Hamel et al., 'Collaborate with Your Competitors – and Win', *Harvard Business Review*, 67 (January–February 1989) 133.

13. P. J. Buckley and M. Casson, 'A Theory of Cooperation in International Business', in *Cooperative Strategies in International Business*, (ed.) F. J. Contractor and P. Lorange (Lexington, MA: Lexington Books, 1988), p. 32.

14. R. Axelrod and R. O. Keohane, 'Achieving Cooperation under Anarchy: Strategies and Institutions', *World Politics*, 38 (1985) 226.

15. R. Gulati, T. Khanna, and N. Nohria, 'Unilateral Commitments and the Importance of Process in Alliances', *Sloan Management Review*, 35 (1994) 61–9; D. J. Teece, 'Profiting from Technological Innovation: Implications, Integration, Collaboration, Licensing and Public Policy', in *The Competitive Challenge*, (ed.) D. J. Teece (Cambridge, MA: Ballinger Publishing, 1987), pp. 185–219.

16. R. Gulati, 'Does Familiarity Breed Trust? The Implications of Repeated Ties for Contractual Choice in Alliances', *Academy of Management Journal*, 38 (1995) 102.

17. T. Volery and S. Mensik, 'The Role of Trust in Creating Effective Alliances: A Managerial Perspective', *Journal of Business Ethics*, 17 (1998) (accessed 16 November 2001); available from ABI/Inform.

18. O. E. Williamson, *Markets and Hierarchies: Analysis and Antitrust Implications* (New York: The Free Press, 1975), p. 255.

19. Buckley and Casson, *Theory of Cooperation*, 34.
20. B. Gomes-Casseres, *The Alliance Revolution: The New Shape of Business Rivalry* (Cambridge, MA: Harvard University Press, 1996), p. 141.
21. Gomes-Casseres, *Alliance Revolution*, 70–96.
22. For example, the US' *National Cooperative Research and Production Act of 1993* was designed to encourage collaboration between competitors in R&D and production, by relaxing antitrust restrictions to companies registered under this Act, and waiving treble damages in case of civil litigation.
23. M. Brewer, Vice President – Alliances, United Airlines, interview by author, 25 October 2000, Medford, MA (via telephone).
24. W. B. Arthur, 'Increasing Returns and the New World of Business', *Harvard Business Review*, 74 (July–August 1996) 100–9.
25. T. K. Das and B. Teng, 'Instabilities of Strategic Alliances: An Internal Tensions Perspective', *Organization Science*, 11 (2000) 84–90.
26. A. O. Hirschman, *Exit, Voice and Loyalty: Responses to Decline in Firms, Organizations and States* (Cambridge, MA: Harvard University Press, 1970).
27. D. Spar, 'Note on Rules', HBS No. 799–013/Rev. 31 March 1999 (Boston: Harvard Business School Publishing, 1999).
28. Game theory addresses a some of the issues faced by firms in alliances. One of the few to combine game theory with multifirm alliances is Hwang and Burgers' work. P. Hwang and W. P. Burgers 'The Many Faces of Multi-Firm Alliances: Lessons for Managers', *California Management Review*, 39 (Spring 1997) 101–17.
29. D. Cush, Vice President – International Planning and Alliances, American Airlines, interview by author, 3 November 2000, Medford, MA (via telephone); S. Khemani and L. Waverman, 'Strategic Alliances: A Threat to Competition?', in *Competition Policy in the Global Economy: Modalities for Cooperation*, (ed.) L. Waverman, W. S. Comanor, and A. Goto (London: Routledge, 1997).

Chapter 3   Power and Interdependence: the Firm's Ability to Act

1. G. H. Snyder, 'Alliance Theory: A Neorealist First Cut,' in *The Evolution of Theory in International Relations: Essays in Honor of William T. R. Fox*, (ed.) R. L. Rothstein (Columbia, SC: University of South Carolina Press, 1991), p. 93.
2. From K. N. Waltz, 'The Myth of Interdependence' in *The International Corporation*, (ed.) C. P. Kindleberger (Cambridge, MA: The MIT Press, 1970), p. 216.
3. Snyder, *Alliance Theory*, 94.
4. D. J. Brass and M. E. Burkhardt, 'Centrality and Power in Organizations', in (eds) N. Nohria and R. G. Eccles, *Networks and Organizations: Structure, Form, and Action* (Boston: Harvard Business School Press, 1992), pp. 194–6.
5. J. Pfeffer and G. R. Salancik, *The External Control of Organizations: A Resource Dependence Perspective* (New York: Harper and Row, 1978), p. 27.
6. R. O. Keohane and J. S. Nye, *Power and Interdependence*, 3rd edn (Boston: Longman, 2001), p. 10.

7. D. A. Baldwin, 'Interdependence and Power: A Conceptual Analysis,' *International Organization*, 34 (1980) 495–8.
8. Keohane and Nye, *Power and Interdependence*, 10.
9. J. S. Nye, 'Soft Power', *Foreign Policy*, 80 (1990) 159–60.
10. A. Tighe, General Manager – Alliances, British Airways, interview by author, 13 October 2000, Harmondsworth, Middlesex, UK.
11. R. Rosecrance, 'Interdependence', in *The Oxford Companion to Politics of the World*, (ed.) J. Krieger (Oxford: Oxford University Press, 1993), pp. 430–2.
12. Keohane and Nye, *Power and Interdependence*, 9.
13. Keohane and Nye, *Power and Interdependence*, 10–16.
14. T. K. Das and B. Teng, 'A Resource-Based Theory of Strategic Alliances', *Journal of Management*, 26 (2000) 53–4.
15. T. K. Das and B. Teng, 'Partner Analysis and Alliance Performance', *Scandinavian Journal of Management*, 19 (2003) 288.
16. Das and Teng, *Partner Analysis*, 290–1.
17. B. Gomes-Casseres, *The Alliance Revolution: The New Shape of Business Rivalry* (Cambridge, MA: Harvard University Press, 1996), pp. 136–41.
18. W. M. Cohen and D. A. Levinthal, 'Absorptive Capacity: A New Perspective on Learning and Innovation', *Administrative Science Quarterly*, 35 (1990) 128–52.
19. D. J. Teece, 'Profiting from Technological Innovation: Implications for Integration, Collaboration, Licensing and Public Policy', in *The Competitive Challenge*, (ed.) D. J. Teece (Cambridge, MA: Ballinger Publishing, 1987), pp. 185–219.
20. A. O. Krueger, 'Are Preferential Trading Arrangements Trade – Liberalising or Trade Protectionist?' *Journal of Economic Perspectives*, 13 (1999) 110; A. O. Krueger, 'NAFTA's Effects: A Preliminary Assessment', *The World Economy*, 23 (2000) 761–75.
21 See Pfeffer and Salancik, *External Control*.

Chapter 4 Microsoft: Power and the Limits of Power

1. J. Heilemann, *Pride Before the Fall: the Trials of Bill Gates and the End of the Microsoft Era* (New York: HarperCollins, 2001), p. 57.
2. US v. Microsoft Corporation, 87 F. Supp. 2d 30 (US Dist. 2000).
3. R. Waters, 'Search Engines, Anti-Virus Software Targeted,' *Financial Times*, 30 September 2004, 28.
4. W. B. Arthur, 'Increasing Returns and the New World of Business', *Harvard Business Review* 74 (July–August 1996) 100–9.
5. For example, there would be significant training costs for users to switch to a different word processing, spreadsheet or presentations programme. They would also be reluctant to change if they could not easily send files to other users because of a lack of an installed base.
6. See J. Bleeke and D. Ernst, 'Is Your Strategic Alliance Really a Sale?' *Harvard Business Review* 73 (January–February 1995) 97–105. Bleeke and Ernst found that in 80% of joint ventures, one partner eventually sold its assets.
7. Price Waterhouse LLP, *Technology Forecast: 1998* (Menlo Park: Price Waterhouse Global Technology Centre, 1998), p. 285.
8. US v. Microsoft Publicly Released Deposition Transcripts, Deposition of Joe Belfiore. Available from www.justice.gov/atr/cases/ms_depos.htm

9. US v. Microsoft Publicly Released Deposition Transcripts, Deposition of John Soyring.
10. From the Testimony of Garry Norris. K. Auletta, *World War 3.0: Microsoft and its Enemies* (New York: Random House, 2001), p. 257.
11. Brinkley and Lohr, *Microsoft*, 229–41; Auletta, *World War 3.0*, 257–9.
12. Heilemann, *Pride*, 146–54; Auletta, *World War 3.0*, 109–12; Brinkley and Lohr, *Microsoft*, 82, 84; US v. Microsoft, Government Exhibits 275–90. Exhibits available from www.justice.gov/atr/cases/ms_exhibits.htm
13. US v. Microsoft, Government Exhibit 278.
14. US v. Microsoft, Government Exhibit 281; Brinkley and Lohr, *Microsoft*, 82.
15. The start-up sequence is what users see as the computer boots, along with the default desktop. The modifications the OEMs made added features such as pop-up windows to the desktop so that users could accept / reject a 'tour' of the PC's features.
    US v. Microsoft, Direct Testimony of John Soyring. Direct Testimony Available from www.justice.gov/atr/cases/ms_testimony.htm. This practice ended in 1998. US v. Microsoft, Government Exhibit 294.
16. US v. Microsoft, Government Exhibits 309, 316.
17. Brinkley and Lohr, *Microsoft*, 235.
18. US v. Microsoft, Deposition of Celeste Dunn.
19. US v. Microsoft, Direct Testimony of James A. Gosling, 11.
20. M. A. Cusumano and D. B. Yoffie, *Competing on Internet Time: Lessons from Netscape and its Battle with Microsoft* (New York: The Free Press, 1998), p. 135.
21. R. H. Reid, *Architects of the Web: 1,000 Days that Built the Future of Business* (New York: John Wiley & Sons, Inc., 1997), p. 2.
22. US v. Microsoft, Direct Testimony of Jim Barksdale, 46.
23. Cusumano and Yoffie, *Competing*, 134.
24. Reid, *Architects*, 31.
25. Cusumano and Yoffie, *Competing*, 136.
26. Government Exhibit 350 Microsoft Report 'Top North American Internet Access Providers'.
27. Cusumano and Yoffie, *Competing*, 134.
28. Brinkley and Lohr, *Microsoft*, 49.
29. US v. Microsoft, Direct Testimony of William H. Harris, 31.
30. US v. Microsoft, Direct Testimony of David M. Colburn, 14.
31. Auletta, *World War 3.0*, 56.
32. There are also allegations that Microsoft sought to preclude ICPs from paying Netscape in return for placement on the Windows desktop. Auletta, *World War 3.0*, 194.
33. US v. Microsoft, Direct Testimony of Jim Barksdale; US v. Microsoft, Government Exhibits 298–301, 649; Brinkley and Lohr, *Microsoft*, 176, 187, 201.
34. US v. Microsoft, Direct Testimony of William H. Harris; Auletta, *World War 3.0*, 121–5; Government Exhibit 1156.
35. US v. Microsoft, Direct Testimony of David M. Colburn; Auletta, *World War 3.0*, 93–6; Brinkley and Lohr, *Microsoft*, 53–9; US v. Microsoft, 84F. Supp. 2d. 9 (US Dist 1999).
36. Direct Testimony of David M. Colburn.
37. Brinkley and Lohr, *Microsoft*, 184.

38. US v. Microsoft, Direct Testimony of Avadis Tevanian, Jr.; US v. Microsoft, 84F. Supp. 2d. 9 (US Dist 1999); Auletta, *World War 3.0*, 96–107; Heilemann, *Pride*, 115–20.
39. US v. Microsoft, 84F. Supp. 2d. 9 (US Dist 1999).
40. Auletta, *World War 3.0*, 232.
41. XML is intended to replace html as the primary language used to format, customize and display content on a webpage, and to challenge Sun's Java. Auletta, *World War 3.0*, 399.
42. M. McCarthy, 'Media Giants Suit Up to Take on Video Games', *USA Today*, 27 August 2004, 5B.
43. R. Waters, 'Microsoft to Pursue Growth in Core Information Systems', *Financial Times*, 30 July 2004, 15.
44. Auletta, *World War 3.0*, 337–8; 'Let the Games Begin' *The Economist*, 19 May 2001, 57.
45. A. Wahl, 'We Got Game', *Canadian Business*, 10 November 2003, 85–91.
46. PricewaterhouseCoopers Technology Centre, *Technology Forecast 2001–2003* (Menlo Park: Pricewaterhouse Coopers, 2001), pp. 344–51.
47. Auletta, *World War 3.0*, 337.
48. Auletta, *World War 3.0*, 387. In the US: $1B for 11.5 per cent of Comcast (1997); $5B in AT&T. In Canada: $400M in Rogers Communications. In Europe: $3B for 30 per cent of Telewest (UK) $500M in NTL (UK); $300M for 8 per cent of United Pan-Europe Communications NV in 1999 (12 countries, including Israel); $40M in Globo Cabo of Portugal (1999). In South America: $126M for 11 per cent of Globo Cabo of Brazil. In Japan 42 per cent of TITUS, the largest cable company; 1/3 of Cable & Wireless' CATV business (June 2000).
49. Auletta, *World War 3.0*, 167.
50. Auletta, *World War 3.0*, 162.
51. Auletta, *World War 3.0*, 391.
52. BBC News, 'Key Cable TV Deal for Microsoft', 9 November 2004, http://news.bbc.co.uk/2/hi/business/3994933.stm; downloaded 9 November 2004.
53. K. Peterson, 'Fuzzy Reception', *The Seattle Times*, 18 August 2003, C1.
54. J. Beauprez, 'Microsoft Dives Into Digital Cable Software,' *Denver Post*, 10 June 2003, C1.
55. T. Kort, et al., *Windows CE Surpasses Palm OS in 3Q04*, (Stamford: Gartner Research, 2004).
56. Ericsson Microsoft Mobil Ventures AB (accessed 10 May 2001); available from www.microsoft.com/PressPass/press/2000/Sept00/EricssonFAQ.asp

Chapter 5   Ballard Power: Shifting Dependence, Changing Structures

1. This chapter is adapted from 'Managing International Technology Alliances: Ballard Power and Fuel Cell Vehicle Development', which won a Best Student Paper award at the *Portland International Conference on Management of Engineering and Technology* in 2001.
2. In electrolysis, when an electric current is applied to water (H_2O), it breaks down into H_2 and O_2. Therefore, putting H_2 and O_2 together generates electricity and H_2O.

3. 'At Last, the Fuel Cell', *The Economist*, 25 December 1997, 89.
4. M. Pencak and N. Stein, *Energy Technology: An Overview* (Toronto: Credit Suisse First Boston, Equity Research, 6 July 2000), (accessed 13 February 2001); available from FirstCall.
5. R. Würster, 'PEM Fuel Cells in Stationary and Mobile Applications: Infrastructural Requirements, Environmental Benefits, Efficiency Advantages, and Economical Implications', (accessed 13 February 2001); available from www.hydrogen.org/Knowledge/biel97.htm, 'At Last, The Fuel Cell', *The Economist*, 25 December 1997, 89–92.
6. M. J. Bradley & Associates and Northeast Advanced Vehicle Consortium, *Future Wheels: Interviews with 44 Global Experts On the Future of Fuel Cells for Transportation and Fuel Cell Infrastructure and A Fuel Cell Primer* (Boston: Northeast Advanced Vehicle Consortium, 2000), 32–3.
7. R. Morrow, *Ballard Power Systems* (Toronto: CIBC World Marks Inc (Canada)- Equity Research, 8 July 1999), (accessed 13 February 2001); available from Investext Group.
8. California's emissions regulations establish several classes of vehicles: transitional low-emission vehicles, low emission vehicles, ultra low-emission vehicles, super ultra low-emission vehicles, and zero emission vehicles. Ballard Power Systems, *Prospectus 23 February 2000* (Burnaby, BC: Ballard Power Systems, 2000), 45.
9. Morrow, *Ballard*, available from FirstCall.
10. J. Ng, Vice President – Autos & Industrials Industry Specialist & Corporate Finance Originator, Citibank, N.A., interview by author, 15 March 2001, New York.
11. D. B. Smith, *Gearing Up GM's Hy-Wire Fuel Cell Vehicle for the Paris Auto Show* (New York: Salomon Smith Barney, 14 August 2002).
12. Pencak and Stein, *Energy Technology*, available from FirstCall.
13. Ballard Power Systems, *Annual Report 1999* (Burnaby, BC: Ballard Power Systems, 2000), 4.
14. Bradley, *Future Wheels*, 6.
15. J. D. Power and Associates, 'Market Segment Summary', *J. D. Power and Associates Sales Report* (July 2004) 8.
16. D. Hakim, 'Automakers Sue to Block Emissions Law in California', *New York Times*, 8 December 2004, C1.
17. D. Smith, *Ballard Power Systems: Honda Internal Development Breakthrough Could Leap Cost Bundle* (New York: Citigroup Smith Barney, 14 October 2003); available from Investext Group.
18. Ballard, *Prospectus*, 29.
19. XCELLSIS and Ecostar have undergone several name changes since then. For simplicity, they will be referred to by their original names, or as the former – throughout this book.
20. C$146M cash, $55M intellectual property, $1M capital assets. Daimler Benz invested a further $200M to start up dbb. J. Leslie, 'Dawn of the Hydrogen Age', *Wired*, October 1997, 140. Ballard received 1/3 interest in dbb for $53.3M in cash and $30M in intellectual property and capital assets.
21. F. Chamoun, Director – Equity Research Analyst, Transportation & Industrial Products, UBS Securities Canada, interview by author, 21 October 2004, Toronto.

22. Industry analysts estimate that the fuel cell stack accounts for 40 per cent of the content of the fuel cell-related aspects of a vehicle, while the electric drive accounts for 20 per cent and systems integration another 40 per cent. D. Smith, *BLDP: Re-Defined Agreement: Shareholder Value Clouded* (New York: Citigroup Smith Barney, 8 July 2004); available from Investext Group.
23. Ng interview.
24. Daimler's passenger vehicle marques include: Mercedes Benz, Chrysler, Jeep, Dodge, Mitsubishi Motors (34 per cent owned) and Smart. G. P. Maxton, *Global Car Forecasts to 2005 – the Outlook for World Car Sales* (accessed 26 February 2001), available from http://just-auto.com/F2K/
25. Maxton, *Global Car*, http://just-auto.com/F2K/

Chapter 6   Global Airline Alliances: Constructing Interdependence

1. P. Hanlon, *Global Airlines: Competition in a Transnational Industry*, 2nd edn (Oxford: Butterworth Heinemann, 1999), p. 2.
2. J. W. Salacuse, 'The Little Prince and the Businessman: Conflicts and Tension in Public International Air Law', *Journal of Air Law and Commerce*, 45 (1980) 812.
3. Hanlon, *Global Airlines*, 86–90; K. Button, K. Haynes, and R. Stough, *Flying Into the Future: Air Transport Policy in the European Union* (Cheltenham: Edward Elgar, 1998), p. 31.
4. Hanlon, *Global Airlines*, 233.
5. S. Holloway, *Straight and Level: Practical Airline Economics* (Aldershot: Ashgate, 1997), pp. 3–24.
6. Hanlon, *Global Airlines*, 13.
7. 'Airlines Slash Thousands of Jobs', *BBC News*, 20 September 2001, http://news.bbc.co.uk/hi/english/business/newsid_1553000/1553416.stm
8. Holloway, *Straight and Level*, 263.
9. T. Oum, J. Park and A. Zhang, *Globalization and Strategic Alliances: the Case of the Airline Industry* (Oxford: Pergamon, 2000), pp. 131, 195–6.
10. S. Holloway, *Changing Planes: A Strategic Management Perspective on an Industry in Transition*, Vol. 1: Situation Analysis (Aldershot: Ashgate, 1998), pp. 125–53.
    Code-sharing occurs when a flight operated by one airline also carries a second, and occasionally a third, carrier's flight number. Where antitrust immunity has been granted, code-shares allow carriers to coordinate schedules to maximize the connections available. In terms of the marketing and sales of code-shared flights, both partners sell their seats individually, and the code-share partner pays the operating partner according to an agreed proration formula. J. E. de Groot, 'Code-Sharing: United States' Policies and the Lessons for Europe', *Air & Space Law*, 19 (1994) 62.
11. S. Holloway, *Changing Planes: A Strategic Management Perspective on an Industry in Transition*, Vol. 2: Strategic Choice (Aldershot: Ashgate, 1998), pp. 126–7.
12. K. O'Toole, 'Sir Michael Bishop: A Stubborn Competitor', *Airline Business*, 16 (August 2000) 38.

13. J. Feldman, 'Alliance Costs Start Building,' *Air Transport World*, 37 (June 2000) 41.
14. Oum, Park and Zhang, *Globalization*, 19.
15. W. W. Suen, 'Firm Power and Interdependence in International Strategic Alliances' (Ph.D. diss., Tufts University, 2002), Appendix II.
16. M. Brewer, Vice President – Alliances, United Airlines, interview by author, 25 October 2000, Medford, MA (via telephone).
17. J. McCulloch, Managing Partner, Oneworld Management Company, interview by author, 17 September 2004, Vancouver.
18. C. Buyck, 'The Target is Not to be the Biggest but to be the Most Profitable', *Air Transport World* (October 2002) 24.
19. While airlines highlight the revenues attributable to their alliances, they never mention the revenues forgone because of these relationships. K. O'Toole, Editor, Airline Business, interview by author, 12 October 2000, Sutton, Surrey, UK.
20. M. Jackson, General Manager – Alliances (Europe & Asia Pacific), British Airways, interview by author, 13 October 2000, Harmondsworth, Middlesex, UK.
21. T. Sattelberger, Executive Vice President, Product & Service, Lufthansa German Airlines presentation at Brandeis University, Graduate School of International Economics & Finance, Waltham, MA, 8 May 2001.
22. O'Toole interview.
23. Travelocity.com search conducted 25 October 2001.
24. Suen, *Power and Interdependence*, Appendix II. These include the carriers in Star, Oneworld, SkyTeam, KLM-NW, and Qualiflyer, as well as several key non-aligned carriers.
25. In contrast, only 38 per cent of BA's traffic is domestic/regional. C. Browning, *Global Airline Benchmark* (New York: Merrill Lynch & Co, 7 June 2000), pp. 2–4.
26. B. Friesen (former) Vice President – Alliances, Canadian Airlines International, interview by author, 16 August 2000, Vancouver.
27. This section is adapted from 'Alliance Strategy and the Fall of Swissair', which was published in the *Journal of Air Transport Management* in September 2002. This paper contains the detailed financial analysis referred to later in this section.
28. M. Jackson, General Manager – Alliances (Europe & Asia Pacific), British Airways, Harmondsworth, Middlesex, UK, 13 October 2000.
29. The airline data in this section come from *Airline Business* magazine's annual alliance surveys and annual Top 150 airline surveys of airline finances and traffic.
30. Brewer interview.
31. Star Alliance Chief Executive Meetings, Common Platform Press Briefing, June 2004. http://www.staralliance.com/star_alliance/star/frame/main_10.html; 23 September 2004
32. D. Field and M. Piling, 'Team Spirit', *Airline Business*, 20 (September 2004) 46.
33. M. Maynard, 'Judge Gives US Airways Authority to Cut Union Pay', *New York Times*, 16 October 2004, C1.
34. 'Thai International's Star Alliance Dilemma', *Aviation Week & Space Technology*, 17 July 2000, 55.

35. 'Thai Wares Pitched to Star Alliance', *Bangkok Post*, 5 December 2000. (accessed 10 December 2000); available from Lexis-Nexis Universe.
36. J. Flottau, 'Swiss Delays Embraer Order; Star Membership Questionable,' *Aviation Daily*, 27 July 2004, 2.
37. McCulloch interview.
38. Field and Piling, *Team Spirit*, 48.
39. Field and Piling, *Team Spirit*, 46.
40. McCulloch interview.
41. M. Lenz, Managing Director – Corporate Planning, American Airlines, interview by author, 30 September 2004, Vancouver (via telephone).
42. McCulloch interview.
43. Brock Friesen estimates that BA generated some 40 per cent of its high-yield traffic on these routes from Canadian-based travellers. Moreover, BA claimed that after Air Canada bought Canadian, it tripled the prorates charged to BA for connecting passengers to BA's Canadian gateways, an allegation backed up by Air France and Cathay Pacific. Friesen interview; L. Wright, 'Airlines Feeling Canadian's Loss', *Toronto Star*, 3 May 2000 (accessed 13 June 2000); available from Lexis-Nexis Universe.
44. 'Where are They?' *Flight International*, 1 July 2003, 34.
45. D. Cush, Vice President – International Planning & Alliances, American Airlines, interview by author, 3 November 2000, Medford, MA (via telephone).
46. Lenz interview.
47. Buecking and Jackson interviews.
48. Cush interview.
49. Cush interview.
50. K. Done and D. Cameron, 'American Looks for Relief Abroad', *Financial Times (London)*, 22 October 2004, p. 16.
51. D. Noyes, Director – Alliances, British Airways, interview by author, 13 October 2000, Harmondsworth, Middlesex, UK.
52. Buyck, *Target*, 24; 'No Room for Swiss in SkyTeam – Air France,' Available from http://news.airwise.com/stories/2004/09/1095588301.html; downloaded 24 September 2004.
53. Field and Piling, *Team Spirit*, 46.
54. C. Baker, 'Joint Vision', *Airline Business*, 20 (July 2004): 36.
55. M. J. Credeur, 'SkyTeam Gives Delta $600M Lift', *Atlanta Business Chronicle*, 26 (28 May 2004), A1.
56. T. Clay, General Manager – Corporate Communications, DeltaAirlines, written responses to questions from author, 13 October 2004.
57. Baker, *Joint Vision*, 36.

Bibliography

Abernathy, W. J., and K. B. Clark. 'Innovation: Mapping the Winds of Creative Destruction' *Research Policy*, 14 (1985) 3–22.

Adams, W., and J. W. Brock. 'Joint Ventures, Antitrust and Transnational Cartelization' *Journal of International Law & Business*, 11 (1991) 433–83.

Agmon, T., and M. A. von Glinow (eds) *Technology Transfer in International Business*. New York: Oxford University Press, 1991.

Airline Business. *The Airline Industry Guide 2001*, (ed.) K. O'Toole. Sutton, UK: Reed Business Information, 2000.

Alamdari, F., and P. Morrell. 'Airline Alliances: A Catalyst for Regulatory Change in Key Markets?' *Journal of Air Transport Management*, 3 (1997) 1–2.

Andaleeb, S. S. 'Dependence Relations and the Moderating Role of Trust: Implications for Behavioral Intentions in Marketing Channels' *International Journal of Research in Marketing*, 12 (1995) 157–72.

Anton, J. J., and D. A. Yao. 'Standard-Setting Consortia, Antitrust, and High-Technology Industries' *Antitrust Law Journal*, 64 (1995) 247–65.

Ariño, A. 'To Do or Not to Do? Noncooperative Behavior by Commission and Omission in Interfirm Ventures' *Group & Organization Management*, 26 (2001) 4–23.

Arthur, W. B. *Increasing Returns and Path Dependence in the Economy* Economics, Cognition, and Society series, (ed.) T. Kuran. Ann Arbor: The University of Michigan Press, 1994.

——. 'Increasing Returns and the New World of Business' *Harvard Business Review*, 74 (July–August 1996) 100–9.

Astley, W. G., and E. W. Zajac. 'Beyond Dyadic Exchange: Functional Interdependence and Sub-Unit Power' *Organization Studies*, 11 (1990) 481–501.

Atik, J. 'Technology and Distribution as Organizational Elements within International Strategic Alliances' *Journal of International Business Law*, 14 (1993) 273–313.

Auletta, K. *World War 3.0: Microsoft and its Enemies*. New York: Random House, 2001.

Axelrod, R. *The Evolution of Cooperation*. New York: Basic Books (HarperCollins), 1984.

——. *The Complexity of Cooperation: Agent-Based Models of Competition and Collaboration*. Princeton: Princeton University Press, 1997.

Axelrod, R., and R. O. Keohane. 'Achieving Cooperation under Anarchy: Strategies and Institutions' *World Politics*, 38 (1985) 226–54.

Ayres, I., and R. Gertner. 'Strategic Contractual Inefficiency and the Optimal Choice of Legal Rules' *Yale Law Journal*, 101 (1992) 729–73.

BBC News. Airlines Slash Thousands of Jobs. 2001. Accessed 20 September 2001. Available from news.bbc.co.uk/hi/english/business/newsid_1553000/1553416.stm.

——. Key Cable TV Deal for Microsoft. 2004. Accessed 9 November 2004. Available from http://news.bbc.co.uk/2/hi/business/3994933.stm.

Baker, C. 'Joint Vision' *Airline Business*, July 2004, 32–6.

——. 'The Quiet Revolutionary' *Airline Business*, September 2000, 45–9.

Baker, G., R. Gibbons, and K. J. Murphy. 'Relational Contracts and the Theory of the Firm' *The Quarterly Journal of Economics*, 117 (2002) 39–83.

Balakrishnan, S., and M. P. Koza. 'Patterns of Cooperative Competition in Global Technological Industries' in *Strategic Management in High Technology Firms*, (ed.) M. Lawless and L. Gomez-Mejia, 12, 97–108. Greenwich, CT: JAI Press, 1990.

Baldwin, D. A. 'Interdependence and Power: A Conceptual Analysis' *International Organization*, 34 (1980) 471–506.

——. *Paradoxes of Power*. New York: Basil Blackwell, 1989.

Balfour, J. 'Airline Mergers and Marketing Alliances – Legal Constraints' *Air and Space Law*, 20 (1995) 112–7.

Ball, D. F. 'The R&D Management Conference 1998. Technology Strategy and Strategic Alliances' *R&D Management*, 29 (1999) 303–11.

Ballard Power Systems. 'Annual Report 1998' Burnaby, BC: Ballard Power Systems, 1999.

——. 'Annual Report 1999' Burnaby, BC: Ballard Power Systems, 2000.

——. 'Annual Report 2000' Burnaby, BC: Ballard Power Systems, 2001.

——. 'Annual Report 2001' Burnaby, BC: Ballard Power Systems, 2002.

——. 'Annual Report 2002' Burnaby, BC: Ballard Power Systems, 2003.

——. 'Annual Report 2003' Burnaby, BC: Ballard Power Systems, 2004.

——. 'Notice of Special Meeting of Shareholders and Proxy Circular with Respect to the Acquisition by Ballard of Xcellsis GmbH and Ecostar Electric Drive Systems L.L.C. From DaimlerChrylser Ag and Ford Motor Company'. Burnaby, BC: Ballard Power Systems, 2001.

——. 'Prospectus' Burnaby, BC: Ballard Power Systems, 2000.

Bamford, J. D., B. Gomes-Casseres, and M. S. Robinson. *Mastering Alliance Strategy: A Comprehensive Guide to Design, Management, and Organization* Business & Management Series. San Francisco: Jossey-Bass, 2003.

Banerjee, P. 'Resource Dependence and Core Competence: Insights from Indian Software Firms' *Technovation*, 23 (2003) 251–63.

Bank, D. *Breaking Windows: How Bill Gates Fumbled the Future of Microsoft*. New York: The Free Press, 2001.

Barney, J., M. Wright, and D. J. Ketchen Jr. 'The Resource-Based View of the Firm: Ten Years after 1991' *Journal of Management*, 27 (2001) 625–41.

Beamish, P. W., and J. P. Killing (eds) *Cooperative Strategies: North American Perspectives*, The Cooperative Strategies Series. San Francisco: The New Lexington Press, 1997.

Beauprez, J. 'Microsoft Dives Into Digital Cable Software' *Denver Post*, 10 June 2003, C1.

Bejesky, R., and O. Valle. 'Consumer Welfare and the Sherman Antititrust Act: Reflecting on the Microsoft-Netscape Browser Competition' *Thomas M. Colley Law Review*, 19 (2002) 37–64.

Bendor, J., and P. Swistak. 'The Evolutionary Stability of Cooperation' *American Political Science Review*, 91 (1997) 290–307.

Berechman, J., and J. de Wit. 'On the Future Role of Alliance' in *Taking Stock of Air Liberalization*, (ed.) M. Gaudry and R. R. Mayes, 257–79. London: Kluwer Academic Publishers, 1999.

Berle, A. A., and G. Means. *The Modern Corporation and Private Property*. New York: Macmillan, 1932.

Bery, V., and T. A. Bowers. 'Rebuilding an Alliance' in *Collaborating to Compete: Using Strategic Alliances and Acquisitions in the Global Marketplace*, (ed.) J. Bleeke and D. Ernst, 67–78. New York: John Wiley & Sons, 1993.

Besen, S. M., and J. Farrell. 'Choosing How to Compete: Strategies and Tactics in Standardization' *Journal of Economic Perspectives*, 8 (1994) 117–31.

Bhagwanani, R., and N. Killisly. 'Counting on Loyalty-Part 1' *Airline Business*, April 2001, 84–6.

——. 'Counting on Loyalty-Part 2' *Airline Business*, May 2001, 84–6.

Birnbirg, J. G. 'Control in Interfirm Co-Operative Relationships' *Journal of Management Studies*, 35 (1998) 421–8.

Bleeke, J., and D. Ernst. 'The Way to Win in Cross-Border Alliances' *Harvard Business Review*, 69 (November–December 1991) 127–35.

—— (eds) *Collaborating to Compete: Using Strategic Alliances and Acquisitions in the Global Marketplace*. New York: John Wiley & Sons, 1993.

——. 'Is Your Strategic Alliance Really a Sale?' *Harvard Business Review*, 73 (January–February 1995) 97–105.

Blois, K. J. 'Trust in Business to Business Relationship: An Evaluation of Its Status' *Journal of Management Studies*, 36 (1999) 197–215.

Boam, C. 'Giving the Phoenix Wings: The Deutsche Telekom/France Telecom/ Sprint Alliance' *The Catholic University of America Commlaw Conspectus*, 5 (1997) 73–96.

Borch, O. J., and M. B. Arthur. 'Strategic Networks among Small Firms: Implications for Strategy Research Methodology' *Journal of Management Studies* 32 (1995) 419–41.

Borys, B., and D. B. Jemison. 'Hybrid Arrangements as Strategic Alliances: Theoretical Issues in Organizational Combinations' *Academy of Management Review*, 14 (1989) 234–49.

Botkin, J. W., and J. B. Matthews. *Winning Combinations: The Coming Wave of Entrepreneurial Partnerships between Large and Small Companies*. New York: John Wiley & Sons, 1992.

Boudon, R. 'Limitations of Rational Choice Theory' *The American Journal of Sociology*, 104 (1998) 817–28.

Brams, S. J. *Negotiation Games: Applying Game Theory to Bargaining and Arbitration*. New York: Routledge, 1990.

Brass, D. J., and M. E. Burkhardt. 'Centrality and Power in Organizations' in *Networks and Organizations: Structure, Form, and Action*, (ed.) N. Nohria and R. G. Eccles, 191–215. Boston: Harvard Business School Press, 1992.

Breslin, J. W., and J. Z. Rubin (eds) *Negotiation Theory and Practice*. Cambridge: The Program on Negotiation at Harvard Law School, 1991.

Bresser, R. K. F. 'Matching Collective and Competitive Strategies' *Strategic Management Journal*, 9 (1988) 375–85.

Brinkley, J., and S. Lohr. *U.S. v. Microsoft*. New York: McGraw-Hill, 2001.

Brown, J. E. 'Technology Joint Ventures to Set Standards or Define Interfaces' *Antitrust Law Journal*, 61 (1993) 921–36.

Browning, C. *Global Airline Benchmark*. New York: Merrill Lynch & Co., Global Securities Research & Economics Group, 7 June 2000.

Browning, C., and M. J. Linenberg. *Global Airline Alliances: Why Alliances Really Matter from an Investment Perspective*. New York: Merrill Lynch, Pierce, Fenner & Smith, 25 September 1998.

———. *Global Airline Alliances: Global Alliances Brands Create Value*. New York: Merrill Lynch, Pierce, Fenner & Smith, 2 June 1999.

Browning, L. D., J. M. Beyer, and J. C. Shetler. 'Building Cooperation in a Competitive Industry: Sematech and the Semiconductor Industry' *Academy of Management Journal*, 38 (1995) 113–51.

Buckley, P. J. *Studies in International Business*. London: Macmillan, 1992.

———. *Cooperative Forms of Transnational Corporation Activity*. Vol. 13 United Nations Library on Transnational Corporations, (ed.) J. H. Dunning. New York: Routledge for United Nations, Transnational Corporations and Management Division, Department of Economic and Social Development, 1994.

Buckley, P. J., and M. Casson. 'A Theory of Cooperation in International Business' in *Cooperative Strategies in International Business*, (ed.) F. J. Contractor and P. Lorange, 31–53. Lexington, MA: Lexington Books, 1988.

Butler, R., and S. Sohod. 'Joint-Venture Autonomy: Resource Dependence and Transaction Costs Perspectives' *Scandinavian Journal of Management*, 11 (1995) 159–75.

Button, K. 'Does the Theory of the 'Core' Explain Why Airlines Fail to Cover Their Long-Run Costs of Capital?' *Journal of Air Transport Management*, 9 (2003) 5–14.

Button, K., K. Haynes, and R. Stough. *Flying into the Future: Air Transport Policy in the European Union*. Cheltenham: Edward Elgar Publishing Limited, 1998.

Buvik, A., and K. Gronhaug. 'Inter-Firm Dependence, Environmental Uncertainty and Vertical Co-Ordination in Industrial Buyer-Seller Relationships' *Omega: the International Journal of Management Science*, 28 (2000) 445–54.

Buyck, C. 'The Target is Not to be the Biggest but to be the Most Profitable' *Air Transport World* (October 2002) 22–4.

Campbell, C. P. 'Fit to Be Tied: How United States v. Microsoft Corp. Incorrectly Changed the Standard for Sherman Act Tying Violations Involving Software' *Loyola of Los Angeles Entertainment Law Review*, 22 (2002) 583–611.

Carlson, R. L. *The Information Superhighway: Strategic Alliances in Telecommunications and Multimedia*. London: Macmillan Business, 1996.

Cauley de la Sierra, M. *Managing Global Alliances: Key Steps for Successful Collaboration* The EIU Series. New York: Addison-Wesley Publishing Company and The Economist Intelligence Unit, 1995.

Chang, Y., and G. Williams. 'Changing the Rules-Amending the Nationality Clauses in Air Services Agreements' *Journal of Air Transport Management*, 7 (2001) 207–16.

Charny, D. 'Nonlegal Sanctions in Commercial Relationships' *Harvard Law Review*, 104 (1990) 375–467.

Chen, F. C., and C. Chen. 'The Effects of Strategic Alliances and Risk Pooling on the Load Factors of International Airline Operations' *Transportation Research Part E*, 39 (2003) 19–34.

Chen, Z., and T. W. Ross. 'Strategic Alliances, Shared Facilities, and Entry Deterrence' *RAND Journal of Economics*, 31 (2000) 326–44.

Cheng, B. 'The Role of Consultation in Bilateral International Air Services Agreements, as Exemplified by Bermuda I and Bermuda II' *Columbia Journal of Transnational Law*, 19 (1981) 183–95.

Cheung, S. N. S. 'The Fable of the Bees: An Economic Investigation' *The Journal of Law and Economics*, 16 (1973) 11–33.

Child, J. , and D. Faulkner. *Strategies of Cooperation: Managing Alliances, Networks, and Joint Ventures*. New York: Oxford University Press, 1998.

Christensen, C. M. *The Innovator's Dilemma: When New Technologies Cause Great Firms to Fail*. Boston: Harvard Business School Press, 1997.

Christensen, T. J., and J. Snyder. 'Chain Gangs and Passed Bucks: Predicting Alliance Patterns in Multipolarity' *International Organization*, 44 (1990) 137–68.

Ciborra, C. 'Alliances as Learning Experiments: Cooperation, Competition and Change in Hightech Industries' in *Strategic Partnerships: States, Firms and International Competition*, (ed.) L. K. Mytelka, 51–77. Madison: Fairleigh Dickinson University Press, 1991.

Clapes, A. L. 'Blinded by the Light: Antitrust Analysis of Computer Industry Alliances' *Antitrust Law Journal*, 61 (1993) 899–920.

Clarke-Smith, J. M. 'The Development of the Monopolistic Leveraging Theory and Its Appropriate Role in Antitrust Law' *Catholic University Law Review*, 52 (2002) 179–205.

Coase, R. H. 'The Nature of the Firm' *Economica*, 4 (1937) 186–205.

——. 'The Lighthouse in Economics' *The Journal of Law and Economics*, 17 (1974) 357–76.

Cohen, A. 'Surveying the Microsoft Antitrust Universe' *Berkeley Technology Law Journal*, 19 (2004) 333–64.

Cohen, W. E. 'Competition and Foreclosure in the Context of Installed Base and Compatibility Effects' *Antitrust Law Journal*, 64 (1996) 535–69.

Cohen, W. M., and D. A. Levinthal. 'Absorptive Capacity: A New Perspective on Learning and Innovation' *Administrative Science Quarterly*, 35 (1990) 128–52.

Comanor, W. S., and P. Rey. 'Competition Policy Towards Vertical Foreclosure in a Global Economy' in *Competition Policy in the Global Economy: Modalities for Cooperation*, (ed.) L. Waverman, W. S. Comanor and A. Goto, 344–60. London: Routledge, 1997.

Compton, C. T. C. 'Cooperation, Collaboration, and Coalition: A Perspective on the Types and Purposes of Technology Joint Ventures' *Antitrust Law Journal*, 61 (1993) 861–97.

Conner, K. R. 'A Historical Comparison of Resource-Based Theory and Five Schools of Thought within Industrial Organization Economics: Do We Have a New Theory of the Firm' *Journal of Management*, 17 (1991) 121–54.

Contractor, F. J., and P. Lorange. *Cooperative Strategies in International Business*. Lexington, MA: Lexington Books, 1988.

——. 'Why Should Firms Cooperate? The Strategy and Economics Basis for Cooperative Ventures' in *Cooperative Strategies in International Business*, (ed.) F. J. Contractor and P. Lorange, 3–30. Lexington, MA: Lexington Books, 1988.

Corley, R. F. D. 'The Competition Act and the Information Economy' in *Canadian Bar Association 5th Annual Competition Law Conference*, (ed.) J. B. Musgrove, 143–85. Aylmer, Quebec: Juris Publishing, 1997.

Costello, R. A., and R. Horak. *Basic Concepts of Communications: An Introduction*. Stamford: Gartner Research, 2003.

Coup, D. 'Toyota's Approach to Alternative Technology Vehicles: The Power of Diversification Strategies' *Corporate Environmental Strategy*, 6 (1999) 258–69.

186 Bibliography

Cowhey, P. F., and J. D. Aronson. *Managing the World Economy: The Consequences of Corporate Alliances*. New York: Council on Foreign Relations, 1993.

Coyne, K. P. 'Sustainable Competitive Advantage – What It Is, What It Isn't' *Business Horizons*, 29 (1986) 54–61.

Craswell, R., and J. E. Calfee. 'Deterrence and Uncertain Legal Standards' *Journal of Law, Economics, and Organization*, 2 (1986) 279–303.

Cravens, D. W., N. F. Piercy, and S. H. Shipp. 'New Organizational Forms for Competing in Highly Dynamic Environments: The Network Paradigm' *British Journal of Management*, 7 (1996) 203–18.

Cravens, K., N. Piercy, and D. Cravens. 'Assessing the Performance of Strategic Alliances: Matching Metrics to Strategies' *European Management Journal*, 18 (2000) 529–41.

Credeur, M. J. 'SkyTeam Gives Delta $600M Lift' *Atlanta Business Chronicle*, 28 May 2004, A1.

Cusumano, M. A., and D. B. Yoffie. *Competing on Internet Time: Lessons from Netscape and Its Battle with Microsoft*. New York: The Free Press, 1998.

Das, S., P. K. Sen, and S. Sengupta. 'Impact of Strategic Alliances on Firm Valuation' *Academy of Management Journal*, 41 (1998) 27–41.

Das, T. K., and B. Teng. 'Risk Types and Interfirm Alliance Structures' in *Academy of Management Best Papers Proceedings 1996*, (ed.) J. B. Keys and L. N. Dosier, 11–15. Cincinnati, OH: Academy of Management, 1996.

——. 'Between Trust and Control: Developing Confidence in Partner Cooperation in Alliances' *Academy of Management Review*, 23 (1998) 491–512.

——. 'Instabilities of Strategic Alliances: An Internal Tensions Perspective' *Organization Science*, 11 (2000) 77–101.

——. 'A Resource-Based Theory of Strategic Alliances' *Journal of Management*, 26 (2000) 31–61.

——. 'Partner Analysis and Alliance Performance' *Scandinavian Journal of Management*, 19 (2003) 279–308.

Davies, W. *Partner Risk: Managing the Downside of Strategic Alliances*. West Lafayette, IN: Purdue University Press, 2001.

Davis, S., and J. Botkin. 'The Coming of Knowledge-Based Business' *Harvard Business Review*, 72 (September–October 1994) 165–70.

Davis, S., and C. Meyer. *Blur: The Speed of Change in the Connected Economy*. Reading, MA: Addison-Wesley, 1998.

de Groot, J. E. C. 'Code-Sharing: United States' Policies and Lessons for Europe' *Air and Space Law Journal*, 19 (1994) 62–74.

Dempsey, P. S. 'Turbulence in the 'Open Skies': The Deregulation of International Air Transport' *Transportation Law Journal*, 12 (1987) 305-88.

Demsetz, H. 'Industry Structure, Market Rivalry, and Public Policy' *Journal of Law and Economics*, 16 (1973) 1–9.

Denton, N., and N. Dennis. 'Airline Franchising in Europe: Benefits and Disbenefits to Airlines and Consumers' *Journal of Air Transport Management*, 6 (2000) 179–90.

Dertouzos, M. L. *What Will Be: How the New World of Information Will Change Our Lives*. New York: HarperEdge, 1998.

Dickson, K. 'How Informal Can You Be? Trust and Reciprocity within Co-Operative and Collaborative Relationships' *International Journal of Technology Management*, 11 (1996) 129–39.

Dingman, R. V. 'Theories of, and Approaches to, Alliance Politics' in *Diplomacy: New Approaches in History, Theory and Policy*, (ed.) P. G. Lauren, 245–66. New York: The Free Press, 1979.

Doganis, R. *The Airline Business in the Twenty-First Century.* London: Routledge, 2001.

———. *Flying Off Course: The Economics of International Airlines.* 3rd edn. London: Routledge, 2002.

Done, K., and D. Cameron. 'American Looks for Relief Abroad' *Financial Times*, 22 October 2004, 16.

Downes, L., and C. Mui. *Unleashing the Killer App: Digital Strategies for Market Dominance.* Boston: Harvard Business School Press, 1998.

Doz, Y. L. 'Technology Partnerships between Larger and Smaller Firms: Some Critical Issues' in *Cooperative Strategies in International Business*, (ed.) F. J. Contractor and P. Lorange, 317–38. Lexington, MA: Lexington Books, 1988.

———. 'The Evolution of Cooperation in Strategic Alliances: Initial Conditions or Learning Processes?' *Strategic Management Journal*, 17 (1996) 55–83.

Doz, Y. L., and G. Hamel. *Alliance Advantage: The Art of Creating Value through Partnering.* Boston: Harvard Business School Press, 1998.

Drake, W. J. (ed.) *The New Information Infrastructure: Strategies for U.S. Policy.* New York: The Twentieth Century Fund Press, 1995.

Dresner, M., S. Flicop, and R. Windle. 'Trans-Atlantic Airline Alliances: A Preliminary Evaluation' *Journal of the Transportation Research Forum*, 35 (1995) 13–25.

Dresner, M., and M. W. Tretheway. 'The Changing Role of IATA: Prospects for the Future' *Annals of Air and Space Law*, 13 (1988) 3–23.

Dresner, M. E., and R. J. Windle. 'Alliances and Code-Sharing in the International Airline Industry' *Built Environment*, 22 (1996) 201–11.

Dunford, R. 'The Suppression of Technology as a Strategy for Controlling Resource Dependence' *Administrative Science Quarterly*, 32 (1987) 512–25.

Dunning, J. H. 'The Eclectic Paradigm of International Production: A Restatement and Some Possible Extensions' *Journal of International Business Studies*, 19 (1988) 1–31.

———. 'Reappraising the Eclectic Paradigm in an Age of Alliance Capitalism' *Journal of International Business Studies*, 26 (1995) 461–91.

———. *Alliance Capitalism and Global Business.* New York: Routledge, 1997.

Dussauge, P., and B. Garrette. 'Determinants of Success in International Strategic Alliances: Evidence from the Global Aerospace Industry' *Journal of International Business Studies*, 26 (1995) 505–30.

Dussauge, P., and B. Garrette. 'Anticipating the Evolutions and Outcomes of Strategic Alliances between Rival Firms' *International Studies of Management and Organization*, 27 (1997) 104–26.

Duysters, G., and J. Hagedoorn. 'Strategic Groups and Inter-Firm Networks in International High-Tech Industries' *Journal of Management Studies*, 32 (1995) 359–81.

Dyer, J. H., and H. Singh. 'The Relational View: Cooperative Strategy and Sources of Interorganizational Competitive Advantage' *Academy of Management Review*, 23 (1998) 660–79.

Dyerson, R., A. Pilkington, and O. Tissier. 'Technological Development & Regulation: Capability Alignment & the Electric Vehicle' in *Portland*

International Conference on Management of Engineering and Technology 2001, Vol. 2: Papers Presented at PICMET. Portland, OR, 2001.

Ebke, W. F., and G. W. Wenglorz. 'Liberalizing Scheduled Air Transport within the European Community: From the First Phase to the Second and Beyond' *Transportation Law Journal*, 19 (1991) 417–52.

Economist, The. 'At Last, the Fuel Cell', 25 December 1997, 89.

——. 'Let the Games Begin', 19 May 2001, 57.

Eisenhardt, K. M., and C. B. Schoonhoven. 'Resource-Based View of Strategic Alliance Formation: Strategic and Social Effects in Entrepreneurial Firms' *Organization Science*, 7 (1996) 136–150.

Elg, U., and U. Johansson. 'Decision Making in Inter-Firm Networks as a Political Process' *Organization Studies*, 18 (1997) 361–84.

Emerson, R. M. 'Power-Dependence Relations' *American Sociological Review*, 27 (1962) 31–41.

Endres, G. 'British Midland Decides on the Star Attraction' *Airline Business*, December 1999, 20.

Faulkner, D. O. *International Strategic Alliances: Co-Operating to Compete*. New York: McGraw-Hill Book Company, 1995.

Faulkner, D. O., and M. de Rond (eds) *Cooperative Strategy: Economic, Business, and Organizational Issues*. Oxford: Oxford University Press, 2000.

——. 'Introduction: Perspectives on Cooperative Strategy' in *Cooperative Strategies: Economic, Business and Organizational Issues*, (ed.) D. O. Faulkner and M. De Rond, 3–39. Oxford: Oxford University Press, 2000.

Fearon, J. D. 'Bargaining, Enforcement, and International Cooperation' *International Organization*, 52 (1998) 269–305.

Feldman, J. 'Alliance Costs Start Building' *Air Transport World*, June 2000, 41–8.

Field, D., and M. Piling. 'Team Spirit' *Airline Business*, September 2004, 46–8.

Flottau, J. 'Swiss Delays Embraer Order; Star Membership Questionable' *Aviation Daily*, 27 July 2004, 2.

Forrest, J. E., and M. J. C. Martin. 'Strategic Alliances between Large and Small Research Intensive Organizations: Experiences in the Biotechnology Industry' *R&D Management*, 22 (1992) 41–53.

Foss, Nicolai J. 'Research in the Strategic Theory of the Firm: "Isolationism" and "Integrationism"' *Journal of Management Studies*, 36 (1999) 725–55.

Freeman, L. C. 'Centrality in Social Networks: Conceptual Clarification' *Social Networks*, 1 (1979) 215–39.

Freidheim, C. F. Jr., 'The Battle of the Alliances' *Management Review*, 88 (1999) 46–51.

Friedman, J. R., C. Bladen, and S. Rosen (eds) *Alliances in International Politics*. Boston: Allyn and Bacon, 1970.

Fruin, W. M. *The Japanese Enterprise System: Competitive Strategies and Cooperative Structures*. Oxford: Clarendon Press, 1992.

Fung, K. K. 'On the Slippery Slope: Conformance vs Defection in a Multi-Party Prisoner's Dilemma' *Journal of Economic Behavior and Organization*, 9 (1988) 325–43.

Gallacher, J. 'Bagging the Benefits' *Airline Business*, July 1994, 44–9.

——. 'Tagging Along' *Airline Business*, July 1994, 25–42.

——. 'A Clearer Direction?' *Airline Business*, June 1996, 22–45.

——. 'Partners for Now' *Airline Business*, June 1997, 26–55.

Gallacher, J., and S. Wood. 'Hold Your Horses!' *Airline Business*, June 1998, 42–81.
——. 'Circling the Globe' *Airline Business*, July 1999, 34–65.
Gambetta, D. (ed.) *Trust: Making and Breaking Cooperative Relations*. New York: Basil Blackwell, 1988.
Gerde, V. W., and R. V. Mahto. 'Disruptive Technology and Interdependence: The Relationships of Biomems Technology and Pharmaceutical Firms' *The Journal of High Technology Management Research*, 15 (2004) 73–89.
Geringer, J. M. 'Strategic Determinants of Partner Selection Criteria in International Joint Ventures' *Journal of International Business Studies*, 22 (1991) 41–62.
Geringer, J. M., and L. Hebert. 'Control and Performance of International Joint Ventures' *Journal of International Business Studies*, 20 (1989) 235–54.
Gerlach, M. L. *Alliance Capitalism: The Social Organization of Japanese Business*. Los Angeles: University of California Press, 1992.
Gertler, Z. J. 'Nationality of Airlines: A Hidden Force in the International Air Regulation Equation' *Journal of Air Law and Commerce*, 48 (1982) 51–88.
Gerybadze, A. *Strategic Alliances and Process Redesign: Effective Management and Restructuring of Cooperative Projects and Networks*. New York: Walter de Gruyter, 1995.
Geyskens, I., J. E. M. Steenkamp, L. K. Scheer, and N. Kumar. 'The Effects of Trust and Interdependence on Relationship Commitment: A Trans-Atlantic Study' *International Journal of Research in Marketing*, 13 (1996) 303–17.
Gillen, D., and A. Lall. 'International Transmission of Shocks in the Airline Industry' *Journal of Air Transport Management*, 9 (2003) 37–49.
Gilroy, B. M. *Networking in Multinational Enterprises: The Importance of Strategic Alliances*. Columbia, SC: University of South Carolina, 1993.
Glaister, K. W. 'Dimensions of Control in UK International Joint Ventures' *British Journal of Management*, 6 (1995) 77–96.
Glaister, K. W., and P. J. Buckley. 'Strategic Motives for International Alliance Formation' *Journal of Management Studies*, 33 (1996) 301–32.
Glaser, C. L. 'Realists as Optimists: Cooperation as Self-Help' *International Security*, 19 (1994) 50–90.
Goldstein, A. 'Discounting the Free Ride: Alliances and Security in the Postwar World' *International Organization*, 49 (1995) 39–71.
Gomes-Casseres, B. 'Group Versus Group: How Alliance Networks Compete' *Harvard Business Review*, 74 (July–August 1994) 62–74.
——. *The Alliance Revolution: The New Shape of Business Rivalry*. Cambridge, MA: Harvard University Press, 1996.
——. 'Competitive Advantage in Alliance Constellations' *Strategic Organization*, 1 (2003) 327–35.
Goodale, J. C. 'The Changing Landscape of Jurisprudence in Light of the New Communications and Media Alliances' *Fordham Intellectual Property, Media and Entertainment Law Journal*, 6 (1996) 427–64.
Gowa, J. 'Anarchy, Egoism, and Third Images: The Evolution of Cooperation and International Relations' *International Organization*, 40 (1986) 167–86.
Grandori, A., and G. Soda. 'Inter-Firm Networks: Antecedents, Mechanisms and Forms' *Organization Studies*, 16 (1995) 183–214.

Grant, R. M. 'The Resource-Based Theory of Competitive Advantage: Implications for Strategy Formulation' *California Management Review*, 33 (1991) 114–35.

Greene, J. 'Microsoft: How It Became Stronger Than Ever' *Business Week*, 4 June 2001, 74–85.

Grieco, J. M. 'Anarchy and the Limits of Cooperation: A Realist Critique of the Newest Liberal Institutionalism' in *Controversies in International Relations Theory: Realism and the Neoliberal Challenge*, (ed.) C. W. Kegley, Jr., 151–71. New York: St. Martin's Press, 1995.

Griffith, D. A., and M. G. Harvey. 'A Resource Perspective of Global Dynamic Capabilities' *Journal of International Business Studies*, 32 (2001) 597–606.

Groth, A. J., and R. G. Randall. 'Alliance Pathology: Institutional Lessons of the 1930s' *Political Science Quarterly*, 106 (1991) 109–21.

Gulati, R. 'Does Familiarity Breed Trust? The Implications of Repeated Ties for Contractual Choice in Alliances' *Academy of Management Journal*, 38 (1995) 85–112.

——. 'Alliances and Networks' *Strategic Management Journal*, 19 (1998) 293–317.

——. 'Network Location and Learning: The Influence of Network Resources and Firm Capabilities on Alliance Formation' *Strategic Management Journal*, 20 (1999) 397–420.

Gulati, R., T. Khanna, and N. Nohria. 'Unilateral Commitments and the Importance of Process of Alliances' *Sloan Management Review*, 35 (1994) 61–69.

Gulati, R., and H. Singh. 'The Architecture of Cooperation: Managing Coordination Costs and Appropriation Concerns in Strategic Alliances' *Administrative Science Quarterly*, 43 (1998) 781–814.

Gutterman, A. S. *The Law of Domestic and International Strategic Alliances: A Survey for Corporate Management*. Westport, CT: Quorum Books, 1995.

Hadfield, G. K. 'Weighing the Value of Vagueness: An Economic Perspective on Precision in the Law' *California Law Review*, 82 (1994) 541–54.

Hagedoorn, J., and B. Sadowski. 'The Transition from Strategic Technology Alliances to Mergers and Acquisitions: An Exploratory Study' *Journal of Management Studies*, 36 (1999) 87–107.

Hakim, D. 'Automakers Sue to Block Emissions Law in California' *New York Times*, 8 December 2004, C1.

Halinen, A., A. Salmi, and V. Havila. 'From Dyadic Change to Changing Business Networks: An Analytical Framework' *Journal of Management Studies*, 36 (1999) 779–94.

Hall, W. *Managing Cultures: Making Strategic Relationships Work*. New York: John Wiley & Sons, 1995.

Ham, R. M., G. Linden, and M. M. Appleyard. 'The Evolving Role of Semiconductor Consortia in the United States and Japan' *California Management Review*, 41 (1998) 137–63.

Hamel, G. 'Competition for Competence and Inter-Partner Learning within Strategic Alliances' *Strategic Management Journal*, 12 (1991) 83–103.

Hamel, G., Y. L. Doz, and C. K. Prahalad. 'Collaborate with Your Competitors – and Win' *Harvard Business Review*, 67 (January–February 1989) 133–39.

Hamel, G., and C. K. Prahalad. *Competing for the Future: Breakthrough Strategies for Seizing Control of Your Industry and Creating the Markets of Tomorrow*. Cambridge: Harvard Business School Press, 1994.

Hanlon, P. *Global Airlines: Competition in a Transnational Industry*. 2nd edn. Oxford: Butterworth-Heineman, 1999.

Harbison, J. R., and P. Pekar Jr. *Smart Alliances: A Practical Guide to Repeatable Success*. San Francisco: Jossey-Bass Publishers, 1998.

Harrigan, K. R. 'Joint Ventures and Competitive Strategy' *Strategic Management Journal*, 9 (1988) 141–58.

——. 'Strategic Alliances and Partner Asymmetries' in *Cooperative Strategies in International Business*, (ed.) F. J. Contractor and P. Lorange, 205–26. Lexington, MA: Lexington Books, 1988.

Hay, G. 'Innovations in Antitrust Enforcement' *Antitrust Law Journal*, 64 (1995) 7–17.

Heilemann, J. *Pride Before the Fall: the Trials of Bill Gates and the End of the Microsoft Era*. New York: HarperCollins, 2001.

Heppenheimer, T. A. *Turbulent Skies: The History of Commercial Aviation*. Sloan Technology Series. New York: John Wiley & Sons, 1995.

Hergert, M., and D. Morris. 'Trends in International Collaborative Agreements' in *Cooperative Strategies in International Business*, (ed.) F. J. Contractor and P. Lorange, 99–109. Lexington, MA: Lexington Books, 1988.

Hill, C. W. L. 'Cooperation, Opportunism, and the Invisible Hand: Implications for Transactions Cost Theory' *Academy of Management Review*, 15 (1990) 500–13.

Hirschman, A. O. *Exit, Voice, and Loyalty: Responses to Decline in Firms, Organizations and States*. Cambridge, MA: Harvard University Press, 1970.

Holloway, S. *Straight and Level: Practical Airline Economics*. Aldershot: Ashgate, 1997.

——. *Changing Planes: A Strategic Management Perspective on an Industry in Transition*. Vol. One: Situation Analysis. Aldershot: Ashgate Publishing, 1998.

Holm, D. B., K. Eriksson, and J. Johanson. 'Business Networks and Cooperation in International Business Relationships' *Journal of International Business Studies*, 27 (1996) 1033–54.

Holsti, O. R., P. T. Hopmann, and J. D. Sullivan. *Unity and Disintegration in International Alliances: Comparative Studies*. Comparative Studies in Behavioral Science, (ed.) R. T. Hold and J. E. Turner. Toronto: John Wiley & Sons, 1973.

Hooper, P., and C. Findlay. 'Developments in Australia's Aviation Policies and Current Concerns' *Journal of Air Transport Management*, 4 (1998) 169–76.

Hovi, J. *Games, Threats and Treaties: Understanding Commitments in International Relations*. London: Pinter, 1998.

Howarth, G., and T. Kirsebom. *The Future of Airline Alliances: Current Thinking, Strategic Direction and Implications*. Sutton, Surrey: Airline Business, 2000.

Howe, J. 'Code-Sharing: Fraud or Favour?' *Interavia Businesss and Technology*, 53 (June 1998) 30.

Hruska, A. C. 'A Broad Market Approach to Antitrust Product Market Definition in Innovative Industries' *The Yale Law Journal*, 102 (1992) 305–31.

Hubley, M. I., and N. J. Muller. *Linux: What Major IT Vendors Are Doing*. Stamford, CT: Gartner Research, 2003.

Hubley, M. I., F. Troni, T. Kort, and W. Clark. *PDA and Smartphone Operating Systems: Technology Overview*. Stamford, CT: Gartner Research, 2004.

Hurwitz, A. 'Organizational Structures for the 'New World Order'.' *Business Horizons*, 39 (May–June 1996) 5–14.

Hwang, P., and W. P. Burgers. 'The Many Faces of Multi-Firm Alliances: Lessons for Managers' *California Management Review*, 39 (1997) 101–17.

Iacobucci, D., and N. Hopkins. 'Modeling Dyadic Interactions and Networks in Marketing' *Journal of Marketing Research*, 29 (1992) 5–17.

Inkpen, A. 'Creating Knowledge through Collaboration' *California Management Review*, 39 (1996) 123–40.

Inkpen, A. C., and J. Ross. 'Why Do Some Strategic Alliances Persist Beyond Their Useful Life?' *California Management Review*, 44 (2001) 132–48.

Ionides, N. 'Two Years Old and Still Growing' *Airline Business*, June 1999, 34–5.

Ireland, R. D., M. A. Hitt, and D. Vaidyanath. 'Alliance Management as a Source of Competitive Advantage' *Journal of Management*, 28 (2002) 413–46.

Itschert, J., and R. ul-Haq. *International Banking Strategic Alliances*. Houndmills: Palgrave Macmillan, 2003.

J. D. Power and Associates. 'Market Segment Summary' *J. D. Power and Associates Sales Report*, July 2004, 8.

James, H. S. Jr., and M. Weidenbaum. *When Businesses Cross International Borders: Strategic Alliances and Their Alternatives*. Westport, CT: Praeger, 1993.

Jarillo, J. C. 'On Strategic Networks' *Strategic Management Journal*, 9 (1988) 31–41.

——. *Strategic Networks: Creating the Borderless Organization*. Oxford: Butterworth Heinemann, 1993.

Jenkins, D. (ed.) *Handbook of Airline Economics*. Falls Church, VA: Aviation Week Group, 1995.

Jensen, M. 'Who Gets Wall Street's Attention? How Alliance Announcements and Alliance Density Affect Analyst Coverage' *Strategic Organization*, 2 (2004) 293–312.

Jensen, M. C., and W. H. Meckling. 'Theory of the Firm: Managerial Behavior, Agency Costs and Ownership Structure' *Journal of Financial Economics*, 3 (1976) 305–60.

Jervis, R. *Perception and Misperception in International Politics*. Princeton: Princeton University Press, 1976.

——. 'Realism, Game Theory, and Cooperation' *World Politics*, 40 (1998) 317–49.

Johanson, J., and L. Mattsson. 'Interorganizational Relations in Industrial Systems: A Network Approach Compared with the Transactions-Cost Approach' in *Markets, Hierarchies and Networks: The Coordination of Social Life*, (ed.) G. Thompson and et al., 256–64. London: SAGE Publications, 1991.

Jorde, T. M. 'Antitrust and the Information Economy: A United States Perspective' in *Canadian Bar Association 5th Annual Competition Law Conference*, (ed.) J. B. Musgrove, 189–94. Aylmer, Quebec: Juris Publishing, 1997.

Jorde, T. M., and D. J. Teece. 'Innovation, Cooperation and Antitrust' *High Technology Law Journal*, 4 (1989) 1–112.

—— (eds) *Antitrust, Innovation, and Competitiveness*. New York: Oxford University Press, 1992.

——. 'Innovation, Cooperation and Antitrust' in *Antitrust, Innovation, and Competitiveness*, (ed.) T. M. Jorde and D. J. Teece, 47–81. New York: Oxford University Press, 1992.

——. 'Introduction' in *Antitrust, Innovation, and Competitiveness*, (ed.) T. M. Jorde and D. J. Teece, 3–28. New York: Oxford University Press, 1992.

——. 'Innovation, Market Structure and Antitrust: Harmonizing Competition Policy in Regimes of Rapid Technological Change' in *Competition Policy in the Global Economy: Modalities for Cooperation*, (ed.) L. Waverman, W. S. Comanor and A. Goto, 289–303. London: Routledge, 1997.

Joshi, A. W., and R. L. Stump. 'Determinants of Commitment and Opportunism: Integrating and Extending Insights from Transaction Cost Analysis and Relational Exchange Theory' *Canadian Journal of Administrative Sciences*, 16 (1999) 334–52.

Kaduck, R. 'Canadian Carrier Strategies and the 1995 Open Skies Agreement' *Journal of Air Transport Management*, 3 (1997) 145–53.

Kahneman, D. 'Maps of Bounded Rationality: Psychology for Behavioral Economics' *The American Economic Review*, 93 (2003) 1449–75.

——. 'A Psychological Perspective on Economics' *AEA Papers and Proceedings*, 93 (2003) 162–6.

Kalhammer, F. R., et al. *Status and Prospects of Fuel Cells as Automobile Engines: A Report of the Fuel Cell Technical Advisory Panel*. Sacramento: State of California Air Resources Board, 1998.

Kalmbach, C. Jr., and C. Roussel. *Dispelling the Myths of Alliances*. Anderson Consulting, 1999. Accessed 16 October 1999. Available from www.ac.com:80/overview/Outlook/special99/over_specialed_strat.html.

Kanter, R. M. *When Giants Learn to Dance: Mastering the Challenge of Strategy, Management, and Careers in the 1990s*. Toronto: Simon and Schuster, 1989.

——. 'Collaborative Advantage: The Art of Alliances' *Harvard Business Review*, 71 (July–August 1994) 96–108.

Kaplan, M. A. *System and Process in International Politics*. Huntington, NY: Robert E. Krieger Publishing Company, 1975.

Kattan, J. 'Antitrust Analysis of Technology Joint Ventures: Allocative Efficiency and the Rewards of Innovation' *Antitrust Law Journal*, 61 (1993) 937–73.

Kegley, C. W. Jr. (ed.) *Controversies in International Relations Theory: Realism and the Neoliberal Challenge*. New York: St. Martin's Press, 1995.

Keohane, R. O., and J. S. Nye. 'Power and Interdependence in the Information Age' *Foreign Affairs*, 77 (1998) 81–94.

——. *Power and Interdependence: World Politics in Transition*. Boston: Little, Brown and Company, 1977.

——. *Power and Interdependence*. 3rd edn Boston: Longman, 2001.

Khanna, T., R. Gulati, and N. Nohria. 'Alliances as Learning Races' in *Academy of Management Best Papers Proceedings 1994*, (ed.) Dorothy P. Moore, 42–6. Dallas: Academy of Management, 1994.

——. 'Competition, Cooperation and Sub-Optimal Behavior in Alliances'. Boston: Harvard Business School, Division of Research, 1995.

Khemani, S., and L. Waverman. 'Strategic Alliances: A Threat to Competition?' in *Competition Policy in the Global Economy: Modalities for Cooperation*, (ed.) L. Waverman, W. S. Comanor and A. Goto, 127–51. London: Routledge, 1997.

Killing, J. P. 'Understanding Alliances: The Role of Task and Organizational Complexity' in *Cooperative Strategies in International Business*, (ed.) F. J. Contractor and P. Lorange, 55–67. Lexington, MA: Lexington Books, 1988.

Kindleberger, C. P. (ed.) *The International Corporation*. Cambridge, MA: The MIT Press, 1970.

Kissling, C. 'Liberal Aviation Agreements-New Zealand' *Journal of Air Transport Management*, 4 (1998) 177–80.

Kleymann, B., and H. Seristo. 'Coalition Dynamics in Service Industries-the Case of Airline Industry Alliances'. *Paper presented at the European International Business Academy-25th Annual Conference*. Manchester, 12–14 December 1999.

——. 'Levels of Airline Alliance Membership: Balancing Risks and Benefits' *Journal of Air Transport Management*, 7 (2001) 303–10.

Knibb, D. 'Virgin Deal Raises Doubts over SIA's Role within Star' *Airline Business*, February 2000, 11.

Kogut, B. 'A Study of the Life Cycle of Joint Ventures' in *Cooperative Strategies in International Business*, (ed.) F. J. Contractor and P. Lorange, 169–85. Lexington, MA: Lexington Books, 1988.

Koppel, T. *Powering the Future: The Ballard Fuel Cell and the Race to Change the World*. Toronto: John Wiley & Sons Canada, Ltd., 1999.

Kor, Y. Y., and J. T. Mahoney. 'Edith Penrose's (1959) Contributions to the Resource-Based View of Strategic Management' *Journal of Management Studies*, 41 (2004) 182–91.

Korczynski, M. 'The Political Economy of Trust' *Journal of Management Studies*, 37 (2000) 1–21.

Korland, L. 'Constellations in the Global Airline Industry, 1998' Waltham: Brandeis University-Graduate School of International Economics & Finance, 1998.

Kort, T., L. Anavitarte, R. Cozza, K. Maita, L. Tay. *Windows CE Surpasses Palm OS in 3Q04*. Stamford, CT: Gartner Research, 5 November 2004.

Krasner, S. D. (ed.) *International Regimes*. Edited by P. Katzenstein, Cornell Studies in Political Economy. Ithaca, NY: Cornell University Press, 1983.

Krauss, M. I. 'Regulation vs. Markets in the Development of Standards' *Southern California Interdisciplinary Law Journal*, 3 (1994) 781–808.

Krueger, A. O. 'Are Preferential Trading Arrangements Trade-Liberalising or Trade Protectionist?' *Journal of Economic Perspectives*, 13 (1999) 105–24.

Krueger, A. O. 'NAFTA's Effects: A Preliminary Assessment' *The World Economy*, 23 (2000) 761–75.

Lane, R. J. 'The Computing Model for the Information Age' in *Blueprint to the Digital Economy: Creating Wealth in the Era of E-Business*, (ed.) Don Tapscott et al., 239–59. New York: McGraw-Hill, 1988.

Lang, J. Temple. 'European Community Antitrust Law: Innovation Markets and High Technology Industries' *Fordham International Law Journal*, 20 (1997) 717–818.

Lawless, M., and L. Gomez-Mejia (eds) *Strategic Management in High Technology Firms*. Vol. 12. Greenwich, CT: JAI Press, 1990.

Lee, M. K., and M. K. Lee. 'High Technology Consortia: A Panacea for America's Technological Competitiveness Problems?' *High Technology Law Journal*, 6 (1991) 335–62.

Leebaert, Derek (ed.) *The Future of the Electronic Marketplace*. Cambridge, MA: The MIT Press, 1998.

Leeds, Douglas D. 'Raising the Standard: Antitrust Scrutiny of Standard-Setting Consortia in High Technology Industries' *Fordham Intellectual Property, Media & Entertainment Law Journal*, 7 (1997) 641–71.

Lei, D., and J. W. Slocum, Jr. 'Global Strategic Alliances: Payoffs and Pitfalls' in *The People Side of Successful Alliances*, (ed.) F. Luthans, 7–25. New York: American Management Association, 1998.

——. 'Global Strategy, Competence-Building and Strategic Alliances' *California Management Review*, 35 (1992) 81–97.

Leslie, J. 'Dawn of the Hydrogen Age' *Wired*, October 1997, 138–48, 191.

Levin, E., and R. V. Denenberg. *Alliances and Coalitions: How to Gain Influence and Power by Working with People*. New York: McGraw Hill, 1984.

Levine, M. E. 'Airline Competition in Deregulated Markets: Theory, Firm Strategy, and Public Policy' *Yale Journal on Regulation*, 4 (1987) 393–494.

Levitt, T. 'The Globalization of Markets' *Harvard Business Review*, 61 (May–June 1983) 92–102.

Li, M. Z. F. 'Distinct Features of Lasting and Non-Lasting Airline Alliances' *Journal of Air Transport Management*, 6 (2000) 65–73.

Liebowitz, S. J., and S. E. Margolis. 'The Fable of the Keys' *The Journal of Law and Economics*, 33 (1990) 1–25.

——. 'Should Technology Choice Be a Concern of Antitrust Policy?' *Harvard Journal of Law & Technology*, 9 (1996) 283–318.

Limerick, D., and B. Cunnington. *Managing the New Organization: A Blueprint for Networks and Strategic Alliances*. San Francisco: Jossey-Bass Publishers, 1993.

Liska, G. *Nations in Alliance: The Limits of Interdependence*. Baltimore: The Johns Hopkins University Press, 1962.

Lockett, A., and S. Thompson. 'Edith Penrose's Contributions to the Resource-Based View: An Alternative Perspective' *Journal of Management Studies*, 41 (2004) 193–203.

Longmuir, S. 'A Decade of Global Airline Alliances: Their Impact on Consumers, Communities, Carriers and Competition' *International Business Lawyer*, 28 (2000) 73–8.

Lorange, P., B. Chakravarthy, J. Roos, and A. Van de Ven (eds) *Implementing Strategic Processes: Change, Learning and Co-Operation*. Cambridge, MA: Blackwell Publishers, 1993.

Lorange, P., and J. Roos. *Strategic Alliances: Formation, Implementation, and Evolution*. Cambridge, MA: Blackwell Publishers, 1993.

Lorenzoni, G., and C. Baden-Fuller. 'Creating a Strategic Center to Management to Manage a Web of Partners' *California Management Review*, 37 (1995) 146–63.

M. J. Bradley & Associates and Northeast Advanced Vehicle Consortium. *Future Wheels: Interviews with 44 Global Experts on the Future of Fuel Cells for Transportation and Fuel Cell Infrastructure and a Fuel Cell Primer*. Boston: Northeast Advanced Vehicle Consortium, 2000, NAVC1099–PG030044.

Madhok, A. 'Opportunism and Trust in Joint Venture Relationships: An Exploratory Study and a Model' *Scandinavian Journal of Management*, 11 (1995) 57–74.

Marks, M. L., and P. H. Mirvis. *Joining Forces: Making One Plus One Equal Three in Mergers, Acquisitions, and Alliances*. San Francisco: Jossey-Bass Publishers, 1998.

Mateiu, R. 'II. Antitrust: B. Clayton Act Violations: 1. Private Antitrust Suit: In Re Microsoft Corp. Antitrust Litigation' *Berkeley Technology Law Journal*, 17 (2002) 295–315.

Matthews, J. C. III. 'Current Gains and Future Outcomes: When Cumulative Relative Gains Matter' *International Security*, 21 (1996) 112–46.

Maxton, G. P. *Global Car Forecasts to 2005 – the Outlook for World Car Sales* (accessed 26 February 2001), available from http://just-auto.com/F2K/.

Maynard, M. 'Judge Gives US Airways Authority to Cut Union Pay' *New York Times*, 16 October 2004, C1.

McCarthy, M. 'Media Giants Suit Up to Take on Video Games', *USA Today*, 27 August 2004, 5B.

McGowan, D. 'The Interface between Intellectual Property Law and Antitrust Law: Has Java Changed Anything? The Sound and Fury of Innovation Litigation' *Minnesota Law Review*, 87 (2003) 2039–62.

McGrath, R. N. 'Effects of Incumbency and R&D Affiliation on the Legitimation of Electric Vehicle Technologies' *Technological Forecasting and Social Change*, 60 (1999) 247–62.

McKnight, L. W., and J. P. Bailey (eds) *Internet Economics*. Cambridge, MA: The MIT Press, 1997.

McKnight, L. W., P. M. Vaaler, and R. L. Katz (eds) *Creative Destruction: Business Survival Strategies in the Global Internet Economy*. Cambridge, MA: The MIT Press, 2001.

Medcof, J. W. 'Why Too Many Alliances End in Divorce' *Long Range Planning*, 30 (1997) 718–32.

Mendoza, A. 'Promoting the Transfer of U.S. Technology across National Borders: The Enemy Within' *North Carolina Journal of International Law & Commercial Regulation*, 20 (1994) 97–113.

Merrill Lynch Global Securities Research & Economics. 'Global Airline Benchmark'. New York: Merrill Lynch & Co., 2000.

Michalet, C. 'Strategic Partnerships and the Changing Internationalization Process' in *Strategic Partnerships: States, Firms and International Competition*, (ed.) L. K. Mytelka, 35–50. Madison: Fairleigh Dickinson University Press, 1991.

Microsoft Corporation. 'Annual Report 1999'. Redmond, WA: Microsoft Corporation, 1999.

——. 'Annual Report 2000'. Redmond, WA: Microsoft Corporation, 2000.

——. *Ericsson Microsoft Mobil Ventures Ab*. Accessed 10 May 2001. Available from www.microsoft.com/PressPass/press/2000/Sept00/EricssonFAQ.asp.

——. Microsoft's Investment Strategy. Accessed 14 May 2001. Available from www.microsoft.com/msft/investphil.htm.

——. *Partnering with Microsoft*. Accessed 15 May 2001. Available from www.microsoft.com/directaccess/partnering/microsoft/.

Miller, R. 'International Airline Alliances – a Review of Competition Law Aspects' *Air and Space Law Journal*, 23 (1998) 125–32.

Milner, H. 'International Theories of Cooperation among Nations: Strengths and Weaknesses' *World Politics*, 445 (1992) 466–96.

Minshall, T. 'A Resource-Based View of Alliances: The Case of the Handheld Computer Industry' *International Journal of Innovation Management*, 3 (1999) 159–83.

Mintzberg, H., J. Jorgensen, D. Dougherty, and F. Westley. 'Some Surprising Things About Collaboration – Knowing How People Connect Makes It Work Better' *Organizational Dynamics*, 25 (1996) 60–71.

Mintzberg, H., and J. Lampel. 'Reflecting on the Strategy Process' *Sloan Management Review*, 40 (1999) 21–30.

Mody, A. *Staying in the Loop: International Alliances for Sharing Technology*, World Bank Discussion Papers # 61. Washington: The World Bank, 1989.

Moore, G. A. *Crossing the Chasm: Marketing and Selling High-Tech Products to Mainstream Customers*. New York: HarperCollins, 1991.

Moore, J. F. *The Death of Competition: Leadership & Strategy in the Age of Business Ecosystems*. New York: Harper Business, 1996.

Morgan, P. M. *Deterrence: A Conceptual Analysis*. London: Sage Publications, 1977.

Morgenthau, H. J. *Politics among Nations: The Struggle for Power and Peace*. 5th edn, Revised edn. New York: Alfred A. Knopf, 1978.

Morrow, R. 'Ballard Power Systems' Toronto: CIBC World Markets (Canada), 8 July 1999.

Mosher, J. S. 'Relative Gains Concerns When the Number of States in the International System Increases' *Journal of Conflict Resolution*, 47 (2003) 642–68.

Mosin, S. 'Riding the Merger Wave: Strategic Alliances in the Airline Industry' *Transportation Law Journal*, 27 (2000) 271–85.

Moxon, R. W., T. W. Roehl, and J. F. Truitt. 'International Cooperative Ventures in the Commercial Aircraft Industry: Gains, Sure, but What's My Share?' in *Cooperative Strategies in International Business*, (ed.) F. J. Contractor and P. Lorange, 255–77. Lexington, MA: Lexington Books, 1988.

Muller, P. M. 'The European Quality Alliance: Co-Operating for the Future' *European Free Trade Association Bulletin*, 31 (July–September 1990) 25–7.

Mytelka, L. K. 'Crisis, Technological Change and the Strategic Alliance' in *Strategic Partnerships: States, Firm and International Competition*, (ed.) L. K. Mytelka, 7–34. Madison: Fairleigh Dickinson University Press, 1991.

—— (ed.) *Strategic Partnerships: States, Firms and International Competition*. Madison: Fairleigh Dickinson University Press, 1991.

National Research Council, Computer Science & Telecommunications Board. *Keeping the U.S. Computer and Communications Industry Competitive*. Washington: National Academy Press, 1995.

Negroponte, N. *Being Digital*. New York: Vintage Books, 1995.

Nicholson, M. *Formal Theories in International Relations*. Vol. 3 Cambridge Studies in International Relations, (ed.) S. Smith, et al. New York: Cambridge University Press, 1989.

Nielsen, R. P. 'Cooperative Strategy' *Strategic Management Journal*, 9 (1988) 475–92.

Nohria, N. 'Is a Network Perspective a Useful Way of Studying Organizations?' in *Networks and Organizations: Structure, Form, and Action*, (ed.) N. Nohria and R. G. Eccles, 1–22. Boston: Harvard Business School Press, 1992.

Nohria, N., and R. G. Eccles (eds) *Networks and Organizations: Structure, Form, and Action*. Boston: Harvard Business School Press, 1992.

Nohria, N., and C. Garcia-Pont. *How Strategic Networks Get Built: The Dynamics of Alliance Formation in the Global Automobile Industry*. Boston, MA: Harvard Business School, 1996.

Nonaka, I., and H. Takeuchi. *The Knowledge-Creating Company: How Japanese Companies Create the Dynamics of Innovation*. New York: Oxford University Press, 1995.

Nooteboom, B. 'Trust, Opportunism and Governance: A Process and Control Model' *Organization Studies*, 17 (1996) 985–1010.
——. *Inter-Firm Alliances: Analysis and Design*. New York: Routledge, 1999.
Nooteboom, B., H. Berger, and N. G. Noorderhaven. 'Effects of Trust and Governance on Relational Risk' *Academy of Management Journal*, 40 (1997) 308–38.
Nordberg, M., A. J. Campbell, and A. Verbeke. 'Can Market-Based Contracts Substitute for Alliances in High Technology Markets?' *Journal of International Business Studies*, 27 (1996) 963–79.
Normann, R., and R. Ramirez. 'From Value Chain to Value Constellation: Designing Interactive Strategy' *Harvard Business Review*, 71 (July–August 1993) 65–77.
Nye, J. S. 'Soft Power' *Foreign Policy*, 80 (1990) 153–71.
OECD. *Electronic Commerce: Opportunities and Challenges for Government*. Paris: OECD, 1997.
——. *Gateways to the Global Market: Consumers and Electronic Commerce*. Paris: OECD, 1998.
Ohmae, K. 'The Global Logic of Strategic Alliances' *Harvard Business Review*, 67 (March–April 1989) 143–54.
Olson, M. *The Logic of Collective Action: Public Goods and the Theory of Groups*. Vol. CXXIV Harvard Economic Series. Cambridge, MA: Harvard University Press, 1971.
Olson, M. Jr., and R. Zeckhauser. 'An Economic Theory of Alliances' *The Review of Economics and Statistics*, 48 (1966) 266–79.
Olson, W. C., and A. J. R. Groom. *International Relations Then and Now: Origins and Trends in Interpretation*. London: HarperCollins, 1991.
O'Toole, K. 'Sir Michael Bishop: A Stubborn Competitor' *Airline Business*, August 2000, 36–9.
——. 'Playing for Position' *Airline Business*, July 2001, 40–70.
O'Toole, K., and H. Ombelet. 'The Airline Rankings 2001' *Airline Business*, September 2001, 59–92.
Oum, T. H. (ed.) *Airlines Economics and Policy: Selected Papers of Tae Hoon Oum*, Transportation Series. Seoul: Korea Research Foundation For the 21st Century, 1995.
Oum, T. H., and J. Park. 'Airline Alliances: Current Status, Policy Issues, and Future Directions' *Journal of Air Transport Management*, 3 (1997) 133–44.
Oum, T. H., J. Park, and A. Zhang. 'The Effects of Airline Codesharing Agreements on Firm Conduct and International Air Fares' *Journal of Transport Economics and Policy*, 30 (1996) 187–202.
——. *Globalization and Strategic Alliances: The Case of the Airline Industry*. New York: Pergamon, 2000.
Oum, T. H., C. Yu, and A. Zhang. 'Global Airline Alliances: International Regulatory Issues' *Journal of Air Transport Management*, 7 (2001) 57–62.
Oum, T. H., and A. Zhang. 'Key Aspects of Global Strategic Alliances and the Impacts on the Future of the Canadian Airline Industry' *Journal of Air Transport Management*, 7 (2001) 287–301.
Oum, T. H., A. Zhang, and Y. Zhang. 'Airline Network Rivalry' *Canadian Journal of Economics*, 28 (1995) 836–57.
Oye, K. A. 'Explaining Cooperation under Anarchy: Hypotheses and Strategies' *World Politics*, 38 (1985) 1–24.

Pantoja, J. A. 'Desirable Economic Cooperation among High-Technology Industries: A Look at Telephone and Cable' *Columbia Business Law Review*, 1994 (1994) 617–64.

Park, J. 'Strategic Airline Alliance: Modelling and Empirical Analysis' PhD, University of British Columbia, 1997.

Park, N. K., and D. Cho. 'The Effect of Strategic Alliance on Performance: A Study of International Airline Industry' *Journal of Air Transport Management*, 3 (1997) 155–64.

Park, S. H. 'Managing an Interorganizational Network: A Framework of the Institutional Mechanism for Network Control' *Organization Studies*, 17 (1996) 795–824.

Parkhe, A. ' "Messy" Research, Methodological Predispositions, and Theory Development in International Joint Ventures' *Academy of Management Review*, 18 (1993) 227–68.

——. 'Strategic Alliance Structuring: A Game Theoretic and Transaction Cost Examination of Interfirm Competition' *Academy of Management Journal*, 36 (1993) 794–829.

Payne, J. L. *Foundations of Empirical Political Analysis*. Chicago: Markham Publishing Company, 1973.

Pekar, P. Jr. 'Alliance Enterprise Strategies Destroying Firm Boundaries' in *Creative Destruction: Business Survival Strategies in the Global Internet Economy*, (ed.) L. W. McKnight, P. M. Vaaler and R. L. Katz, 119–44. Cambridge, MA: The MIT Press, 2001.

Pels, E. 'A Note on Airline Alliances' *Journal of Air Transport Management*, 7 (2001) 3–7.

Pencak, M., and N. Stein. 'Energy Technology: An Overview' Toronto: Credit Suisse First Boston Corporation-Equity Research, 6 July 2000.

Penrose, E. *The Theory of the Growth of the Firm*. 3rd edn. Oxford: Oxford University Press, 1995.

Perrow, C. 'Markets, Hierarchies and Hegemony' in *Perspectives on Organization Design and Behavior*, (ed.) A. H. Van de Ven and W. F. Joyce, 371–86. Toronto: John Wiley & Sons, 1981.

——. 'Small-Firm Networks' in *Networks and Organizations: Structure, Form, and Action*, (ed.) N. Nohria and R. G. Eccles, 445–70. Boston: Harvard Business School Press, 1992.

Peterson, K. 'Fuzzy Reception', *The Seattle Times*. 18 August 2003, C1.

Pfeffer, J., and G. R. Salancik. *The External Control of Organizations: A Resource Dependence Perspective*. New York: Harper and Row, 1978.

Phillips, N., T. B. Lawrence, and C. Hardy. 'Inter-Organizational Collaboration and the Dynamics of Institutional Fields' *Journal of Management Studies*, 37 (2000) 23–43.

Pilkington, A., R. Dyerson, and O. Tissier. 'Patent Data as Indicators of Technological Development: Investigating the Electric Vehicle' in *Portland International Conference on Management of Engineering and Technology 2001*, Vol. 2: Papers Presented at PICMET. Portland, OR, 2001.

Piraino, T. A., Jr. 'Reconciling Competition and Cooperation: A New Antitrust Standard for Joint Ventures' *William and Mary Law Journal*, 35 (1994) 871–941.

——. 'The Antitrust Analysis of Network Joint Ventures' *Hastings Law Journal*, 47 (1995) 5–59.

Pogue, L. W., and J. Marshall Pogue. 'The International Civil Aviation Conference (1944) and Its Sequel the Anglo-American Bermuda Air Transport Agreement (1946)' *Annals of Air and Space Law*, 19 (1994) 1–49.

Porter, M. E. *Competitive Advantage: Creating and Sustaining Superior Performance.* New York: The Free Press, 1985.

——. 'The Competitive Advantage of Nations' *Harvard Business Review*, 68 (March–April 1990) 73–93.

Porter, M. E., and M. B. Fuller. 'Coalitions and Global Strategy' in *Competition in Global Industries*, (ed.) M. E. Porter, 315–43. Boston: Harvard Business School Press, 1986.

Poundstone, W. *Prisoner's Dilemma.* Toronto: Doubleday, 1992.

Powell, R. 'Absolute and Relative Gains in International Relations Theory' *The American Political Science Review*, 85 (1991) 1303–20.

——. 'Anarchy in International Relations Theory: The Neorealist-Neoliberal Debate' *International Organization*, 48 (1994) 313–44.

Price Waterhouse Global Technology Centre. *Technology Forecast 1998.* Menlo Park, CA: Price Waterhouse LLP, 1998.

PricewaterhouseCoopers Technology Centre. *Technology Forecast 2001–2003 Mobile Internet: Unleashing the Power of Wireless.* Menlo Park, CA: Pricewaterhouse Coopers LLP, 2001.

Priem, R. L., and J. E. Butler. 'Tautology in the Resource-Based View and the Implications of Externally Determined Resource Value: Further Comments' *Academy of Management Review*, 26 (2001) 57–65.

Pucik, V. 'Technology Transfer in Strategic Alliances: Competitive Collaboration and Organizational Learning' in *Technology Transfer in International Business*, (ed.) T. Agmon and M. A. von Glinow, 121–38. New York: Oxford University Press, 1991.

Puckett, A. L. 'European Competition Law: Managing the 'Chameleon' of Antitrust-Technology Joint Ventures' *Maryland Journal of International Law & Trade*, 19 (1995) 47–79.

Pustay, M. W. 'Long Journey to Free Trade in U.S.–Canada Airline Services' *Canadian-American Public Policy*, 29 (1997) 1–58.

Rackham, N., L. Friedman, and R. Ruff. *Getting Partnering Right: How Market Leaders Are Creating Long-Term Competitive Advantage.* New York: McGraw-Hill, 1996.

Reich, R. B., and E. D. Mankin. 'Joint Ventures with Japan Give Away Our Future' *Harvard Business Review*, 64 (March–April 1986) 78–86.

Reid, R. H. *Architects of the Web: 1,000 Days That Built the Future of Business.* New York: John Wiley & Sons, 1997.

Renzi, S., and R. Crawford. 'Powering the Next Generation Automobile: DaimlerChrysler's Venture into Fuel Cell Technology' *Corporate Environmental Strategy*, 7 (2000) 38–50.

Rhoades, D. L., and H. Lush. 'A Typology of Strategic Alliances in the Airline Industry: Propositions for Stability and Duration' *Journal of Air Transport Management*, 3 (1997) 109–14.

Richardson, G. B. 'The Organisation of Industry' *The Economic Journal*, 82 (1972) 883–96.

Riker, W. H. *The Theory of Political Coalitions.* New Haven: Yale University Press, 1962.

Ring, P. S., and A. Van de Ven. 'Developmental Processes of Cooperative Interorganizational Relationships' *Academy of Management Review*, 19 (1994) 90–118.

Rivoli, P., and Eugene S. 'Foreign Direct Investment and Investment under Uncertainty' *Journal of International Business Studies*, 27 (1996) 335–57.

Rockart, J. F. 'Towards Survivability of Communication-Intensive New Organization Forms' *Journal of Management Studies*, 35 (1998) 417–20.

Root, F. R. 'Some Taxonomies of International Cooperative Arrangements' in *Cooperative Strategies in International Business*, (ed.) F. J. Contractor and P. Lorange, 69–80. Lexington, MA: Lexington Books, 1988.

Rosecrance, R. 'Interdependence' in *The Oxford Companion to Politics of the World*, (ed.) J. Krieger (Oxford: Oxford University Press, 1993), 430–2.

Rosecrance, R., and A. Stein. 'Interdependence: Myth or Reality' *World Politics*, 26 (1973) 1–27.

Rousseau, D. L. 'Motivations for Choice: The Salience of Relative Gains in International Politics' *Journal of Conflict Resolution*, 46 (2002) 394–426.

Rugman, A. M., and A. Verbeke. 'A Final Word on Edith Penrose' *Journal of Management Studies*, 41 (2004) 205–17.

Rumelt, R. P. 'How Much Does Industry Matter?' *Strategic Management Journal*, 12 (1991) 167–85.

Russett, B. 'Dimensions of Resource Dependence: Some Elements of Rigor in Concept and Policy Analysis' *International Organization*, 38 (1984) 481–99.

Russett, B. M. 'Components of an Operational Theory of International Alliance Formation' *Conflict Resolution*, 12 (1968) 285–301.

Safarian, A. E. 'Trends in the Forms of International Business Organization' in *Competition Policy in the Global Economy: Modalities for Cooperation*, (ed.) L. Waverman, W. S. Comanor and A. Goto, 40–65. London: Routledge, 1997.

Salacuse, J. W. 'The Little Prince and the Businessman: Conflicts and Tensions in Public International Air Law' *Journal of Air Law and Commerce*, 45 (1980) 807–44.

——. 'Renegotiations in International Business' in *Negotiation Theory and Practice*, (ed.) J. W. Breslin and J. Z. Rubin, 341–47. Cambridge: The Program on Negotiation at Harvard Law School, 1991.

Salbu, S. R. 'The Decline of Contract as a Relationship Management Form' *Rutgers Law Review*, 47 (1995) 1273–1360.

Salbu, S. R., and R. Brahm. 'Planning Versus Contracting for International Joint Venture Success: The Case for Replacing Contract with Strategy' *Columbia Journal of Transnational Law*, 31 (1993) 283–317.

Sampson, A. *Empires of the Sky: The Politics, Contests and Cartels of World Airlines*. London: Hodder and Stoughton, 1984.

Sarkar, M., S. Tamer Cavusgil, and C. Evirgen. 'A Commitment-Trust Mediated Framework of International Collaborative Venture Performance' in *Cooperative Strategies: North American Perspectives*, (ed.) P. W. Beamish and J. P. Killing, 255–85. San Francisco: The New Lexington Press, 1997.

Saxton, T. 'The Effects of Partner and Relationship Characteristics on Alliance Outcomes' *Academy of Management Journal*, 40 (1997) 443–61.

Schanzenbach, M. 'Network Effects and Antitrust Law: Predation, Affirmative Defenses, and the Case of U.S. v. Microsoft' *Stanford Technology Law Review* 2002 (2002). Available on Lexis-Nexis.

Schelling, T. C. *The Strategy of Conflict.* Paperback, with new Preface edn. Cambridge, MA: Harvard University Press, 1980.

Schere, F. M. *Competition Policies for an Integrated World Economy.* Washington: The Brookings Institution, 1994.

Schlender, B. 'The Beast Is Back' *Fortune,* 11 June 2001, 74–86.

Schmalansee, R. 'Antitrust Issues in Schumperterian Industries' *The American Economic Review,* 90 (2000) 192–6.

Sebenius, J. K. 'Challenging Conventional Explanations of International Cooperation: Negotiation Analysis and the Case of Epistemic Communities' *International Organization,* 46 (1992) 323–65.

Segil, L. *Intelligent Business Alliances: How to Profit Using Today's Most Important Strategic Tool.* New York: Random House, 1996.

Shankar, B. *Alliance for Fixed-Mobile Convergence Needs More Members.* Stamford, CT: Gartner Research, 21 July 2004.

Shapiro, C. 'The Theory of Business Strategy' *RAND Journal of Economics,* 20 (1989) 125–37.

Shapiro, C., and H. R. Varian. *Information Rules: A Strategic Guide to the Network Economy.* Boston: Harvard Business School Press, 1998.

——. 'The Art of Standards Wars' *California Management Review,* 41 (1999) 8–32.

Sheppard, B. H., and D. M. Sherman. 'The Grammar of Trust: A Model and General Implications' *Academy of Management Review,* 23 (1998) 422–37.

Shibata, K. 'Motives for Mega-Alliances between US Ex-Trunk Carriers and European Flag Carriers' *Journal of Air Transport Management,* 7 (2001) 197–206.

Shubik, M. *Games for Society, Business and War: Towards a Theory of Gaming.* New York: Elsevier, 1975.

Simons, M. S. 'Global Airline Alliances – Reaching out to New Galaxies in a Changing Competitive Market – the Star Alliance and Oneworld' *Journal of Air Law and Commerce,* 65 (2000) 313–25.

Singh, K., and W. Mitchell. 'Precarious Collaboration: Business Survival after Partners Shut Down or Form New Partnerships' *Strategic Management Journal,* 17 (1996) 99–115.

Siverson, R. M., and H. Starr. 'Regime Change and the Restructuring of Alliances' *American Journal of Political Science,* 38 (1994) 145–61.

Sivinski, G. A. 'International Airline Alliances: Competition Policy and Procedure' *International Business Lawyer,* 28 (2000) 66–71.

Slowinski, G., E. R. Oliva, and L. J. Lowenstein. 'Medusa Alliances: Managing Complex Interorganizational Relationships' *Business Horizons,* 38 (1995) 48–52.

Smith, D. *Ballard Power Systems: Honda Internal Development Breakthrough Could Leap Cost Bundle.* New York: Citigroup Smith Barney, 14 October 2003.

——. *BLDP: Re-Defined Agreement: Shareholder Value Clouded.* New York: Citigroup Smith Barney, 8 July 2004. Available from Investext Group.

Smith, D. B. *Gearing Up GM's Hy-Wire Fuel Cell Vehicle for the Paris Auto Show.* New York: Salomon Smith Barney, 14 August 2002.

Smith, K. G., S. J. Carroll, and S. J. Ashford. 'Intra- and Interorganizational Cooperation: Toward a Research Agenda' *Academy of Management Journal,* 38 (1995) 7–23.

Smith, S. 'Linking Fuel Cell Technology with Environmental Strategy: The Plug Power Story' *Corporate Environmental Strategy,* 6 (1999) 270–7.

Snidal, D. 'Relative Gains and the Pattern of International Cooperation' *American Political Science Review*, 85 (1991) 701–26.

Snow, C. C., and J. B. Thomas. 'Building Networks: Broker Roles and Behaviours' in *Implementing Strategic Processes: Change, Learning and Co-operation*, (ed.) P. Lorange, et al. 217–38. Cambridge, MA: Blackwell Publishers, 1993.

Snyder, G. H. 'Alliance Theory: A Neorealist First Cut' in *The Evolution of Theory in International Relations: Essays in Honor of William T.R. Fox* (ed.) R. L. Rothstein, 83–103. Columbia, SC: University of South Carolina Press, 1991.

Spar, D. L. *The Cooperative Edge: The Internal Politics of International Cartels*. Ithaca: Cornell University Press, 1994.

——. 'Note on Rules' HBS Note 799-013/Rev 31 March 1999. Boston: Harvard Business School Publishing, 1999.

Spekman, R. E., T. M. Forbes III, L. A. Isabella, and T. C. MacAvoy. 'Alliance Management: A View from the Past and a Look to the Future' *Journal of Management Studies*, 35 (1998) 747–72.

Spekman, R. E., L. A. Isabella, T. C. MacAvoy, and Theodore Forbes III. 'Creating Strategic Alliances Which Endure' *Long Range Planning*, 29 (1996) 346–57.

Staniland, M. 'Conference Report: University of Pittsburgh Conference on "the Future of E.U.–U.S. Aviation Relations"' *Journal of Air Transport Management*, 6 (2000) 245–7.

Star Alliance. *Star Alliance Chief Executive Meetings, Common Platform Press Briefing*, June 2004. Available from http://www.staralliance.com/stara_alliance/star/frame/main_10.html.

Stein, A. 'Coordination and Collaboration: Regimes in an Anarchic World' *International Organization*, 36 (1982) 299–324.

Stobaugh, R., and L. T. Wells, Jr. (eds) *Technology Crossing Borders: The Choice, Transfer, and Management of International Technology Flows*. Boston: Harvard Business School Press, 1984.

Suen, W. W. 'Managing International Technology Alliances: Ballard Power and Fuel Cell Vehicle Development' in *Portland International Conference on Management of Engineering and Technology 2001*, Vol. 2: Papers Presented at PICMET. Portland, OR, 2001.

Suen, W. W. 'Alliance Strategy and the Fall of Swissair' *Journal of Air Transport Management*, 8 (2002) 355–63.

Suen, W. W. 'Firm Power and Interdependence in International Strategic Alliances' PhD, Tufts University, 2002.

Sullivan, L. A., and A. I. Jones. 'Monopoly Conduct, Especially Leveraging Power from One Product Market to Another' in *Antitrust, Innovation, and Competitiveness*, (ed.) T. M. Jorde and D. J. Teece, 165–84. New York: Oxford University Press, 1992.

Tapscott, D. *The Digital Economy: Promise and Peril in the Age of Networked Intelligence*. New York: McGraw-Hill, 1996.

Tapscott, D., et al. *Blueprint to the Digital Economy: Creating Wealth in the Era of E-Business*. New York: McGraw-Hill, 1998.

Teece, D. J. (ed.) *The Competitive Challenge*. Cambridge, MA: Ballinger Publishing, 1987.

——. 'Profiting from Technological Innovation: Implications for Integration, Collaboration, Licensing and Public Policy' in *The Competitive Challenge*, (ed.) D. J. Teece, 185–219. Cambridge, MA: Ballinger Publishing, 1987.

——. 'Competition, Cooperation and Innovation: Organizational Arrangements for Regimes of Rapid Technological Progress' *Journal of Economic Behavior and Organization*, 18 (1992) 1–25.

——. 'Information Sharing, Innovation, and Antitrust' *Antitrust Law Journal*, 62 (1994) 465–81.

Teece, D. J., and M. Coleman. 'The Meaning of Monopoly: Antitrust Analysis in High-Technology Industries' *The Antitrust Bulletin*, 43 (1998) 801–57.

'Thai International's Star Alliance Dilemma' *Aviation Week & Space Technology*, 17 July 2000, 55.

'Thai Wares Pitched to Star Alliance' *Bangkok Post*, 5 December 2000. Available from Lexis-Nexis.

Thompson, J. D. *Organizations in Action: Social Science Bases of Administrative Theory*. Toronto: McGraw-Hill, 1967.

Thornton, D. Weldon. *Airbus Industries: The Politics of International Industrial Collaboration*. New York: St. Martin's Press, 1995.

Thurow, L. *Head to Head: The Coming Economic Battle among Japan, Europe, and America*. New York: Warner Books, 1992.

Tomkins, C. 'Interdependencies, Trust and Information in Relationships, Alliances and Networks' *Accounting, Organizations and Society*, 26 (2001) 161–91.

Touval, S. 'Multilateral Negotiations: An Analytic Approach' in *Negotiation Theory and Practice*, (ed.) J. W. Breslin and J. Z. Rubin, 351–65. Cambridge: The Program on Negotiation at Harvard Law School, 1991.

Tretheway, M. W., and T. H. Oum. *Airline Economics: Foundations for Strategy and Policy*. Vancouver: Centre for Transportation Studies, University of British Columbia, 1992.

Troni, F., and R. Cozza. *Personal Digital Assistants: Overview*. Stamford, CT: Gartner Research, 2004.

Tucker, J. B. 'Partners and Rivals: A Model of International Collaboration in Advanced Technology' *International Organization*, 45 (1991) 83–120.

Tyson, L. D. *Who's Bashing Whom? Trade Conflict in High Technology Industries*. Washington: Institute for International Economics, 1992.

United States v. Microsoft, 84F. Supp. 2d. 9 (U.S. Dist. 1999).

United States v. Microsoft, 87F. Supp. 2d 30 (U.S. Dist. 2000).

United States v. Microsoft, Government Exhibits. Available from *www.justice.gov/atr/cases/ms_exhibits.htm*.

United States v. Microsoft, Direct Testimony. Available from *www.justice.gov/atr/cases/ms_testimony*.

United States v. Microsoft, Depositions. Available from *www.justice.gov/atr/cases/ms_depos.htm*.

United States v. Microsoft Corporation Publically Released Deposition Transcripts: Depositions taken between July 9, 1998 and February 4, 1999 (Redacted on CD-ROM). Washington: United States Government Printing Office, May 1999.

Updegrove, A. 'Forming and Representing High-Technology Consortia: Legal and Strategic Issues' *The Computer Lawyer*, 11 (1994) 8–17.

Urban, S., and S. Vendemini. *European Strategic Alliances: Co-Operative Corporate Strategies in the New Europe*. Translated by R. Ingleton. Oxford: Blackwell Publishers, 1992.

Vamos-Goldman, A. 'The Stagnation of Economic Regulation under Public International Law: Examining Its Contribution to the Woeful State of the Airline Industry' *Transportation Law Journal*, 23 (1996) 425–70.

Van de Ven, A. H., and W. F. Joyce (eds) *Perspectives on Organization Design and Behavior*. Toronto: John Wiley & Sons, 1981.

Varadarajan, P. Rajan, and Margaret H. Cunningham. 'Strategic Alliances: A Synthesis of Conceptual Foundations' *Journal of the Academy of Marketing Science*, 23 (1995) 282–96.

Vernon, R. 'International Investment and International Trade in the Product Cycle' *Quarterly Journal of Economics*, 80 (1966) 190–207.

——. *Sovereignty at Bay: The Multinational Spread of U.S. Enterprises*. New York: Basic Books, 1971.

Viner, J. 'Power Versus Plenty as Objectives of Foreign Policy in the Seventeenth and Eighteenth Centuries' *World Politics*, 1 (1948) 1–29.

Volery, T., and S. Mensik. 'The Role of Trust in Creating Effective Alliances: A Managerial Perspective' *Journal of Business Ethics*, 17 (1998) 987–94.

Wahl, A. 'We Got Game' *Canadian Business*, 10 November 2003, 85–91.

Walker, G. 'Network Analysis for Cooperative Interfirm Relationships' in *Cooperative Strategies in International Business*, (ed.) F. J. Contractor and P. Lorange, 227–240. Lexington, MA: Lexington Books, 1988.

Waller, S. W. 'Understanding and Appreciating EC Competition Law' *Antitrust Law Journal*, 61 (1992) 55–77.

Walt, S. 'The Relation between Competition and Cooperation' *Harvard Journal of Law & Public Policy*, 15 (1992) 733–45.

Walt, S. M. *The Origins of Alliances*. Ithaca: Cornell University Press, 1987.

——. 'Why Alliances Endure or Collapse' *Survival*, 39 (1997) 156–79.

Waltz, K. N. 'The Myth of National Interdependence' in *The International Corporation*, (ed.) C. P. Kindleberger, 205–23. Cambridge, MA: The MIT Press, 1970.

Ward, M. D. *Research Gaps in Alliance Dynamics*. Vol. 19 Monograph Series in World Affairs. Denver: University of Denver, 1982.

Waters, R. 'Microsoft to Pursue Growth in Core Information Systems' *Financial Times*, 30 July 2004, 15.

——. 'Search Engines, Anti-Virus Software Targeted' *Financial Times*, 30 September 2004, 28.

Waverman, L., W. S. Comanor, and A. Goto (eds) *Competition Policy in the Global Economy: Modalities for Cooperation*, Routledge Studies in the Modern World Economy. London: Routledge, 1997.

Weber, M., and J. Dinwoodie. 'Fifth Freedoms and Airline Alliances: The Role of Fifth Freedom Traffic in an Understanding of Airline Alliances' *Journal of Air Transport Management*, 6 (2000) 51–60.

Weinstein, S. Noah. 'II. Antitrust: A. Sherman Act Violations: 1. Monopolization: A) Tying: United States v. Microsoft Corp.' *Berkeley Technology Law Journal*, 2002 (2002) 273–94.

'Where are They?' *Flight International*, 1 July 2003, 34.

Williams, G. *The Airline Industry and the Impact of Deregulation*. Aldershot: Ashgate Publishing Limited, 1993.

Williamson, O. E. *Markets and Hierarchies: Analysis and Antitrust Implications – a Study in the Economics of Internal Organization*. New York: The Free Press, 1975.

——. 'Transaction-Cost Economics: The Governance of Contractual Relations' *The Journal of Law and Economics*, 22 (1979) 253–61.

——. 'Credible Commitments: Using Hostages to Support Exchange' *The American Economic Review*, 73 (1983) 519–40.

—— (ed.) *Organization Theory: From Chester Barnard to the Present and Beyond*. New York: Oxford University Press, 1990.

——. 'Comparative Economic Organization: The Analysis of Discrete Structural Alternatives' *Administrative Science Quarterly*, 36 (1991) 269–96.

——. 'Calculativeness, Trust and Economic Organization' *Journal of Law and Economics*, 36 (1993) 453–86.

Williamson, O. E., and S. G. Winter (eds) *The Nature of the Firm: Origins, Evolution, and Development*. New York: Oxford University Press, 1991.

Wilson, K. A. 'The Fuel Cell Sell' *Autoweek*, 3 March 1997, 12–4.

Winters, R. K. 'A Look at New Technologies Set to Revolutionize Power Generation for Markets Such as Transportation, Stationary Power, Back-up/Standby Power & Portable Power'. New York: Bear, Stearns & Co. Equity Research, 4 April 2000.

Wright, L. 'Airlines Feeling Canadian's Loss' *Toronto Star*, 3 May 2000 (accessed 13 June 2000); available from Lexis-Nexis Universe.

Würster, R. *PEM Fuel Cells in Stationary and Mobile Applications: Infrastructural Requirements, Environmental Benefits, Efficiency Advantages, and Economical Implications*. 1997. Accessed 13 February 2001. Available from www.hydrogen.org/Knowledge/biel97.htm.

Yergin, D., R. H. K. Vietor, and P. C. Evans. *Fettered Flight: Globalization and the Airline Industry*. Cambridge, MA: Cambridge Energy Research Associates, 2000.

Yoffie, D. B. (ed.) *Competing in the Age of Digital Convergence*. Boston: Harvard Business School Press, 1997.

Yoshino, M. Y., and U. S. Rangan. *Strategic Alliances: An Entrepreneurial Approach to Globalization*. Boston: Harvard Business School Press, 1995.

Young, J. 'Airline Alliances – Is Competition at the Crossroads?' *Air and Space Law Journal*, 24 (1999) 287–93.

Young-Ybarra, C., and M. Wiersema. 'Strategic Flexibility in Information Technology Alliances: The Influence of Transaction Cost Economics and Social Exchange Theory' *Organization Science*, 10 (1999) 439–59.

Youssef, W., and M. Hansen. 'Consequences of Strategic Alliances between International Airlines: The Case of Swissair and SAS' *Transportation Research – An International Journal Part A: Policy & Practice*, 28A (1994) 415–31.

Zacher, M., and B. Sutton. *Governing Global Networks: International Regimes for Transportation and Communication*. Vol. 44 Cambridge Studies in International Relations. Cambridge: Cambridge University Press, 1996.

Zaheer, A., and N. Venkatraman. 'Relational Governance as an Interorganizational Strategy: An Empirical Test of the Role of Trust in Economic Exchange' *Strategic Management Journal*, 16 (1995) 373–92.

Interviews

Brewer, M., Vice President – Alliances, United Airlines. Interview by author, 25 October 2000, Medford, MA (via telephone).

Buecking, P., Managing Partner – Oneworld Management Company Ltd. Interview by author, 16 August 2000, Vancouver.

Chamoun, F. Director – Equity Research Analyst, Transportation & Industrial Products, UBS Securities Canada. Interview by author, 21 October 2004, Toronto.

Clay, T. General Manager – Corporate Communications, Delta Airlines. Written responses to questions from author, 13 October 2004.

Cush, F. Vice President – International Planning and Alliances, American Airlines. Interview by author, 3 November 2000, Medford, MA (via telephone).

Friesen, B. (Former) Vice President – Alliances, Canadian Airlines. Interview by author, 16 August 2000, Vancouver.

Jackson, M. General Manager – Alliances (Europe and Asia Pacific), British Airways. Interview by author, 13 October 2000, Harmondsworth, Middlesex, UK.

Lenz, M. Managing Director – Corporate Planning, American Airlines. Interview by author, 30 September 2004, Vancouver (via telephone).

McCulloch, J. Managing Partner – Oneworld Management Company, interview by author, 17 September 2004, Vancouver.

Ng, J. Vice President – Autos & Industrials Industry Specialist & Corporate Finance Originator, Citibank N. A. Interview by author, 15 March 2001, New York.

Noyes, D. Director – Alliances, British Airways. Interview by author, 13 October 2000, Harmondsworth, Middlesex, UK.

O'Toole, K. Editor – Airline Business. Interview by author, 12 October 2000, Sutton, Surrey, UK.

Pilkington, M. Manager – Airline Alliances, Virgin Atlantic Airways. Interview by author, 18 October 2000, Medford, MA (via telephone).

Stabile, R. Associate – Institutional Equity Research, CIBC World Markets. Interview by author, 14 October 2004, Toronto.

Taub, S. Associate Director – North America Energy, Cambridge Energy Research Associates. Interview by author, 1 March 2001, Cambridge, MA.

Tighe, A. General Manager – Alliances, British Airways. Interview by author, 13 October 2000, Harmondsworth, Middlesex, UK.

Zaarour, R. Manager – Star Alliance Development, Air Canada. Interview by author, 8 August 2000, Vancouver (via telephone).

Zelewski, T. Managing Director – Oneworld Business Development, American Airlines. Interview by author, 28 November 2000, Medford, MA (via telephone).

Index

208